D0931517

*The Paradox of
Continental Production*

A volume in the series

Cornell Studies in Political Economy

EDITED BY PETER J. KATZENSTEIN

A full list of titles in the series appears at the end of the book.

The Paradox of Continental Production

NATIONAL INVESTMENT POLICIES
IN NORTH AMERICA

BARBARA JENKINS

CORNELL UNIVERSITY PRESS

Ithaca and London

First published 1992 by Cornell University Press.

International Standard Book Number 0-8014-2676-6
Library of Congress Catalog Card Number 92-52761
Printed in the United States of America
Librarians: Library of Congress cataloging information
appears on the last page of the book.

⊗ The paper in this book meets the minimum requirements
of the American National Standard for Information Sciences—
Permanence of Paper for Printed Library Materials, ANSI Z39.48-1984.

For Harriet Louise Jenkins

Contents

Preface   ix
1. The Interaction between the State and the Market   1
2. Regulating Foreign Direct Investment   38
3. The Regulation of Foreign Direct Investment in the
   United States   74
4. Canada: A Small State with a Hegemon's Mentality   110
5. Mexico's *Apertura*   155
6. Policy Alternatives   193
   Appendix 1. Canadian Decisions on Foreign-Investment
   Applications by Sector, 1978–1985   225
   Appendix 2. Areas Restricted to Foreign Investors
   in Mexico   226
   Index   231

Preface

This book grew out of a desire to examine the potential for state intervention in a global economy. My interest in this issue was heightened by the implementation of the Canada–U.S. Free Trade Agreement (FTA) in 1989 and the initiation of free trade talks with Mexico in 1991. As states willingly relinquished their control over policy tools such as tariffs and performance requirements, the potential for effective state intervention seemed greatly diminished. Despite the willingness of neo-liberal governments in all three countries to give more play to market forces, however, I found that political forces played a greater role than ever in continental trade and investment relations. Curiously, the harder states tried to extract themselves from continental market interactions, the more politicized trade and investment issues became. The signing of the FTA seemed only to fuel trade disputes between the United States and Canada in areas such as beer, autos, carpets, pork, and softwood lumber, and the proposal to expand the agreement to Mexico led to an explosion of political opposition in both of Mexico's northern neighbors.

The reason is that meticulously negotiated trade rules devised by governments do little to abate the fears, insecurities, or grievances felt by such political actors as business and labor. Indeed, exposing them more broadly to market forces often exacerbates their perceived grievances and encourages unprotected interests to battle out their differences even more furiously. Paradoxically, therefore, one

of the best ways to promote a freer trade and investment environment is for the state to protect these interests—not in the traditional
sense of offering quotas or tariff barriers but by enhancing available
adjustment measures. These measures would involve the implementation of state-led programs to train and retrain workers, coordinate R&D, provide sufficient unemployment insurance, and help
firms adapt to global competition. Yet as these three countries reduced their trade barriers, they simultaneously cut many of the
programs that might provide their citizens with greater adjustment
security. I conclude that despite the current emphasis on market
forces and globalization, the need for effective national and subnational state policies is greater than ever.

The announcement of a North American Free Trade Agreement
(NAFTA) in August 1992 came as this book was in its late stages of
production. Nonetheless, it was written in anticipation of such a
pact, and its conclusions are relevent in the context of the political
debates sure to ensue in all three countries as the agreement passes
through their legislatures. Comprehensive investment strategies addressing the concerns of both workers and firms will encourage
greater continental cooperation while avoiding a downward spiral to
the lowest common denominator.

Many people assisted me in the writing of this book, and I thank
the dozens of government officials, academics, and corporate execu-
tives in all three countries who gave precious time to discuss my
project. I extend special thanks to Ari Abonyi, Oliver Avens, David
Cameron, Bruce Campbell, Manuel Gameros, Monty Graham,
Chris Howell, Mike Kelley, Jeanne Laux, Kate McFate, Gaston
Melo-Medina, Lynn Mytelka, Paul Pierson, Helen Shapiro, Claire
Sjolander, Miriam Smith, Murray Smith, Christopher Wilkie, and
Glen Williams. In addition, I thank Roger Haydon and Peter Katzenstein for their good spirits and patience throughout this publishing endeavor. Joanne Hindman of Cornell University Press deserves
particular mention for patiently enduring the travails caused by my
correcting the manuscript while in Argentina, and Joanne Ains-
worth deserves mention for her fine editing skills. Nancy Drozd and
Rena Ramkay both provided superb research assistance.

Finally I could not have written this book without the support of my family and friends. Trisha Craig, Susan Kelley, Nicola Shilliam, and Kevin Wannamaker deserve particular mention. Their excellent humor and steadfast disinterest in my work helped me keep the importance of this project in perspective. Last but not least, I note the influence of my ninety-three-year-old grandmother, Harriet Louise Jenkins, to whom the book is dedicated.

BARBARA JENKINS

Ottawa, Ontario

The Paradox of
Continental Production

CHAPTER ONE

The Interaction between the State and the Market

One of the central issues countries face is how to encourage investment in their economies. Yet as states slide with surprising ease into regional trade blocs and continentalized economies, we hear much talk of tariffs, financial integration, and policy harmonization and very little of concrete investment policies. Negotiators have spent countless hours agonizing over the minute details of trade agreements, and trade policy is currently one of the most highly politicized issues for both developed and developing countries. But when one assesses the arguments for and against free trade or managed trade, the key questions often come down to investment flows. How can a country attract foreign investors, opponents of free trade argue, without forcing them to jump a tariff barrier? Why would multinational enterprises (MNEs) invest in an economy that does not have tariff-free access to contiguous markets, proponents of free trade reply? What is to induce international companies to source components locally if performance requirements are not allowed, ask the advocates of managed trade?

Investment issues were at the forefront of the international political economy (IPE) debates of the 1970s but took a back seat to trade and financial issues in the 1980s as states increased foreign borrowing and began to negotiate bilateral or regional trade agreements. The current trend back to equity financing in developing countries, however, combined with the clear implications new trading arrangements have for investors, guarantees that investment issues will reappear on the IPE agenda. And the complex and often contradictory nature of these questions ensures that the debates of the 1990s will be as highly charged as those of the 1970s.

In this book I propose to reintroduce the investment debate by focusing on the investment policies of the three countries that make up the greater North American continent: Canada, the United States, and Mexico. It is an attempt to analyze investment policies in their entirety. One of the central lessons will be that investment policies are not about state bureaucrats facing off with the anonymous global markets of international firms. Rather, they are integrated into the political economy of each country and reflect the institutional capacities of the state, the interests of social actors (including international firms), *and* the constraints of the market. Thus, this book is an attempt to "people" the market operations of international firms and reveal the extensive space available for political action. It is an effort to lay bare the true paradox of continental production: that the more international markets become, the more essential government efforts to control and maintain those markets are. Despite the many warnings about the "globalization" or "continentalization" of economies, state strategies at the national, regional, and local level are more important than ever.

The reasons for this importance will be developed in greater detail below, but the basic rationale involves a more complex understanding of the market than is invoked in most neo-liberal policy prescriptions. Focusing on economic efficiency purely in terms of market interactions ignores political factors that can sabotage or destabilize market operations. A broader and more political view of the market indicates that free market solutions can ultimately be extremely inefficient because they are inherently dysfunctional in a political sense.

The Canada–U.S. Free Trade Agreement (FTA), for example, consists of a complex set of rules to govern trade and investment practices and a dispute settlement mechanism designed to adjudicate trade problems. The excessively legalistic and economistic nature of the agreement, however, ignores some of the fundamental political conflicts that underlie current trade disputes. Therefore, it provides only post hoc, short-term solutions for deeply entrenched trade problems. Not surprisingly, since the implementation of the

FTA in 1989, bitter trade disputes between Canada and the United States have arisen in the beer, automobile, softwood lumber, pork, and carpet industries.

A more complete effort to encourage continental free trade would have to acknowledge explicitly the political problems underlying trade disputes, and address these issues directly via state-led adjustment policies for threatened workers and firms. Adjustment policy and investment policy are directly linked because some of the most important forms of adjustment assistance are also effective tools in attracting and nurturing investment. State policies designed to retrain workers, encourage R&D, or assist local firms in adapting to international competition not only can reduce protectionist pressures but also affect the quantity and quality of domestic investment.

At present, none of the three countries involved in the North American Free Trade Agreement (NAFTA) negotiations have effective investment policies: Canada and Mexico have transformed any semblance of investment policy that might have existed into strategies more akin to an advertising campaign, and the growing interest of the United States in monitoring foreign investment is more accurately described as nationalistic reaction rather than a concrete investment strategy. Since the investment policies of each country are largely proscribed by the FTA and NAFTA, they fall prey to the same criticisms listed above. Rule-making is a necessary but not sufficient condition for effective trade and investment policies and provides at best a superficial response to pressing economic issues. Indeed, one of the most trenchant critiques by opponents of the FTA and NAFTA contends that the major goal of these agreements is not to lower tariffs but rather to reduce government regulation and cut social overhead payments that supposedly make firms uncompetitive. In addition, many of the neo-liberal policies evident in Canada, the United States, and Mexico expressly limit some of the most effective methods of trade adjustment, such as unemployment insurance, worker retraining, and industrial policies that might help firms adjust. Again, the short-term nature of these policies is obvious, since they only exacerbate trade tensions by eliminating many of the adjustment programs available to injured parties.

A related factor is that state policies to insulate domestic constituents from the market have historically played an integral role in the legitimation of governments in the two small states considered here, Canada and Mexico. In contrast to the laissez-faire, free trade strategies characteristic of hegemons, both these countries traditionally made use of interventionist policies to protect domestic firms and specific regions from excessive exposure to the winds of international competition. In this context, the neo-liberal state strategies in vogue in both Canada and Mexico since the mid-1980s are extremely risky, since they threaten one of the fundamental sources of government legitimacy.

Consideration of these more political aspects of continental integration reveals significant contradictions in the current trajectory of trade and investment strategies in all three states. The trade and investment agendas defined in the FTA and the negotiations for NAFTA are destined to *increase* rather than reduce hostilities between the three trade partners because they focus on quantitative concerns, such as "getting the prices right," rather than on more fundamental qualitative issues, such as how to increase productivity. Consequently, they invite political battles over distributional questions both within and between states. Briefly, there are five areas where conflicts are likely to arise. The first is in the area of exchange rates; all three countries have relied on the devaluation of their currencies to increase competitiveness in the past. Obviously, exchange rates are important only in a relative sense, however, and all three cannot have a cheaper currency than the others. One or more countries will have to concede, and the battles over which ones will compromise are bound to be acrimonious.

Similar arguments are likely to arise in the second and third areas of contention: wages and corporate taxes. The prices of these two items are also important in a comparative sense, and the downward pressure on both wages and taxes that will result from continental integration in its current form is destined not only to spark furious distributional debates within each country, but to create further economic woes for all three. Lower wages result in poorer consumers and a consequent diminishing of potential markets, and low corporate taxes have already exacerbated the yawning budget deficits with which these countries are struggling. To date, the neo-liberal governments in place in all three have responded to the budget deficits with cuts in social spending.

These spending cuts in turn create a fourth area of potential conflict: as states withdraw from the kinds of "cushioning" roles they have played in the past they are more likely to be faced with protectionist pressures from their populace. As mentioned above, the easiest way to diffuse a protectionist backlash is to guarantee threatened workers or firms assistance in the restructuring that is supposed to accompany the dismantling of tariffs and investment restrictions. Yet neo-liberal policies are focused on cutting precisely the kinds of expenditure that would provide such guarantees and enhance structural adjustment.

A fifth and final area of potential hostilities of more direct interest for our purposes is the question of investment incentives and subsidies. As I completed the writing of this book, an agreement on subsidies had not been reached in either the FTA or NAFTA negotiations. In the absence of such an agreement, the reduction of tariffs and investment regulations will inevitably increase the temptation for states to lure companies into their economies through subsidies and other handouts. Without tariffs to protect the market share of foreign investors or comprehensive investment strategies that make an economy a particularly attractive investment site, the only alternative left for states is to bribe investors with subsidies, tax cuts, or real estate deals. The result is a continental bidding war in which both national and regional governments try to best each other in their concessions to corporations.

The five factors listed—devalued exchange rates, reduced wages costs, low corporate taxes, cuts in social expenditures, and higher investment incentives—are key elements of the national corporate agendas in all three states. Since they will continue to be of importance whether or not a NAFTA is negotiated, one of the purposes of the three case studies included in this book is to outline the role of corporate interests in creating contemporary trade and investment policies, and to illustrate the highly political nature of the continentalization agenda. Still, this agenda is shortsighted even with respect to capital's wishes. Apart from the destabilizing economic impact lower wages and higher budget deficits can have, business has typically been the first to complain about "overvalued" currencies or the lack of government assistance. Ironically, therefore, one of the major forces in a future protectionist reaction to continentalization could be business interests themselves.

Clearly, ignoring the political implications of the continental free trade agenda will create major contradictions for all three parties involved. Yet the neo-classical concept of the market implicit in the rationale for a continental free trade area excludes political factors by definition. Rather than being viewed as part of the market, political elements are considered only to the extent that they create aberrations of market logic. Therefore, a rethinking of this neo-classical conception of the market is warranted. States and politics are not extraneous to markets; on the contrary, they are an integral part of everyday market operations. In this light, the idea that state intervention in the market will disrupt some intricate balance of market forces reveals a fundamental misunderstanding of what markets are. There is no such thing as a single, abstract market logic that snaps in to punish states once they cross an invisible Maginot Line of non-market-conforming policies. Politics are part of markets, and political manipulations of market operations have important consequences for the welfare of domestic firms and for the shape of international competition.

Underlying this analysis is a message for policymakers: markets unquestionably place structural constraints on all market actors, including states. But focusing on the factors constraining a state's involvement in the market obscures the potential for political action. States play a significant role in molding the contours of competition in international markets and in legitimizing and supporting such markets once they are in operation. Ignoring this political side of market operations and emphasizing the constraints on state actions creates a sense of futility and underestimates the potential for effective state policies. Moreover, ignoring the role states play in cushioning their constituents from the harsh impact of international competition simply invites a nationalist reaction. Such reactions can ultimately undermine any benefits that a gentler approach to internationalization might have brought.

By focusing on this more political aspect of markets, we can dispell some of the more common myths about state policies toward foreign investors. For example, it is commonly assumed that given the fierce competition between countries to attract foreign direct investment, states must reduce their controls on MNEs or risk losing potential investors. Any attempt to make demands on international companies, it is thought, will simply drive them away. The evidence provided here shows that this argument is a vast oversimplification and that countries often regulate international firms with relative impunity. This is not to say that such regulation is always necessary. Indeed, I will raise some major issues about foreign-investment review. It is merely to emphasize that the exigencies of market competition do not dictate a uniform, noninterventionist response by states. A state's role in the market is unquestionably affected by technology and changes in the nature of competition, but the way it eventually acts is a question of politics. It is influenced by the interests of domestic political actors and state institutions and by how they respond to various policy options.

The remainder of this chapter emphasizes the importance of bringing politics into our theoretical understanding of the nature of international markets. Before I proceed, one caveat is necessary, however. When I refer to international firms, or MNEs, I am not referring only to companies of foreign origin. Most of the theoretical analysis focuses on bargaining relations between states and foreign MNEs because there is a large literature to draw on relevant to our discussion. Similarly, because foreign investors have been the focus of investment policy in all three countries, they will also be the focus of my policy histories. But there is no reason to believe that investment policies should be directed any more at foreign firms than at domestic ones. As long as there are firms with international operations, whether they be of domestic or foreign origin, the question of how to make their investments work in the national interest will arise.

The Paradox of International Production

Reading through the international relations literature of the 1960s and 1970s, one gains the impression, especially from the voluminous literature on international production, that the internationalization of national economies creates an inescapable paradox for states. For the state, the movement of national firms abroad means that the likelihood for inducing firms to help achieve national economic goals is reduced. Foreign direct investment by definition means that the MNE is the subject of at least two sovereign jurisdictions—those of the home and the host state. National plans that include a role for domestic firms in industrial policy, for example, may be stymied by incentives of host countries that make it more profitable for MNEs to make their investments abroad. The movement of assembly lines to developing countries to make use of cheap labor and tax incentives in export enclaves is one example. Also, states desiring to protect nascent domestic industries from international competition by the use of tariffs may be constrained in doing so by fear of retaliation in kind from potential export or investment markets. For firms with offshore assembly operations, such tariffs may be self-defeating if they impose duties on the company's own products.

More generally, once a firm's production becomes global, there is no guarantee that it will show greater concern for its operations in the home country than for those elsewhere. If an investment in Ireland would fit an American firm's global strategy better than an investment in Iowa, the MNE has little incentive to increase its investment in its home economy. And if investment conditions are inappropriate in one host market, the MNE frequently will simply pick up and move elsewhere. International investment also creates a paradox for firms. After all, individual firms rely on their respective states to protect them with measures such as tariffs and procurement policies or promote them through subsidies or other support mechanisms. The more restricted the state's capacity to provide such services, the less firms will be able to count on it for assistance.

From this perspective, the expansion of international markets seems to lead to an irreversible erosion of state power, as global economic forces relentlessly push forward to obliterate national boundaries. Paradoxically, states have an interest in encouraging the internationalization of domestic firms—in some cases, it may be the only way these companies can remain competitive. Firms in industries with economies of scale or learning need to become international in order to find new markets to sell their goods and to keep competitors from usurping potential customers. In addition, building a complex organization that spans many countries not only allows firms to take advantage of the comparative advantages of each state, it also creates organizational synergies which can lower overall costs. Also, the larger a firm becomes, the more able it is to create barriers to the entry of future competitors, whether through access to cheaper finance capital, the creation of economies of scale, or the ability to fund major research and development (R&D) projects. Yet by encouraging domestic firms to become international, states seem to be creating the seeds of their own destruction in that internationalization reduces their control over the national economy.

This was the predominant view presented in the IPE literature of the 1960s and 1970s, whether of liberal, Marxist, or radical origin. From a liberal perspective, Richard Cooper persuasively argued that the growing inability of states to separate their national markets severely constrained the possibility for national fiscal and monetary control. Charles Kindleberger startled everyone with his announcement that "the nation-state is just about through as an economic unit."[1] On behalf of the radicals, the authors of *Global Reach* illustrated the immense power of the rising multinational corporation by quoting the president of International Business Machines (IBM) as saying, "For business purposes, the boundaries that separate one nation from another are no more real than the equator." World systems theorists such as Immanuel Wallerstein and André Gunder Frank argued that state policies were to a large extent determined by the position they held in a capitalist world economy divided into core, periphery, and semiperiphery.[2] Marxist authors such as Robin Murray systematically enumerated the ways in which the internationalization of capital weakened the national state.[3] Generally, the prospects for state intervention seemed grim.

Given the spectacular growth of multinational enterprises and international trade in this period, it is not surprising that the IPE literature reflected the overwhelming influence these changes were having on the world. But in their desire to document the impact of the economic changes, these scholars largely bypassed the role that states and political factors played in the emerging postwar political

1. Richard Cooper, "Interdependence and Foreign Policy in the Seventies," *World Politics* 24, no. 2 (1972); Charles Kindleberger, *American Business Abroad* (New Haven: Yale University Press, 1969).

2. Richard J. Barnet and Ronald Muller, *Global Reach* (New York: Touchstone, 1974), p. 14; Immanual Wallerstein, *The Modern World System*, 2 vols. (New York: Academic Press, 1974 and 1980); and André Gunder Frank, *Capitalism and Underdevelopment in Latin America* (London: Modern Paperbacks, 1969).

3. Robin Murray, "The Internationalization of Capital and the Nation State," *New Left Review*, no. 67 (May–June 1971).

economy.[4] In this respect, the work of this period, including that of the Marxists and radicals, reflected a singularly liberal understanding of the nature of markets. That is, they conceived of the market as primarily a private economic institution, where anonymous buyers and sellers gathered to exchange goods. This is not to say that they had no appreciation of the political *implications* of markets, but rather that they did not consider the political nature of markets themselves. If there was a criticism of liberal arguments about market operations, it was that they ignored market imperfections. Thus considerable emphasis was placed on the concept of market power and the dominance of monopolies or oligopolies in international markets.[5]

Theorists who emphasize the overwhelming impact international markets and international firms have on national political power are missing an important aspect of economic interactions. They ignore how global markets came into being in the first place, and how states determine the shape of competition in international markets. In essence, they omit a central characteristic of capitalist markets: the role of states in creating, shaping, and legitimating market operations. The *true* paradox of international production is not that states push for the creation of an international institution (the market) that ultimately creates the seeds of their own destruction. Rather, it is that an institution that appears to be so clearly and consummately global has such a fundamentally national foundation. Understanding why this is so necessitates a more in-depth analysis of the relationship between states and markets.

THE INTERACTION BETWEEN THE STATE AND THE MARKET

The Market as Prison

The perception in the international political economy literature that the internationalization of markets makes nation-states increas-

4. Two notable exceptions are Robert Gilpin's *U.S. Power and the Multinational Corporation* (New York: Basic Books, 1975) and Raymond Vernon's *Sovereignty at Bay* (New York: Basic Books, 1974). While the title of Vernon's book might lead one to believe he is describing the demise of the nation-state, in fact one of his central arguments is how national political reactions were affecting bargaining relations between states and MNEs.

5. See especially Stephen Hymer, *The International Operations of National Firms* (Cambridge: MIT Press, 1976).

ingly obsolete is similar to an argument presented across a wide ideological spectrum in the comparative politics literature. Essentially, the argument is that a state's participation in any market, whether national or international, restricts its opportunities for intervention in the economy. Some argue further that state intervention disrupts efficient market operations. For example, those on the neo-conservative right maintain that the slower growth, stagflation, and high budget deficits of the 1970s and 1980s were due to the Keynesian policies implemented after World War II.[6] Throughout the 1980s, many governments accepted the neo-conservative argument that extensive state intervention in the economy was the source of these ills and embarked upon a series of privatizations and programs involving reduced social spending.

This argument is not restricted to the Right, however. Numerous authors on the Left have also argued that there is a fundamental conflict between state intervention in the economy and the smooth operation of capitalism. Many of these theorists focus on the contradiction inherent in the state's need to legitimate while at the same time accumulate. They argue that in order to legitimate itself, the state must give in to the demands of various constituencies for increased social spending. These expenditures—in the form of both welfare policies and subsidies to private capital—build steadily over time as they become cumulative. As the bill for these programs mounts, sources of funds must be expanded, or a fiscal crisis will ensue. A catch-22 situation for the state results: demands on the state for increased spending continue, but the resources to fund these expenditures can be provided only through increased taxation of constituents—the very groups demanding state assistance. The result is a legitimation crisis for the state, a reflection of the futility of attempts to intervene in the operation of capitalist markets.[7]

A related variant of this argument is espoused by both Marxist and more mainstream theorists. Essentially, their goal is to illustrate how

6. For variants of the neo-conservative argument, see George Gilder, *Wealth and Poverty* (New York: Basic Books, 1981); Bruce Scott, "Can Industry Survive the Welfare State?" *Harvard Business Review* 60, no. 5 (1982); and R. Bacon and W. Eltis, *Britain's Economic Problems: Too Few Producers* (London: Macmillan, 1978).

7. See James O'Connor, *The Fiscal Crisis of the State* (New York: St. Martin's, 1973); Alan Wolfe, *The Limits of Legitimacy* (New York: Free Press, 1978); and Samuel Bowles and Herbert Gintis, "The Crisis of Liberal Democratic Capitalism," *Politics and Society* 11, no. 1 (1982).

the imperatives of a market economy *constrain* state policymaking. In contrast to the leftist theories focusing on legitimacy, this body of work emphasizes the influence of capital on state policy, and the manner in which that influence is exerted. In a persuasive essay discussing the interaction between the market and politics, Charles Lindblom argues that the market in fact acts as a "prison," channeling ideas and policies in a way that conforms to market prerogatives.[8] He maintains that a critical aspect of market economies is that key actors in the economy, namely business people, have to be "induced" to perform their functions. If a national economy is to thrive, it is critical that businesses perform the important functions of investing, innovating, and employing. Because such functions have an effect on jobs, prices, the standard of living, and general economic security, government officials cannot help but be concerned with how well business performs them. If business decides that investment conditions are not appropriate and that sufficient profits will not accrue, it will refuse to invest. The adverse economic conditions that would result could bring down a government. Therefore, it is in the interest of states to ensure that business is sufficiently motivated.

Since macroeconomic policies implemented by the state concerning taxes, interest rates, and the like have an impact on investment decisions, it follows that states have an interest in providing investment policies which secure business approval. Business actors thus hold a privileged position: "Any change in their position that they do not like is a disincentive, an anti-inducement, leading them not to perform their function or to perform it with less vigor. Any change or reform they do not like brings to all of us the punishment of unemployment or a sluggish economy."[9]

Other theorists have argued in a similar fashion, albeit from a different perspective. Like Lindblom, Fred Block maintains in his early work that state managers pursue policies that are in the general interest of capital because they are dependent on a reasonable level of economic activity. State managers rely on a growing economy both

8. Charles Lindblom, "The Market as Prison," reprinted in Thomas Ferguson and Joel Rogers, eds., *The Political Economy: Readings in the Politics and Economics of American Public Policy* (Armonk, N.Y.: M. E. Sharpe, 1984).

9. Ibid., p. 6.

as a source of income (through taxation or borrowing) and as a source of political legitimation. State measures that contradict the general wishes of capital are feasible, but they come only as a result of intense political struggle on the part of the working class.[10] Similarly, Claus Offe argues that advanced capitalist states rely on capital both to maintain capital accumulation and to help legitimize state activities by ensuring the sustainability of the exchange process. Capital controls the volume, timing, and nature of the exchange process. Thus Offe claims, "Every interest the state (or the personnel of the state apparatus, its various branches and agencies) may have in their own stability and development can only be pursued if it is in accordance with the imperative of maintaining accumulation; this fundamental dependency upon accumulation functions as a selective principle upon state policies."[11]

Finally, in an article designed to show the inevitable dilution of socialist policies once social democratic parties enter into electoral politics, Adam Przeworski notes, "the very electoral support for any particular government depends upon actions of capitalists. People do not vote exclusively for 'public goods' when they vote for a party: they vote against the incumbent government when their personal income falls or unemployment increases. Hence any party is dependent upon private capital even for its electoral survival in office."[12]

The common thread throughout all these arguments is how the market restricts state options in capitalist economies. It is important to note, however, that there is a difference between the argument that state intervention in the economy *impairs* the operation of capitalism and the position that policymaking is *constrained* by market imperatives. Advocates of the first thesis (such as Bruce Scott, George Gilder, James O'Connor, and Alan Wolfe) see state involvement in the economy as inevitably leading to crisis and contradiction. In contrast, those focusing on the constraints markets place on

10. Fred Block, "The Ruling Class Does Not Rule," *Socialist Review* 7 (May–June 1977).

11. Claus Offe, "The Theory of the Capitalist State and the Problem of Policy Formation," in Leon Lindberg, Robert Alford, Colin Crouch, and Claus Offe, *Stress and Contradiction in Modern Capitalism* (Lexington, Mass: D. C. Heath, 1973), p. 126.

12. Adam Przeworski, *Capitalism and Social Democracy* (Cambridge: Cambridge University Press, and Paris: Editions de la Maison des Science de Homme, 1985), p. 42.

policymaking (like Block, Lindblom, Przeworski, and Offe) allow that state intervention is necessary and feasible but argue that the room for maneuver is highly restricted.

There is considerable evidence to confirm the idea that intervention does not disrupt the normal functioning of capitalist markets. In fact, many have shown that there is no necessary relation between interventionist social democratic policies and economic disruption. For example, in a study of nineteen countries David Cameron shows that there is no direct connection between high inflation, low growth, and increased levels of public spending. Others have argued that market solutions are not always the most efficient response to economic problems.[13] Still others have maintained that the failure of social democratic policies is often due to poor or inappropriate policy choices, rather than to some inevitable tendency to policy dilution.[14]

But the notion that the market acts as a "prison," constraining our actions and ideas, has considerably more empirical and analytical merit. Who could deny the punishment doled out to transgressors of international market logic such as the French Socialists during 1981–82, or Ortega's Nicaragua, or Allende's Chile? Governments seeking to carve out a socialist path in an interdependent capitalist world economy have confronted all the predictable market reactions: capital flight, sinking currencies, investment strikes, and sometimes the political wrath of defenders of the capitalist system (such as the United States).

Despite the evidence to support the market-as-prison argument, however, there are numerous counterexamples of instances where states have implemented policies that appear to defy the interests of capital with relative impunity. We will see in Chapter 2, for example, that regulations on foreign direct investors do not deter foreign investment as such an argument would predict. In fact, foreign investment regulatory policies seem to have little or no impact

13. See David Cameron, "The Limits of the Public Economy," *Annals of the American Political Science Association*, January 1982, and Block, "Rethinking the Political Economy of the Welfare State," in Fred Block, Richard Cloward, Barbara Ehrenreich, and Frances Fox Piven, *The Mean Season: The Attack on the Welfare State* (New York: Pantheon Books, 1987).

14. Gosta Esping-Anderson, *Politics against Markets: The Social Democratic Road to Power* (Princeton: Princeton University Press, 1985), and David Cameron, "The Colors of a Rose" (Paper presented at the American Political Science Association Meeting, Washington, D.C., August 1986).

on investment flows. Similarly, according to a study conducted by the Organization for Economic Co-operation and Development (OECD), redistributive tax policies do not have a significant impact on labor supply or savings and investment rates.[15] More recently, Przeworski has shown that there are numerous ways for states to influence income distribution without reducing investment, and that governments can counteract the irrationality of capitalist markets through fiscal policies, public or cooperative ownership structures, and social policies.[16] Indeed, countries such as Norway, Austria, and Sweden have pursued such policies for decades without witnessing massive capital flight, even though it meant that domestic firms turned less of a profit than those in other countries.[17]

How can we account for these apparent exceptions to the rule? The answer lies in examining a less emphasized aspect of the market-as-prison argument. In addition to their structural economic arguments, these authors provide important insights into the political aspects of market operations. Lindblom explicitly notes the political nature of markets. He remarks that in principle, "governments can redistribute income and wealth and repeat the redistribution as frequently as wished. Their disinclination to do so requires a political explanation rather than reference to market forces."[18] Lindblom further notes that business and government are in constant dispute over issues such as tax rates and regulatory policies. He postulates a continuum of possible combinations of business and government control ranging from an extreme form of laissez-faire to a complete lack of business autonomy. While the extreme positions on this continuum are not disputed, some narrow range of disagreement

15. Peter Saunders and Frederich Klau, *The Role of the Public Sector: Causes and Consequences*, OECD Economic Studies, no. 4 (Paris: OECD, 1985).

16. Adam Przeworski and Michael Wallerstein, "Structural Dependence of the State on Capital," *American Political Science Review* 82, no. 3 (1988), and Adam Przeworski, "Could We Feed Everyone? The Irrationality of Capitalism and the Infeasibility of Socialism," *Politics and Society* 19, no. 1 (March 1991).

17. For example, in 1985, ten cents of every dollar of value-added in manufacturing was consumed by companies in Austria and Norway, as opposed to about forty cents by companies in the United States and the United Kingdom. World Bank data cited in Przeworski, "Could We Feed Everyone?" p. 21.

18. Charles Lindblom, *Politics and Markets* (New York: Basic Books, Inc., 1977), p. 44.

between them is. Over the past several decades, he argues, this range has slowly shifted toward increasing authority for governments.[19]

Block addresses this issue by posing the question, "If the state is unwilling to risk a decline in business confidence, how is it then that the state's role has expanded inexorably throughout the twentieth century?"[20] He argues that in its attempts to protect itself from the ravages of the market, the working class has applied critical political pressure to increase state services and state regulation of the economy. For Block, pressure for state involvement in the economy also comes from state managers. As their powers expand along with the growing state, state managers have an interest in increasing their influence by pushing for higher levels of economic intervention. He maintains that the likelihood of expanding state involvement is particularly high in times of economic crisis, when the potential for influence from capital is low. In his later work, Block argues that many barriers to state intervention in the economy are political and ideological and can be overcome given the political will to do so.[21]

Block challenges the notion that states that institute extensive social programs experience capital flight because of the efficiency implications of such government policies. In fact, he argues, redistributive policies might strengthen the domestic market and create even more investment opportunities. But domestic and international businesses do not wait around to see the potential benefits of such policies—instead, they pick up their investment dollars and take flight, fearing that they will face higher taxes and an increasingly powerful labor force.[22] He notes that arguing that state intervention automatically disrupts the functioning of markets "mistakes the political preferences of an extremely powerful interest group for the fundamental logic of an economic system."[23]

The cases examined here corroborate Block's argument that state

19. Ibid., chap. 13.

20. Block, "Ruling Class," p. 20.

21. Fred Block, "Beyond Relative Autonomy: State Managers as Historical Subjects," in Ralph Miliband and John Saville, eds., *The Socialist Register 1980* (London: Merlin Press, 1980), and Block, "Political Choice and the Multiple Logics of Capital," *Theory and Society* vol. 15, nos. 1 and 2 (1986).

22. Block, "Political Choice," pp. 185–86.

23. Ibid., p. 189.

intervention does not decrease national competitiveness. On the contrary, they show how the lack of effective state intervention in Canada and the United States has had an adverse effect on economic welfare. But evidence from these case studies shows that we can go further than Block to argue that, often, highly interventionist policies do not even result in capital flight. The Mexican case in particular reveals that although capital may complain about state intervention, such policies frequently have little or no impact on investment.

In fact, state intervention is often taken at the behest of capital. Lindblom was correct to note that business has a privileged position in the political battles surrounding state intervention. That interventionist policies commonly appear because capital supports them may in itself offer small comfort to those who wish to implement policies that might counter the interests of capital or, in other words, that are not market conforming. There are, however, a wide variety of market-conforming policies. The cases studies show that the interests of capital are in reality quite malleable and that business can often be persuaded to put up with the nuisance of policies that benefit labor or the greater community simply because it perceives the advantages of such policies for itself. This allows states considerable leeway in their approaches to market intervention.

The relationship between state policies and economic actors is obviously very complex. To understand the nature of markets, we must examine the political machinations involved in persuading capital and other social actors to buy into such policies. Market relationships reflect a tangled web of social and political influences as much as they do economic exigencies. Market forces are thus far less immutable than they first appear, I argue, because states have both a reactive and a proactive relationship to the market that is historically determined and therefore will vary across and even within states.

State Reaction to the Market

Up to this point, I have described the state as a sort of billiard ball that acts and reacts in response to the market. This viewpoint is no longer tenable. If we are to understand how various states interact with the market, we must see how the market is internalized within the domestic political economy of each country. This exercise will illustrate that state intervention in the market is as constrained politically as it is economically and that social and political relations shape state interactions with the market as much as anonymous exchange relationships do.

An extensive literature on comparative politics has amply illustrated the importance of examining domestic political factors to find an explanation for the differences in state intervention across countries.[24] These studies focus on the different responses of states to a single international shock, or on the varying approaches countries have to organizing and directing their economies. They provide an important contribution to an understanding of state relations with the market because they emphasize the capacity for politics in market relations. Domestic political forces form an essential element of state power, acting as both an enabling and a constraining force in terms of state intervention in the market. If political coalitions supporting state intervention exist, a state's ability to implement such policies will be enhanced. The absence of domestic political support, however, does not augur well for effective state intervention. But integrating domestic politics into the study of relations between the state and international markets presupposes some understanding of the relationship, first, between national political forces and the international market, and second, between these political forces and the state.

International market forces influence national political forces to the extent that they become woven into class relations of each country. One of the most significant contributions of the dependency theorists was their contention that the international market has an influence not just at a policymaking level but also at a more basic social and political level. For example, once an MNE invests in a host country's economy, the international market takes a concrete form domestically as international capital forms lobbying groups that pressure for policies reflecting its global outlook and enters into

24. See, for example, Peter Katzenstein, ed., *Between Power and Plenty* (Madison: University of Wisconsin Press, 1978); John Goldthorpe, ed., *Order and Conflict in Contemporary Capitalism* (Oxford: Clarendon Press, 1984); John Zysman, *Governments, Markets, and Growth* (Ithaca: Cornell University Press, 1983); and Andrew Shonfield, *Modern Capitalism* (Oxford: Oxford University Press, 1958).

alliances with various domestic interests. Furthermore, the presence of international capital in an economy can affect the interests of labor, creating divisions between workers employed by international firms and those working for domestic companies. Similarly, it can create divisions among domestic sources of capital—for example, between companies that benefit from contact with international firms and those that are threatened by new and formidable global competitors.

Peter Gourevitch also shows how participation in the international political economy affects patterns of class conflict and cooperation domestically, as alliances between international and domestic elements of capital rise and fall in response to events such as economic depression.[25] Consequently, class interests are in part determined by each group's relationship to the international market. For example, fractions of capital that are domestically oriented will have a different perspective on state policies such as tariffs from that of fractions of capital that rely on access to external markets. In a sense, the international market becomes institutionalized domestically, becoming a part of the political-economic flora of each state. This point is particularly important for the Mexicans, as they seek to integrate their economy continentally. Such integration is bound to redirect the interests of both domestic and international capital away from the Mexican economy to the broader continental economy. A similar phenomenon occurred in Canada, with significant political implications for the feasibility of its investment policies and for the quality of its economic development.

But the interests of domestic political groups or classes are not determined solely with regard to the international market. They are also determined by the relation of such groups to one another and by their interactions with the institutions that make up the state. The complex interactions of social actors with one another and with the state constitute an interpretive web of political and economic relations that affects the way market realities are translated in the domestic political economy. The unique way in which the market combines with the political interests present in any particular coun-

25. Peter Gourevitch, *Politics in Hard Times* (Ithaca: Cornell University Press, 1986).

try will affect the kinds of policies that domestic political groups lobby for and that states deem appropriate. Thus it is not always possible to generalize about the interests of various social actors, nor to predict the way capital (including international capital) will react to attempts by the state to intervene in the market.

One cannot assume, for example, that international companies will rebel when states try to regulate them. Capital's attitude toward such regulations will vary according to its perception of the costs and benefits involved. Will protests against foreign-investment regulations affect the firm's political relationship with the host government or with other fractions of capital? Can it derive any economic benefits from such measures? As we will see in each case study, even the most international of firms will support state intervention in the market if they feel threatened by foreign competitors or think it will protect their market share.

Similarly, domestic capital's reaction to regulations on foreign investment will depend on the extent to which it needs protection from foreign competitors and the degree to which it benefits from the presence of MNEs within the domestic market. Even within domestic capital, myriad divisions exist that reflect varying relations both to the state and to foreign capital. In addition, the institutional capacities of each state and the ideological affiliations of state managers will affect the extent to which individual states can intervene in their markets. The absence of state institutions that are ready and willing to implement interventionist policies forms a serious constraint on the ability of a state to intervene effectively.[26]

Domestic political considerations such as class interests, state capacities, party politics, and ideology have a major impact on the role the state plays in the domestic economy and therefore must be included in our notion of what the term "market constraint" means. Each of the case studies to follow includes detailed analyses of how these factors affect the state's ability to intervene. Examining specific

26. For studies emphasizing the importance of state institutions in the United States, see Stephen Skowroneck, *Building a New American State: The Expansion of National Administrative Capacities* (Cambridge: Cambridge University Press, 1979), and *International Organization* 42, no. 1 (Winter 1988). For a comparative perspective see Peter B. Evans, Dietrich Rueschemeyer, and Theda Skocpol, *Bringing the State Back In* (Cambridge: Cambridge University Press, 1985).

instances of state intervention in different countries will provide a fuller understanding of the variations in state responses to the market and what it means to say that market constraints are in part politically determined. I show that it is impossible to assess the feasibility of state intervention in the economy without considering these political forces. Regardless of how necessary or how feasible state intervention is in an abstract or theoretical sense, if domestic political capacities do not exist to support such policies, state action will not be forthcoming. Conversely, if domestic political groups do support state intervention and the state in question has the institutional capacity to intervene, interventionist policies can sometimes be implemented *even if* economic conditions mitigate against such action.

But studying a state's reaction to the market reveals only half of the reality of state-market interactions. Many comparative politics studies portray the state as presented with objective market conditions to which they must *react*. This view is important in that it emphasizes that state power does not emerge from thin air—a state's position in the market is in part determined by social forces. But the state interacts with the market in other ways as well. What remains to be examined is the state's *proactive* relation to the market.

The State's Proactive Relation to the Market

In practice, it is often difficult to distinguish between a state's proactive and reactive relation to the market. One person's attempt to structure international markets through state interventions is another's attempt to react to the exigencies of global market competition, because the complex dialectic between the state and the market makes the separation of proactive and reactive relations difficult if not impossible.

Assume for heuristic purposes that the market can be divided into two layers. Imagine that the first layer is the "invisible hand" version of the market presented by Adam Smith—an anonymous institution comprised of individual decision makers acting from the profit motive. This is the interpretation of the market presented in neoclassical economics. In this part of the market, decision making is atomistic, and each individual makes her own decisions from self-interest. As these individuals act on their decisions, they create objective market forces that are larger than themselves and to which they are in turn subject. This market of atomistic individuals is highly constraining because it is beyond the control of any single actor. The lack of control stems in part from the absence of information. Because they are in competition with each other, individuals have no incentive to share information. The result is high levels of uncertainty and decentralized control.[27]

The second layer of the market is a much more amorphous web of relations that interconnects individual market participants. In this part of the market, efforts are made to compensate for uncertainty by improving access to information. This is done in two ways. The first method is for firms to internalize markets. To cope with market imperfections or communications problems, many companies reduce transaction costs by integrating upstream or downstream activities or both, thus turning the market into a hierarchy.[28] The second approach is to create informal relationships between firms through what Arthur Okun refers to as an "invisible handshake."[29] This approach involves the creation of cooperative relations between firms that ensure continuity between buyers and sellers. Here reference is usually made to networks between firms such as those found in Japan and South Korea, where trust and cooperation play a major role in inter firm relations.[30] Such relationships are increasingly appearing between firms in other countries in the form of strategic alliances and cooperative R&D agreements.[31]

Of course, in reality these two layers cannot be fully separated. For example, Diane Elson argues that the search for company competitive advantage, dictated by the atomized marketplace, limits this cooperation by placing constraints on sharing and reciprocity.[32] To

27. For an excellent analysis of neo-classical conceptions of the market, see Diane Elson, "Market Socialism or Socialization of the Market?" *New Left Review*, no. 172 (November–December 1988).

28. See Oliver Williamson, *Markets and Hierarchies* (New York: Free Press, 1975).

29. Arthur Okun, *Price and Quantities: A Macroeconomic Analysis* (Washington: Brookings Institution, 1981), cited in Elson, "Market Socialism."

30. Elson, "Market Socialism," p. 22.

31. See Lynn Krieger Mytelka, ed., *Strategic Partnerships and the World Economy* (London: Pinter Publisher, 1991).

32. Elson, "Market Socialism," p. 15.

a certain degree, she is correct. But she ignores the extensive role the state plays in creating this web of informal relationships and the potential for the state to coordinate the quest for competitive advantage. It is here that the concept of a state's proactive relation to the market is so important. By involving itself in the organization of domestic markets, the state can play a critical role in determining the competitive advantages of individual firms by shaping and directing the nature of competition. In this regard, state policy can have a major impact on the international competitiveness of domestic industries as well as of specific firms.

For example, Japan is frequently cited as a country where a special relationship between the state and domestic companies has resulted in spectacular international economic success. Through a process of "reciprocal consent," the Japanese state and private firms have created a negotiated structure of political and market decision making that has had a significant effect on corporate performance.[33] It is true that Japan's economic success is in part a result of high tariff policies designed to protect domestic firms. But by far the most important form of Japanese state intervention is its role in monitoring and shaping competition in the domestic market by encouraging firms to collaborate on particular products and technologies and by guaranteeing a market for these goods through state procurement policies. The web of relations created between firms and the state is a form of state intervention fundamentally different from the implementation of policies such as tariffs, because it affects the very shape and nature of the market.

This phenomenon is not restricted to Japan—in almost any country one can find ways in which states assist domestic firms through subsidies, procurement policies, or tariff barriers. Of course, some states are more skillful at assisting domestic firms than others. But there is no question that considerable opportunities exist for the state to intervene to decrease market uncertainty and to shape market competition.

Such opportunities are particularly prevalent in imperfect markets. For example, a growing body of strategic trade literature shows that through calculated interventions, states can affect the dynamic

33. Richard J. Samuels, *The Business of the Japanese State: Energy Markets in Comparative and Historical Perspective* (Ithaca: Cornell University Press, 1987).

of competition in oligopolistic markets.[34] The authors show that in industries marked by economies of scale or economies of learning, strategic subsidies or protection can affect a domestic firm's welfare in other markets. If, for example, by producing large quantities of goods a firm moves along a learning curve that allows it to produce more efficiently, guaranteed access to a large domestic market will help it move down that curve more rapidly, thus making it more competitive in foreign markets.[35] Protected markets can offer national firms a foundation from which they can spring out into the international economy. Chapter 5 outlines how Mexico's regulation of foreign investors garnered the support of MNEs by providing them with market shares that were protected from other competitors.

More generally, states can have an important impact on corporate strategies and firm competitiveness through R&D policies. By working closely with domestic companies and providing R&D subsidies, states can affect the pace of technological development within the national industry. Naturally, more rapid technological development will help domestic firms both at home and abroad. In addition, production subsidies can affect a firm's ability to ride out a period of uncertainty whereas under normal market conditions it might choose to leave the market. In industries where a large market share is necessary to recoup production or R&D costs, for example, the willingness of a state to underwrite a firm's losses until optimal market share is reached will encourage the company to stay in the market. Conversely, because the subsidized firm's ability to wait out short-term falls in profits is so credible, foreign competitors not benefiting from subsidies may leave the market, thus increasing the subsidized company's potential market share.[36]

34. See, for example, Paul Krugman, *Strategic Trade Policy and the New International Economics* (Cambridge: MIT Press, 1986); Barbara Spencer and James Brander, "International R&D Rivalry and Industrial Strategy," *Review of Economic Studies* 50 (October 1983).

35. Paul Krugman, "Import Protection as Export Promotion," in H. Kierzkowski, ed., *Monopolistic Competition and International Trade* (Oxford: Oxford University Press, 1984).

36. James Brander, "Rationales for Strategic Trade and Industrial Policy," in Krugman, *Strategic Trade Policy*, and Paul Krugman, "Is Free Trade Passé?" *Economic Perspectives* (Chicago: Federal Reserve Bank, Fall 1987).

Finally, in electronics industries such as computers and telecommunications, states can help firms acquire economies of scale by creating common standards across markets so companies can sell their products abroad. In the telecommunications industry, cooperative state efforts such as the Research and Development for Communication in Europe (RACE) program are important attempts to compensate for the fragmented nature of European markets.

Most important, political actions by the state have an impact on a firm's conception of what is "rational" action in the market. Insofar as state actors affect market incentives, they affect market rationality. As Peter Hall argues, "Even if we regard firms as strategic actors we must recognize that their most rational course of behavior cannot be derived a priori. It will be determined, in large measure, by the set of inducements that confront them within a particular complex of market institutions. Market rationality is a historically specific form of rationality."[37]

But states do far more than affect the shape of competition in the market. In many cases, international markets would not exist were it not for the ongoing efforts of states to construct them.

Economic historians have long contested the idea that markets spring spontaneously from the anonymous needs of various buyers and sellers. Marxist historians such as Maurice Dobb have shown the persistent importance of state actions in the construction of domestic and international markets. From the beginning, capitalist markets required careful nurturing and monitoring by the state. For example, Dobb shows the indispensable role of political intervention in the long, laborious road to Britain's capitalist development. Along this tortuous path, political intervention—whether by towns, the monarchy, or Parliament—prodded and molded the development of competitive markets. Although the enclosure of feudal landholdings began in the fifteenth century, it was the legislation of the general Enclosure Act of 1801 that finally drove peasants off feudal landholdings into the cities, providing a potential labor force for nascent capitalist operations. As early capitalists expanded their

---

37. Peter Hall, *Governing the Economy: The Politics of State Intervention in Britain and France* (New York: Oxford University Press, 1986), p. 36.

productive capacities throughout the sixteenth and seventeenth centuries, they repeatedly called for political intervention to remove the restrictive craft guild and mercantile monopolies that prohibited them from freely trading their goods. Parliament gained its first victory in this regard through bills introduced in 1601 and 1604, which abolished all monopoly privileges in foreign trade.[38]

Even as these actions gradually pushed Britain toward freer and more competitive trade, extensive state intervention in the workings of the market was assumed and accepted. As Dobb notes, "The free trade that was sought was a conditional and limited free trade conceived, not as a general principle, as was to be the case in the nineteenth century but as *ad hoc* proposals to remove certain specific restrictions that bore down upon the complainants. Neither in internal affairs nor in foreign trade did the movement against monopolies imply any general abrogation of control by the State or by trading and industrial companies."[39]

Of course, the extent of this intervention was reduced considerably during the free trade era of the nineteenth century. Dobb argues, however, that even the free trade that formed such an essential ingredient of nineteenth-century British capitalism was but a brief, historically specific period of British capitalist development. "Even in the native land of *Smithianismus* and Manchester liberalism, the tide was beginning to turn in favour of monopolistic privilege and regulation before the nineteenth century drew to its close."[40]

Similarly, Block shows how the spread of the international trade and investment nexus after World War II was a direct result of efforts by the American state to ensure the free flow of goods and capital between the advanced industrialized economies of Europe and North America. In order to ensure markets for U.S. exports to Western Europe, the Americans had to expand the capacity of European economies so they could earn the foreign exchange necessary to purchase such goods. The U.S. government transferred billions of dollars to Europe through the Marshall Plan to ensure that Euro-

38. Maurice Dobb, *Studies in the Development of Capitalism* (New York: International Publishers, 1963).
39. Ibid., p. 164.
40. Ibid., p. 193–94.

peans earned enough dollars through private transactions to balance their multinational trade.[41] Block argues that the Marshall Plan was designed to ensure free access to European markets in the face of an upsurge of European forces that opposed multilateralism, favoring instead a set of national capitalisms joined by bilateral trade arrangements.

In order to encourage the Europeans to deal with the U.S., the Americans had to help European companies become more competitive. Part of the plan was to create an integrated European market. By doing so, the United States hoped to encourage the growth of economies of scale, technological advances, and the abandoning of tariffs. Yet, while the Americans encouraged some level of cooperation in Europe, their support for the Treaty of Rome was conditional on a guarantee of national treatment for American-owned subsidiaries in European markets.[42]

In fact, one of the most prominent examples of states purposefully creating a supranational market was the founding of the European Community (EC). Not surprisingly, the EC is also a primary example of an economic institution that is constantly overshadowed by political considerations. It was not giant European firms that urged their respective states to move toward the enlargement of their markets. Rather, it was state actors that conceived and orchestrated the building of a common market that was perceived to a large degree as a counterweight to the American challenge.

In addition to expanding the size of European markets, individual states also worked toward creating larger national firms and encouraging collaboration between them in an effort to increase their competitiveness in international markets. In Germany and France, a series of mergers and joint ventures were sponsored directly by the state. In Germany, firms were frequently encouraged to cooperate by both the state and privately owned banks. Particularly in high-technology industries and in steel, companies often entered into government-initiated voluntary collaborative agreements with im-

---

41. Fred Block, *The Origins of International Economic Disorder* (Berkeley: University of California Press, 1977), chap. 4.

42. Gilpin, *U.S. Power and the Multinational Corporation*, p. 108.

munity from the Cartel Act.[43] In France, the state actively promoted mergers and collaboration in the 1950s and 1960s in an attempt to create an internationally competitive industrial sector.[44] As Bill Warren notes, "The idea of national states cowering before the [large corporations] of this world is wholly fanciful: the reality is national states deliberately encouraging the creation of gigantic competitive units."[45]

Karl Polanyi's distinction between laissez-faire and economic liberalism is appropriate here. Polanyi defines economic liberalism as the organizing principle of a society in which the economy is based on the institution of a self-regulating market. He maintains that while it is true that once a market system is in operation less intervention is needed, that "markets" and "intervention" are nevertheless not mutually exclusive terms. As long as the market is not established or needs support, economic liberals must and will call for the intervention of the state to ensure its operation. Hence he claims, "The accusation of interventionism on the part of liberal writers is thus an empty slogan. . . . The only principle economic liberals can maintain without inconsistency is that of the self-regulating market, whether it involves them in interventions or not."[46]

This point is of critical importance for the cases examined here. Those who advocate free continental trade, including corporations, identify free trade with laissez-faire government policies. Yet, as we will see, this belief is a contradiction in terms. Minus a prominent state role in providing for adjustment and ensuring the competitiveness of individual firms, the practice of free trade is highly threatened. Free traders must understand that the terms "free trade" and "state intervention" are not mutually exclusive. The continental economy that is the focus of this book is also a political creation. It would be tempting to characterize it as the natural outgrowth of the burgeoning U.S. economy, the result of giant American firms spill-

43. Georg Keister, "Germany," in Raymond Vernon, ed., *Big Business and the State: Changing Relations in Western Europe* (Cambridge: Harvard University Press, 1974), pp. 75–77.

44. Charles-Albert Michalet, "France," in Vernon, *Big Business*.

45. Bill Warren, "How International Is Capital?" in Hugo Radice, ed., *International Firms and Modern Imperialism* (London: Penguin Books, 1975), p. 137.

46. Karl Polanyi, *The Great Transformation* (Boston: Beacon Press, 1944), p. 149.

ing over state boundaries in the relentless push for globalization. Yet this is not the way it happened. United States firms were content simply to export northward until Canada's National Policy tariffs forced manufacturers to produce locally for the Canadian market. These firms were further beckoned by the promise of tariff-free access to the Commonwealth through the system of empire preferences devised in the early twentieth century. Production ties between Canada and the United States were cemented in World War II through various production sharing agreements and policies designed to enhance the continental integration of resource industries. Once these production relationships were created, trade increased correspondingly. About 70 percent of U.S. trade with Canada takes the form of intrafirm transactions. United States–Canada integration is currently in its third stage of consolidation, via the Free Trade Agreement initiated in 1989.[47]

Similarly, Mexico–United States integration was actively encouraged by state policies such as Mexico's *maquiladora* industry (foreign-owned assembly plants that operate duty-free), which offered incentives for U.S. firms to set up assembly operations on its northern border. This program was made feasible by the U.S. policy of letting the products enter the United States with tariffs only on the value added in Mexico. A devalued peso aided this reorientation of production by cheapening Mexican inputs, such as labor. In contrast, few economic links exist between Canada and Mexico. About 1.3 percent of Canada's imports come from Mexico, as opposed to 65.2 percent from the United States. And only about 1.6 percent of FDI in Mexico comes from Canada.[48] This lack of integration is not surprising; until NAFTA talks began in 1991, no specific policies existed to encourage trade and investment between the two countries.

States also play an important part in legitimizing international

47. Janine Brodie, *The Political Economy of Canadian Regionalism* (Orlando: Harcourt Brace Jovanovich, 1990)

48. Trade figures are from Michael Hart, *A North American Free Trade Agreement* (Halifax: Center for Trade Policy and Law, 1990), p. 68. Investment figures are from *Th. Opportunities and Challenges of North American Free Trade: A Canadian Perspective"* (Ottawa: Investment Canada, 1991), table 10.

markets. I am referring not to the ideological role states play in this regard but rather to their capacity to "protect" national constituents from the ravages of the international market. Again, I draw on Polanyi and his description of the instinctive "protective" reaction of states to the unwanted intrusions of international markets. He identifies a "double movement" of modern society, defined as follow:

> It can be personified as the action of two organizing principles in society, each of them setting itself specific institutional aims, having the support of definite social forces and using its own distinctive methods. The one was the principle of economic liberalism, aiming at the establishment of a self-regulating market, relying on the support of the trading classes, and using largely *laissez-faire* and free trade as its methods; the other was the principle of social protection aiming at the conservation of man and nature as well as productive organization, relying on the varying support of those most immediately affected by the deleterious action of the market and using protective legislation, restrictive associations, and other instruments of intervention as its methods.[49]

Polanyi argues that in response to the efforts of liberal economists to create an unhampered self-regulating market, spontaneous collective and protectionist actions on the part of the state began to appear. Thus he claims, "For a century the dynamics of modern society was governed by a double movement: the market expanded continuously but this movement was met by a countermovement checking the expansion in definite directions."[50] This spontaneous movement peaked in the 1870s and 1880s with the appearance of factory laws, the creation of central banks, social insurance, public utilities, tariffs, cartels and trusts, and so on. In Polanyi's view, there is no question that these collectivist actions occurred as a manifestation of the weaknesses of a self-regulating market system; this view, he maintains, is proven by the fact that these actions were taken rapidly, spontaneously, and simultaneously on a number of different issues and in states that had little or no ideological similarities.

49. Polanyi, *The Great Transformation*, p. 132.
50. Ibid., p. 139.

Furthermore, these actions were advocated by economic liberals themselves.[51]

Such actions were taken to protect society, and the self-regulating market itself, from the self-destructive tendencies of economic liberalism. These protectionist reactions, or "disruptive strains" as Polanyi describes them, were "more than the usual defensive behavior of a society faced with change; it was a reaction against a dislocation which attacked the fabric of society, and which would have destroyed the very organization of production that the market had called into being."[52] If capital simply flowed from one branch of the economy to another as the market required, people's lives and social organization would be destroyed in the process. Land that was used until it no longer remained profitable or was polluted beyond repair would be decimated. Furthermore, productive organization would be threatened as well. If prices fell, and production costs did not fall proportionately, going concerns would be bankrupted, even though the fall in prices may merely have been due to the manner in which the monetary system was organized. In order to keep the society from self-destruction, it was necessary for the state to intervene.

As John Gerard Ruggie argues, this protectionist reaction to the international market created a regime of so-called embedded liberalism in the post-World War II period. After the economic and political disasters of the 1930s, Western government leaders agreed that a multilateral trading and investment system was an essential element of national economic growth. This multilateralism was to be predicated, however, upon domestic interventionism. For example, while international institutions such as the General Agreement on Tariffs and Trade (GATT) were created to encourage the international flow of goods, numerous exceptions to the rules of these institutions were granted in order to allow states to protect national interests. In general, the principle of safeguarding domestic stability and national social policies formed an integral part of the building of postwar multilateral institutions.[53]

---

51. Ibid., pp. 145–48.
52. Ibid., p. 130.
53. John Gerard Ruggie, "International Regimes, Transactions, and Change: Embedded Liberalism in the Postwar Economic Order," *International Organization* 36, no 2 (Spring 1982).

The important role states play in "protecting" constituents from the international market is emphasized repeatedly in the three case studies. An almost predictable reaction to significant and rapid inflows of FDI, for example, is a nationalist backlash by domestic actors threatened by foreign investment. Canada and Mexico experienced a backlash in the 1970s, as did the United States in the 1980s and 1990s. Most neo-liberal economists abhor such nationalist reactions, considering them pure alarmism. Nonetheless, they are real and almost guaranteed to occur. The only way to diffuse this nationalism is to have adjustment policies that cushion the companies and workers that are threatened. Failing to do so will only invite a more extreme reaction. Those who advocate free trade have given this reality very little consideration, despite the fact that by ignoring adjustment policies, they are virtually ensuring that free trade will be politically unfeasible.

This point is extremely important not only in considering the state's proactive relationship to the market but in understanding its reactive one as well. State reactions to the market must be "legitimate," and although ensuring this legitimacy sometimes means withdrawing from the market, often such extractions are not politically feasible because they leave important domestic groups too exposed to market exigencies. The case studies show, for example, that the laissez-faire role of the state in Canada and the United States is a reflection of political, economic, and ideological conditions that make such a role politically legitimate. This is not true of Mexico, where the state must carefully balance the interests of domestic capital and rising political threats on the Left and the Right. States must be careful to provide an appropriate investment environment for firms, but "appropriate" does not necessarily translate into a neo-classical heaven. Some of the most attractive investment environments are those that "protect" firms by guaranteeing them market share, provide them with a skilled labor force, or reduce the costs of social overhead through programs such as socialized health care.[54]

54. For an example of the impetus for state intervention in the aircraft industry, even in the face of extensive privatization, see Jeanne Kirk Laux, "Limits to Liberalism," *International Journal* 46, no. 1 (Winter 1990–91).

The Market Is Not a Prison

It is clear that political actions form an integral part of the growth, nature, and legitimation of markets. In my explanation, however, I had to make a false dichotomy by dividing the state's interaction with the market into two distinct relations: a proactive and a reactive one. In fact, the relation between these two elements is complex and takes a much more interactive form. States play a proactive role in the sense that the national policies they adopt significantly affect the nature of competition in international markets. Over time, however, the actions of individual states and other market actors combine to create something that is larger than themselves. This is the so-called objective market reality that they face and to which they must subsequently react. Obviously, it is very difficult to distinguish between these two relations without degenerating into a chicken-and-egg argument that misses the point being made.

The notion that a state has a proactive relation to the market is important, not in the sense that it denotes a specific "stage" in the state's interaction with the market, but because it emphasizes another aspect of the state-market relationship. Clearly, we must focus on the political nature of markets themselves as well as on the "objective market realities" to which a state must react. Looking at both of these interactions provides a fuller understanding of the state's role in the market, one that has several implications for our analysis.

First, this perception of the market emphasizes that state intervention in the market is not only feasible but is a basic reality of market operations. Moves by the state to intervene, or not to intervene, affect the very dynamic of market competition itself. Even our perception of a state's reaction to the market must change, however, once we accept the notion that market logic is historically specific and is composed of various social and state actors. State reactions must be socially legitimate, and the notion of legitimacy will vary from state to state and over time.

Second, it means a more sanguine acceptance of the idea that states are somehow helpless in the face of international market mechanisms. Rather than looking at the market as a deus ex machina that punishes those who violate some imaginary limit, one must look at the interaction between state and market. Actually, the market is a historically determined social relation. It is the culmination of inputs from individual buyers and sellers as well as state actions informed by the interests of domestic social and political actors. As Paul Auerbach, Meghnad Desai, and Ali Shamsavari argue, "markets, like other economic forms, are a *product* of human action and human consciousness as manifested in acts of planning, and *not* entities whose necessary existence can be postulated away from the sphere of planning and decision-making."[55] In this light, assuming that states will not continue to play an active role in markets once they become international or highly competitive ignores the historical foundations of these institutions. As Block adroitly notes, "The specific organization of [the] world economy can never be 'above' politics. It *is* politics."[56]

Third, and perhaps most important, once one perceives that state actions affect market logic, the neo-classical image of the market as a structure made up of autonomous buyers and sellers collapses. One then realizes that what we are dealing with is not an anonymous economic institution that cannot be tampered with for fear of disturbing a delicate equilibrium. Just as economists such as Joan Robinson have emphasized the fallacy of freely competitive markets and the influence of large economic actors in oligopolistic markets, political economists must stress that markets are in part political institutions influenced by ever-changing coalitions of social actors and state actors. This new perception requires a more nuanced view of market logic and acceptance of the fact that market rationality is historically specific and state specific. It also means that appeals by neo-liberal economists that the state should stay out of the market reflect a fundamental misunderstanding of what markets are.

TESTING THE ARGUMENT

The above discussion of the nature of markets makes several points relevant to our investigation of national investment polices.

55. Paul Auerbach, Meghnad Desai, and Ali Shamsavari, "The Transition from Actually Existing Capitalism," *New Left Review*, no. 170 (July–August 1988), p. 73.
56. Block, *Origins*, p. 213.

First, despite the global, or in this case continentalized, nature of production, there is plenty of space for national policies. States are definitely constrained by international competition between firms and by competition with other countries trying to attract these firms. Rather than making national investment policies obsolete, however, this competition makes them more important than ever. If we consider that the competition between states in itself constitutes a market, the way any single country shapes its national economy is key not only because of the way it affects the configuration of competition but also because of the impact it will have on national competitiveness.

Shaping a domestic market and making it an attractive place to invest does not mean simply offering companies cash grants or cheap inputs, however. As Michael Porter has shown, factor inputs are only one aspect of national competitiveness that also includes related and supporting industries, demand conditions and the structure of competition in specific industries.[57] And as Robert Reich argues, it also involves creating a skilled and motivated work force that can be one of a nation's true natural resources.[58] Such national conditioning does not pervert market logic; indeed, it creates it.

A second relevant point is that the role states play in the market can have serious political ramifications. The importance of Polanyi's notion of a protectionist reaction is emphasized in Chapter 2 and reappears in each of the case studies. Cold exposure to the international market, whether via trade or investment flows, will lead to a major backlash if threatened constituents feel that they are not adequately protected. This does not necessarily mean protection through tariffs, as it is generally conceived. Rather, it means adjustment through labor market policies, social policies, and industrial strategies that give assistance to workers and firms in return for contributions to the economy. By ignoring the need to cushion threatened actors, economic liberals in effect sabotage their own projects by guaranteeing that they will not be politically acceptable. In addition, the three case studies show that by paying attention to

57. Michael Porter, *The Competitive Advantage of Nations* (New York: Free Press, 1990).

58. Robert Reich, *The Work of Nations* (New York: Knopf, 1991).

purely economic factors, such as exchange rates, cheap labor, and lower social overhead—in other words, getting the prices right—the governments of all three countries have set themselves on a collision course. Obviously, prices are important only in a relative sense, and if all three countries simply seek to make themselves attractive in terms of cost, the result can only be a self-defeating cycle of downward bidding.

Finally, it is important to understand the political battles involved in "protecting" companies and workers. If we take seriously the idea that the market is a political construction, we realize that there are major political and institutional barriers to attaining such strategies. Therefore, it is extremely important that we understand the broader political economy surrounding investment policies in each state so that we are aware of the constraints and opportunities they present. Such an understanding will also reveal the importance of Block's notion of "institutional fit."[59] Since state institutions form an integral part of the market, having appropriate institutional structures is essential in both an absolute and a relative sense. A lack of institutional capacity or inappropriate state relationships with business or labor will make the fulfillment of adjustment policies impossible, which can be disastrous if the institutions of competitors are more capable. In the United States, especially, inappropriate institutional structures have led to some very nasty trade wars, investment disputes, and enormous resentment, because Americans believed that competitors were more protected by their states than they were.

To illustrate the relevance of these three points to investment policies, in the next four chapters we will look at the interaction between states and the internal markets of international firms in North America. In Chapter 2 I focus on the bargaining literature on relations between states and MNEs and attempt to discern any broad, generalizable patterns in this interaction. The next three chapters are in-depth case studies concerning the political economy of investment policies in each of the three countries. The complexity of the interaction between states and MNEs may prove unsatisfying to some because, as the case studies show, it is difficult to generalize

59. Fred Block, *Postindustrial Possibilities* (Berkeley: University of California Press, 1990), chap. 2.

about the relationship, other than to say that it varies according to the particular social, political, economic, and ideological configurations of each state.

Rather than deny this complexity, however, I attempt to address it directly. The challenge is to separate the standard components in relations between states and MNEs, from the specificities of individual cases. Alain Lipietz compares this task to that of Umberto Eco's character William de Baskerville in *The Name of the Rose*. De Baskerville sets out to solve a series of murders taking place in a medieval abbey, supposedly perpetrated by a mysterious Antichrist. As Lipietz notes:

> He solved the mystery by looking for a chain of causes and for relations between signs, but he also realized each situation was specific. It is true to say that in one sense all the murders were caught up in the contradictions of the same Benedictine institution and that, in a very specific sense, those contradictions did tend to generate an Antichrist. As to whether or not the hand of Satan was *directly* . . . involved that depends which murders we are talking about.[60]

Whether one considers an analogy between Satan and the market appropriate is an ideological question. But the relation between the hand of that Satan and each individual case is an empirical one. It is to this endeavor that I now turn.

60. Alain Lipietz, *Mirages and Miracles* (London: Verso, 1987), p. 20.

CHAPTER TWO

Regulating Foreign
Direct Investment

States desiring to regulate multinational enterprises are faced with two direct challenges to their ability to intervene effectively. First, by definition, MNEs are international as opposed to national entities. Because their survival depends on successful operation in more than one national market, they fall under the jurisdiction of more than one state. This characteristic reduces the ability of any single state to exert control over an MNE, even if the parent company is based in the domestic economy. Second, the global internal markets of MNEs pitch international economic exigencies against national political initiatives. The MNE's economic rationale is international and may or may not correspond with the political imperatives of any single state. Attempts by states to assert national priorities that do not suit the interests of MNEs may simply lead firms to relocate. These dilemmas apply to both host and home countries. If a multinational company feels its home country is not providing an appropriate investment environment, it can just as easily move. My goal in this and the next three chapters is to examine what role remains for states as these conflicting imperatives clash (at times furiously) above their heads.

Qualitative changes in the nature of foreign direct investment flows since the early 1970s have greatly affected the ability of host countries to regulate multinationals. Rather than building an entire product in situ to service the domestic market, multinational enterprises began building global networks in the 1970s that made use of subcontracting, or rationalization, strategies.[1] In such forms of investment, the MNE essentially internalizes the comparative advantages of different countries within the company's international network. For example, the MNE may farm out the manufacture of various components or the assembly of those components to subsidiaries in countries with cheap labor resources that serve as export platforms in the firm's global network. Alternatively, a subsidiary may make use of a country's R&D expertise or infrastructure to manufacture a single component or product in the MNE's network, thereby gaining expertise or economies of scale.

The result has been the development of what Michael Porter calls "global industries," defined as industries "in which a firm's competitive position in one country is significantly influenced by its position in other countries. Therefore, the international industry is not merely a collection of domestic industries but a series of linked domestic industries in which the rivals compete against each other on a truly worldwide basis."[2] Such strategies are designed not only to improve the overall efficiency of the firm but also to increase its flexibility. As Porter argued, the coordination of production in different countries gives firms flexibility in responding to competitors by allowing them to respond in one country to a challenge in another. It also increases the firm's leverage with host governments, since it is able to expand activities in one country at the expense of others.[3] Thus it is not surprising that Porter concludes, "A country must be viewed as a platform and not as the place where all a firm's activities are performed."[4] Under such competitive conditions, a host country must be constantly alert to government regulations that may encourage a firm to move production elsewhere. This obviously has an impact on each "platform's" ability to regulate FDI.

With the introduction of robotics and the growing knowledge intensity of production, international investment strategies are once

1. For changes in the nature of international production, see Folker Frobel, Jurgen Heinrichs, and Otto Kreye, *The New International Division of Labour* (Cambridge: Cambridge University Press, 1980).

2. Michael Porter, "Changing Patterns of International Competition," *California Management Review* 29, no. 2 (Winter 1986), p. 12.

3. Ibid., pp. 21–22.

4. Ibid., p. 26.

again changing. Many offshore assembly operations relying on cheap labor have become redundant or been repatriated, as production becomes less labor intensive. Also, firms are increasingly engaging in strategic partnerships or joint ventures in order to share the costs and risks involved in knowledge-intensive production.[5] This trend is a significant change in the nature of FDI, because in the past, U.S. multinational enterprises in particular tended to invest abroad in the form of wholly owned subsidiaries. Stephen Hymer argues that since a major motivation for foreign investment was the possession of an advantage, MNEs did not want to risk losing this advantage and creating potential competitors by taking on joint venture partners or licensing the product to a local firm.[6] This stance is rapidly changing as MNEs increasingly get involved in joint ventures, R&D collaboration, and marketing and distribution agreements with other firms.

Companies are joining forces because in many industries market conditions are changing so rapidly that it is impossible for any one firm to keep up with product and process innovations. And as Japanese and European firms have grown to challenge U.S. multinationals, competition has intensified. Consequently, it is important that new products be commercialized and distributed worldwide immediately to cover costs and prevent competitors from usurping the firm's market share. Even the largest MNEs may need help in this regard. In some cases, companies that compete in one product have banded together to develop and distribute goods in another segment of the market.

These new investment strategies have significant implications for states. Some argue that security interests can be threatened by strategic partnerships, since domestic companies collaborating with foreign firms may transfer strategic technology abroad—technology that has often been heavily subsidized by the state. In addition, they may make knowledge-hungry firms more willing to decentralize their R&D capacities in order to bring them closer to future customers or to take advantage of local talent. This decentralization is

5. Lynn Krieger Mytelka, ed., *Strategic Partnerships and the World Economy* (London: Pinter Publishers, 1991).
6. Stephen Hymer, *The International Operations of National Firms* (Cambridge: MIT Press, 1976).

potentially good for host governments, who have complained in the past that MNEs have been unwilling to conduct R&D outside of the parent company. It means that states with trained researchers or a critical mass of innovative firms in high-technology industries stand a good chance of attracting knowledge-intensive industries to their economies. It poses a threat for home countries, however, who risk losing the benefits associated with the centralization of R&D in the home economy.

These new concerns are simply added to a long list of factors that have tempted states to regulate international companies. Canada, the United States, and Mexico have made very similar complaints about the impact of FDI on their economies. All three states have felt pressure to regulate foreign investors because of perceived threats to their national economic and political sovereignty. Corporate strategies dictated by parent company headquarters abroad, for example, can affect national balance-of-payments positions. It is often argued that large volumes of FDI in a domestic economy have an adverse effect on a country's trade balance, since if left to their own devices, MNEs tend to import components rather than source locally. Similarly, parent companies often restrict their foreign subsidiaries from exporting. Because many subsidiaries are designed to service the local market, exporting abroad could increase market competition with the company's other subsidiaries.[7] Economists in all three countries have argued that MNEs have distorted trade patterns by increasing imports, decreasing exports, and (in the case of Canada) limiting exports to raw materials. In addition, national current-account difficulties can result from repatriated profits and payments for services provided by the MNEs. Mexico in particular has accused MNEs of having a negative impact on its balance of payments by drawing capital out of the economy in the form of profits, royalties, and management fees.

Countries also worry about the broader economic impact of foreign investment. For example, MNEs may displace local producers, resulting in oligopolistic or even monopolistic markets. Or, if MNEs

7. This has been a particular problem in Canada, where subsidiaries were traditionally created to jump tariff barriers to service the domestic market. See Glen Williams, *Not for Export*, updated ed. (Toronto: McClelland and Stewart, 1986).

borrow locally, they may crowd out local investors. Scarce domestic capital then becomes more expensive, and one of the touted advantages of FDI—that it brings fresh capital into the domestic economy—is negated. This problem is of particular concern in Canada, where approximately 80 percent of the investment capital of foreign investors is raised locally. And one of the most trenchant critiques of MNEs in Canada and Mexico is that they do not carry out R&D in the host economy, thereby limiting the potential for innovation and technology transfer.

Another common complaint is the challenge MNEs present to political sovereignty. In particular, governments charge that MNEs use intrafirm transfer payments to avoid national tax laws. Multinational enterprises can direct profits among their subsidiaries through transfer payments, and thereby avoid concentrating their profits in high-tax countries. This tactic is also used in countries where restrictions on profit repatriation apply, since profits can be taken out of the country through increased charges on management fees and the like.

Political sovereignty is further threatened by the extraterritorial application of home country laws. In the 1960s, the United States infuriated Canada by refusing to allow Canadian subsidiaries of U.S. companies to sell transportation equipment to Cuba and China. The U.S. Trading with the Enemy Act continues to be an irritant in relations between the two countries in the 1990s. The United States has also applied its antitrust laws extraterritorially—although it did so especially in the 1950s. A more serious threat is the impact that home country controls on the outflow of FDI can have on the economy of a country that depends on high levels of incoming FDI. In the 1970s Canada was eventually exempted from mandatory capital export restraints implemented by the United States that were designed to discourage foreign investment in developed countries. Since U.S. foreign investment comprises such a large percentage of investment in Canada, the Canadian government was alarmed at the potential effect this could have on the economy and lobbied heavily to be exempted.

Many of these issues have also been raised in the United States, but the only truly influential argument for the regulation of FDI there to date has been national security. United States proponents of foreign-investment review have argued that subsidiaries of foreign firms could act as a fifth column within the U.S. economy should the United States ever go to war with the MNE's home country. Alternatively, a severing of relations between the parent company and the U.S. subsidiary during hostilities could inhibit the ability of the subsidiary to produce goods critical to the U.S. war effort. Critics argue that militarily vital technologies should remain in the hands of domestic firms or at minimum that subsidiary operations in sensitive industries should be integrated (connected with domestic industry) or relatively self-contained within the United States.[8] Increasingly, however, "R&D" and "high technology" have become the new buzzwords for proponents of investment review in the United States. As foreign companies continue to challenge U.S. technological superiority, and as strategic partnerships that involve the sharing of R&D with foreign firms grow more common, national security and R&D issues become intertwined.

All these factors convinced Canadian, Mexican, and U.S. policymakers at one point or another that MNEs must be watched more carefully. But how successful have they been in these pursuits? The remainder of this chapter examines the kinds of factors that affect a state's ability to implement investment strategies it believes are in the national interest. In the next section a review of the literature on relations between MNEs and states reveals that a myriad of factors can affect the power of states in both positive and negative ways. In the section following, a schematic comparison of the impact of investment review of foreign investment in Canada and Mexico indicates that there is no direct relationship between state regulations and FDI flows; increasing the regulation of MNEs does not necessarily divert foreign investment, nor does reducing controls necessarily attract FDI. Rather, FDI flows more closely follow the boom and bust cycles of the economy, regardless of state regulations. When investment slumps occur as a result of regular economic

8. These issues are summarized in Edward M. Graham and Paul R. Krugman, *Foreign Direct Investment in the United States* (Washington: Institute for International Economics, 1989), chap. 5. See also Linda Spencer, *Foreign Investment in the United States: Unencumbered Access* (Washington: Economic Strategy Institute, 1991), and Theodore Moran, "The Globalization of America's Defense Industries," *International Security* 15, no. 1 (Summer 1990).

downturn, however, many states deregulate foreign investors for fear that they have alienated them. Because almost all states react this way, fierce competition ensues to attract investors, as each state scrambles to offer lucrative incentives.

The comparison between Canada and Mexico also shows that some states are more prone to reducing their controls on FDI in times of slump than others. Mexico is much more resistant to fluctuations in capital flows than Canada is. The reasons for this difference, discussed in Chapters 4 and 5, also are important in the U.S. case study in Chapter 3. In all three cases it is clear that the relationship between the expanding continental economy and national investment policies is complex, dialectical, and definitely not unidirectional.

THEORIES OF BARGAINING RELATIONS

Political scientists and others have offered several explanations for changes in bargaining power between multinational enterprises and host governments. In general, their works can be divided into three broad categories: (1) those of the traditional "bargaining" school that focus on the specific advantages each actor brings to the negotiating table (henceforth referred to as the Bargaining school); (2) those that focus on institutional factors, such as the centralization or decentralization of investment review boards (the Institutionalist school); and (3) those that focus on domestic politics and attempt to explain how alliances among domestic capital, MNEs, and the state affect host government power (the Political Economy school). I will examine each of these approaches in turn.

The Bargaining school focuses on firm-specific or country-specific factors that can tip the bargaining scales toward one party or the other. The authors show that for the MNE, bargaining strength derives from technological, operational, or managerial complexity. If the MNE has unique technological capacities unavailable to the host, or if the host does not have the production knowledge necessary to run the company, naturally bargaining power will shift toward the MNE. The degree to which a subsidiary is integrated into the MNE's global network—in other words, its trade dependence—

also affects bargaining power. If the subsidiary is dependent on inputs from or sales to other parts of the MNE's network, the host government will be reluctant to nationalize the subsidiary for fear of disrupting supply lines that affect the local subsidiary's well-being or of reducing sales to downstream subsidiaries. In addition, the contribution the subsidiary makes to the local economy will affect the willingness of the host government to press demands that could force the MNE to move elsewhere. Finally, numerous studies have found that the degree of advertising intensity and product differentiation of particular goods can affect the MNE's power. Specific name brands hold a particular appeal for consumers, thus enhancing the position of the MNE.[9]

According to these studies, host governments gain bargaining power when competition between MNEs increases. This is particularly true if the host has a large domestic market in which to sell. Alternatively, other host advantages, such as skilled or cheap labor or natural resources, can enhance the country's desirability as an investment site. Finally, a host government's bargaining power will increase if it can offer financial incentives or protectionist barriers to attract foreign investors. If host countries can make an investment financially lucrative, or ensure market share for the MNE once it has invested, it will increase its attractiveness in the eyes of the investor.

The Bargaining school studies have the advantage of focusing on sector, firm, or even product-specific advantages that can affect state-firm relations. By emphasizing micro level influences on bargaining power, they force a detailed and sophisticated analysis of specific negotiations between the state and MNEs. And as we shall see, understanding corporate strategy and the role a subsidiary

---

9. Studies outlining these factors include Nathan Fagre and Louis T. Wells, Jr., "Bargaining Power of Multinationals and Host Governments," *Journal of International Business Studies* 13, no. 2 (Fall 1982); Donald Lecraw, "Bargaining Power, Ownership, and Profitability of Transnational Corporations in Developing Countries," *Journal of International Business Studies* 15, no. 1 (Spring/Summer 1984); Thomas A. Poynter, *Multinational Enterprises and Government Intervention* (New York: St. Martin's Press, 1985). For useful summaries of this literature, see Stephen Kobrin, "Testing the Bargaining Hypothesis in the Manufacturing Sector in Developing Countries," *International Organization* 41, no. 4 (Autumn 1987), and Dennis Encarnation and Louis T. Wells, Jr., "Sovereignty en garde: Negotiating with Foreign Investors," *International Organization* 39, no. 1 (Winter 1985).

plays in the global network of international firms is a critical element of an effective state investment policy. This approach does have its pitfalls, however. First, the dependent variable, or indicator of state power, tends to be the degree of equity ownership an MNE holds in local subsidiaries. An increase in the participation of local capital in an MNE's operations is considered to indicate increasing host bargaining power.

But, as authors in this school are well aware, using equity ownership as the dependent variable provides at best an indirect measure of state bargaining power. As many have shown, lower levels of equity ownership by MNEs do not necessarily mean less control over their foreign subsidiaries.[10] Thus while Donald Lecraw found a correlation between higher levels of host government equity ownership and factors that should increase government bargaining power, such a relationship did not exist between apparent increases in government equity ownership and actual control over MNE behavior.[11] Furthermore, given the increasing propensity of MNEs to enter into joint ventures abroad of their own free will and without the prodding of host governments, it is dubious whether this measure is any longer a valid estimate of host power.[12]

The second and more important weakness in the Bargaining school approach is that these studies are so microlevel they ignore larger forces that can affect a state's bargaining power. For example, they do not include domestic politics or divisions between state bureaucracies that can enhance or hinder a state's ability to mount a coherent challenge to the MNE. Also, these studies touch only indirectly on the effect of international factors on negotiations, such as increases or decreases in global investment flows or international business cycles.

Institutionalist school theories go a step toward remedying this situation insofar as they focus on the role of bureaucratic politics

10. See Thomas J. Biersteker, *Multinationals, the State, and Control in the Nigerian Economy* (Princeton: Princeton University Press, 1987), and Lecraw, "Bargaining Power."

11. Lecraw, "Bargaining Power."

12. See Mytelka, *Strategic Partnerships*; Kenichi Ohmae, *Triad Power* (New York: Basic Books, 1985); and Karen Hladlick, *International Joint Ventures: An Economic Analysis of U.S.-Foreign Business Partnerships* (Lexington, Mass.: Lexington Books, 1986).

and institutional organization in increasing or decreasing state power.[13] In particular, a debate has ensued regarding the relative desirability of centralized versus decentralized foreign-investment review organizations. Sanjaya Lall and Paul Streeten argue that a more centralized review body increases the bargaining power of a state government by preventing MNEs from playing one particular government ministry against another. Ministries and departments often see things differently and act in contradictory ways, whereas the MNE generally acts as a coherent unit. Thus, the authors maintain, a centralized review agency enables the host government to reduce interagency squabbling and produce a coherent front.[14]

Dennis Encarnation and Louis T. Wells have challenged this notion, arguing that host governments who wish to attract foreign investors often have centralized investment review boards in order to simplify the review process. In addition, they emphasize the impact of bureaucratic politics on bargaining outcomes, arguing that various government units can assert themselves at the implementation stage regardless of what the review board has negotiated with foreign investors. For example, a ministry of Finance may refuse to honor tax concessions or tariff exemptions granted by an investment review board.[15]

These theories are improvements in that they look at environmental factors beyond the firm. They still define domestic politics narrowly, however, looking primarily at institutional factors. For example, Encarnation and Wells focus on the implications of the structure of the review process itself rather than the reasons for the nature of that structure. While they show that a host wishing to attract investment might adopt a one-stop review process and a host more wary of FDI will decentralize the process, they do not aim in their work to explain such basic questions as why a host state decides it wants to attract foreign investment in the first place.

In light of these criticisms, the Political Economy school presents a more complete analysis of the politics surrounding the bargaining

13. See Encarnation and Wells, "Sovereignty en garde," and Sanjaya Lall and Paul Streeten, *Foreign Investment, Transnationals, and Developing Countries* (London: Macmillan, 1977).

14. Lall and Streeten, *Foreign Investment*, p. 74.

15. Encarnation and Wells, "Sovereignty en garde," p. 61.

process. Typically, the authors look at a particular sector or industry in a single country over time, concentrating on the role domestic politics plays in bargaining power configurations. In doing so, they provide detailed historical accounts of the nature of bargaining power between host governments and MNEs, allowing a greater understanding of several layers of factors that can influence each party's power.[16] In addition to sector- or firm-specific factors such as technological expertise, these studies often include factors such as intrastate disputes or domestic political issues. Although they place their studies in the context of the international industry involved, the authors examine domestic-level factors primarily, such as alliances between MNEs and national classes or interest groups and changes in these alliances over time.

Two subgroups exist within this school. The first subgroup concentrates on the politics of economic nationalism within the host country as a determinant of bargaining relations between MNEs and the state. Known as the theory of the obsolescing bargain, this argument predicts that once an MNE has made a large investment in a country, bargaining power begins to shift from the firm to the host country. As host countries become resentful of the foreign dominance of their economies and gain technical expertise, the desire to make a show of strength in the form of expropriation becomes more feasible and more politically attractive. As economic nationalism spirals within the country, a strong stand toward foreign investors is guaranteed to increase government popularity. Thus for these theorists, there is an inexorable tendency for the initial bargain MNEs have struck with host governments to "obsolesce" over

16. For studies of this nature, see Biersteker, *Multinationals* (this study is not sector-specific); David Becker, *The New Bourgeoisie and the Limits of Dependency: Mining, Class, and Power in "Revolutionary" Peru* (Princeton: Princeton University Press, 1983); Gary Gereffi, "Drug Firms and Dependency in Mexico: The Case of the Steroid Hormone Industry," *International Organization* 32, no. 1 (Winter 1978); Douglas Bennett and Kenneth Sharpe, *Transnational Corporations versus the State: The Political Economy of the Mexican Auto Industry* (Princeton: Princeton University Press, 1985); Theodore Moran, *Multinational Corporations and the Politics of Dependence: Copper in Chile* (Princeton: Princeton University Press, 1974); Peter Evans, *Dependent Development: The Alliance of Multinational, State, and Local Capital in Brazil* (Princeton: Princeton University Press, 1979); and Joseph Grieco, *Between Dependency and Autonomy: India's Experience with the International Computer Industry* (Berkeley: University of California Press, 1984).

time.[17] Although this theory was originally applied to investments in natural resources in Third World countries by Raymond Vernon, it has since been applied to developed countries and to the manufacturing sector.[18]

The other subgroup in the Political Economy school is devoted to showing that despite some gains in bargaining power on the part of host governments, their ability to control or regulate MNEs is highly constrained.[19] As Thomas J. Biersteker notes, multinationals have responded to the nationalism of the 1970s with protective measures of their own. "Direct foreign investment was a phenomenon of the 1960s, just as economic nationalism, efforts to control multinationals, and mandatory joint ventures were phenomena of the 1970s. Multinationals were able to develop a complex variety of countervailing measures, but they have also simultaneously reduced the flow of their investments to the developed world."[20] Using the same methodological approach as the obsolescing bargain theorists, these authors show how tactics on the part of MNEs, broad trends in international industries, and alliances between political groups within the host country can work to reduce the bargaining power of the state.

It may appear curious to consider two groups of theorists that come to such drastically different conclusions about state bargaining power in the same category of theories. I would submit it is necessary to do so in order to obtain an accurate, overall picture of relations between states and MNEs. One's perception of whether a state's bargaining power is increasing or decreasing relative to

17. For examples of this argument in natural resources sectors, see Raymond Vernon, *Sovereignty at Bay* (New York: Basic Books, 1971), and Theodore Moran, *Multinational Corporations and the Politics of Dependence*. For a similar argument in the manufacturing sector, see Grieco, *Between Dependency and Autonomy*. For studies questioning the applicability of this model, see Barbara Jenkins, "Re-examining the Obsolescing Bargain: A Study of Canada's National Energy Program," *International Organization* 40, no. 1 (Winter 1986), for natural resources, and Kobrin, "Testing," for manufacturing.

18. For an application of this theory in manufacturing, see Grieco, *Between Dependency and Autonomy*. For an application to developed countries, see Fred Bergsten, Thomas Horst, and Theodore Moran, *American Multinationals and American Interests* (Washington: Brookings Institution, 1978).

19. Bennett and Sharpe, *Transnational Corporations versus the State*; Biersteker, *Multinationals*; and Gereffi, "Drug Firms and Dependency in Mexico."

20. Biersteker, *Multinationals*, p. 293–95.

MNEs depends to a large extent on the case one chooses to look at. In some cases the obsolescing bargain theorists are correct in arguing that host country power is increasing. In other cases, it is clear that state bargaining power is constrained.

The three case studies examined here reinforce this point. Two countries (Canada and Mexico) are deregulating, while the third (the United States) is increasing regulations. Even the varying approaches of Canada and Mexico to this deregulation reveal genuine differences in bargaining power for each state. Canada has almost completely abdicated formal control over foreign investors, while Mexico continues to bargain with foreign investors on a quid pro quo basis (although this may change should a NAFTA be negotiated). The individual political, institutional, and ideological configurations of these countries simply make for different capacities to regulate FDI.

Indeed, the common thread between the two subgroups within the Political Economy school is their emphasis on the impact of domestic politics on state bargaining power. In particular, they stress, the role of domestic and foreign capital in the formulation of state policy is critical to understanding state bargaining relations with MNEs. The three case studies that follow demonstrate that domestic capital's attitude toward the regulation of MNEs is an especially important element of state policy. David Becker's description of the attitudes of domestic capital provides a useful starting point for our purposes. Using Richard Sklar's notion of the "doctrine of domicile," Becker identifies a "corporate national bourgeoisie" that is at once nationalist and developmentalist but that also advocates internationalist ideals. He argues that the corporate national bourgeoisie asserts these nationalist and internationalist interests complementarily. At times it will emphasize nationalist aspects in order to claim equality with foreign capital in the domestic economy. But this nationalism will last only until proximate equality is attained. Once attained, internationalist interests are more likely to prevail.[21]

Becker's formulation is important in that he captures a key char-

21. Becker, *The New Bourgeoisie*, pp. 331–35. Richard Sklar's theory of the doctrine of domicile is outlined in Sklar, *Corporate Power in an African State: The Political Impact of Multinational Mining Companies in Zambia* (Berkeley: University of California Press, 1975).

acteristic of domestic capital: that it is a swing group that can side either with nationalist or internationalist interests. As Theodore Moran notes, "alliances or rivalries on the basis of self-interest are extremely diverse."[22] In some cases, domestic capital may ally with foreign capital against interventionist state efforts to control MNEs. This was the case in the Mexican pharmaceutical industry, where Gary Gereffi found that an alliance between multinational pharmaceutical companies and domestic business formed a strong barrier to the reorganization of the sector by Proquivemex, a state firm. Biersteker found that in Nigeria, the support of local capital for the first indigenization decree bolstered the state's ability to implement it, while its opposition to the second indigenization decree made it impossible for the state to implement the program effectively.[23] On the other hand, Peter Evans's study of Brazil notes that local capital can coexist peacefully with *both* state and foreign investors.[24]

The three cases examined here confirm the schizophrenic nature of domestic capital. "Schizophrenic" is an inappropriate adjective in the sense that it implies that domestic capital's actions are irrational. On the contrary, domestic capital's support for state regulation of foreign-investment fluctuates because it is based on a calculation of this group's concrete interests at any particular point in time. As these interests change, so will domestic capital's attitude toward the desirability of foreign investment regulation. Thus, we see certain factions of Mexican business moving from fairly strong support of regulation in the 1970s to greater opposition in the 1980s. In Canada, domestic capital never strongly supported investment regulation. Its more vocal opposition to it in the 1980s, however, was important in the dismantling of the regulatory regime. In the United States, confusion reigns, as some very internationalist firms suddenly take a nationalist U-turn. It is important to note that in all cases, domestic capital is frequently divided in its attitude toward state regulation of FDI. Particularly in Mexico and the United States, major divisions between capital still exist.

Obviously, the attitudes of foreign investors to FDI regulation

22. Theodore Moran, "Multinational Corporations and the Developing Countries: An Analytical Overview," in Moran, ed., *Multinational Corporations: The Political Economy of Foreign Direct Investment* (Lexington, Mass.: Lexington Books, 1986), p. 15.
23. Biersteker, *Multinationals*, p. 297.
24. Evans, *Dependent Development*.

matter as well. Intuitively, one would assume that foreign capital would be opposed to such measures, since they can constitute significant restrictions on its actions. Yet this is not always the case. Foreign investors who comply with the regulations of the host government often support their continuation for three reasons. First, once they have agreed to host government demands, they do not want to see these regulations dismantled in a way that will give an advantage to competitors who follow them into the market. Second, foreign-investment regulations often provide significant barriers to entry for potential competitors, allowing those who comply to ensconce themselves comfortably into the market with relatively little competition. Third, many foreign investors learn to live with investment regulations and oppose home government efforts to force their dismantling for fear of alienating their hosts. These points are particularly instructive in the Mexican case, where multinationals are extremely ambivalent about their positions on deregulation.[25]

This consideration leads to an apparently perverse conclusion. In contrast to the ambivalence of MNEs investing in Mexico, foreign investors in Canada wholeheartedly support the free flow of investment and have consistently opposed foreign-investment regulations, partly because the concessions demanded by Canada have not been significant enough to provide any real barriers to entry to potential competitors. One could quite rationally conclude that the higher the barriers, the better chance states have to garner MNE support for them. Conversely, relatively low barriers merely constitute a nuisance and are less likely to sway MNEs from their traditional free trade positions. In any case, these factors certainly make one question whether states are giving more help to national citizens or to foreign firms by their foreign-investment review policies.

In the three case studies, I draw from all three schools reviewed

---

25. Evans also notes this situation in the Brazilian computer industry, where U.S MNEs did not wholeheartedly back American efforts to dismantle Brazil's computer policy. Having gone along with Brazil's demands, U.S. companies such as IBM had adapted to the situation and feared a nationalist backlash should the American government push too hard. See Peter Evans, "Declining Hegemony and Assertive Industrialization: U.S.-Brazil Conflicts in the Computer Industry," *International Organization* 43, no. 2 (Spring 1989).

here, but I use the methodology of the Political Economy school. In the process, I demonstrate that state power can vary considerably over time and space, primarily because in some cases states do have greater bargaining power over MNEs. In other cases they have less. As discussed in Chapter 1, many of the constraints on a state's ability to regulate foreign investors are largely domestic political inventions, and thus vary with the political economy of each state. Often it is not that a state *cannot* regulate international firms but rather that it *will* not.

Does this mean there are no broader economic constraints on state capacity to regulate MNEs? Definitely not—broader economic factors such as business cycles also have an influence on bargaining power and can result in some predictable patterns as they interact with national political configurations. The changing corporate strategies of the MNEs also form a constraint on state policies. These two factors, economic cycles and corporate strategies, do not necessarily prohibit state intervention but rather comprise the broad parameters within which state policies must be conceived. States devising investment policies must have a strategic sense of timing and an awareness of corporate planning. As we will see, however, when investment policies are formulated with these factors in mind, broader economic influences present as many opportunities as they do constraints.

Obviously, state investment policies are a complex matter that must be formulated with numerous contextual factors in mind. For now, however, I will simply establish some of the regularities in the state-MNE relationship by comparing the experiences of Canada and Mexico, two countries with long histories of investment review. In doing so, we can see if there are any predictable reactions by either states or multinationals over time.

Trends or Regularities in Bargaining Relations

The economic impact of regulating foreign investors, argued the former U.S. secretary of commerce Malcolm Baldrige, was amply illustrated by the Canadian experience with FIRA (Foreign Investment Review Agency). "That was not a question of chilling investment," he claimed. "That put U.S. investment [in Canada] in a deep freeze and slowed it way down."[26] Such accusations are common by those who oppose foreign-investment review. Particularly as competition between host governments for foreign investment grows, it is generally assumed that any increase in regulation by individual countries will cause foreign investors to take their money elsewhere. Consequently, throughout the 1980s a trend toward deregulation occurred, with many host governments liberalizing FDI policies. This deregulation was accompanied by a battle to attract investors with investment incentives.

Regulation Does Not Divert FDI Flows

The notion that regulation deflects investment away from host countries is a vast overgeneralization. While it is true that extreme or sudden policy changes may at times create uncertainty in the investment environment that may lead to a slowdown in FDI, overall, there is little evidence that regulatory schemes have much impact on investment flows. After all, let us not forget that despite Baldrige's claim, Canada continues to have more FDI as a percentage of its gross domestic product (GDP) than any other OECD country. Similarly, the *deregulation* of foreign capital flows does not appear to have a positive impact on FDI inflows. Thus, although investment regulations may affect FDI flows on the margin, it is a very weak independent variable. If regulatory policies do not have a significant impact on international direct investment flows, what does? The largest single influence is economic cycles—the normal boom and bust of the economy. We can learn more about FDI flows by looking at GDP growth than at regulatory trends. I will consider each of these points in turn.

According to Figure 1, foreign-investment inflows in Mexico were relatively stable until 1976–77, when a slight decline occurred. Investment levels rebounded in 1978–79, when inflows began to build again. This upward trend was sharply disrupted in 1982, with a

26. Testimony of Secretary of Commerce Malcolm Baldrige, in U.S. Senate, *Acquisitions by Foreign Companies*, Hearing before the Committee on Commerce, Science, and Technology, 100th Congress, 1st session, June 10, 1987, p. 7.

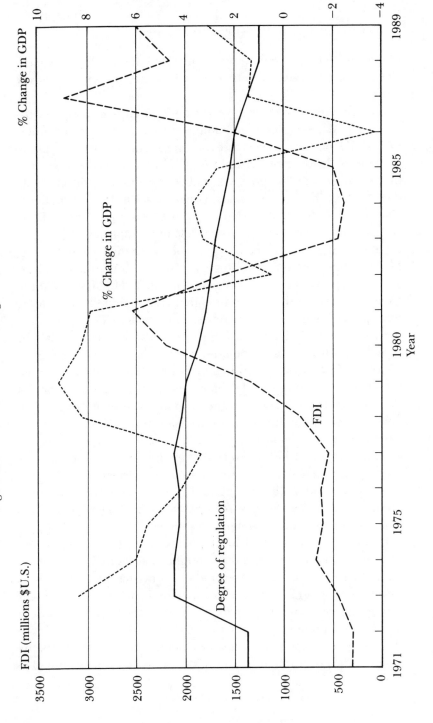

Figure 1. FDI flows and investment regulation in Mexico

Source: United Nations Conference on Trade and Development Data Base, 1971–1989, based on Banco de Mexico figures.

plunge of −63.2 percent in foreign-investment growth. Investment levels were not restored until 1986, when they began to rise once more.

The wide solid line in Figure 1 is a rough approximation of the pattern of Mexico's FDI regulation over time. Since it is impossible to quantify increases or decreases in regulation, this line is simply an attempt to illustrate regulatory trends. If regulations become relatively stricter, the line goes up, if they are relaxed, the line goes down. This schematic approach is hardly scientific, but it should give us some idea of the relationship between regulations and investment flows. For example, the single most important increase in regulation of FDI occurred in 1973, when both the Law to Promote Mexican Investment and to Regulate Foreign Investment and the Technology Transfer Law were implemented. The first law stipulated among other things that foreign investors could hold no more than 49 percent ownership in Mexican enterprises. Thus, the graph portrays this as a significant jump in regulation. Yet, despite the severity of this law, investment levels grew in 1974 and remained relatively stable until 1977, when investment dropped slightly (Figure 1). Even allowing for a lag time between the implementation of the 1973 investment laws and the drop in investment in 1977, it is not clear that the regulations had a major impact. While they may have stalled investment flows for a few years, it is significant that even in 1977, FDI inflows were higher than in the preregulatory years of 1972 and 1973. Moreover, the even sharper drop in FDI in 1982 corresponded with the beginning of the *sexenio* of Miguel dc la Madrid, a president widely recognized as holding an open and flexible attitude toward foreign investment.[27]

In 1984 the government instituted its first round of regulatory reforms, introducing sectoral promotion policies and new regulations designed to cut red tape, and encouraging investment in its *maquiladora* program. This relaxation of investment regulations brought no response until 1986, when FDI inflows picked up once more. It is tempting to see this upswing as a time-lagged response to these (relatively minor) regulatory changes, but in fact it was the result of the government's debt capitalization program instituted in

27. *Sexenio* refers to the six-year term of Mexican presidents.

April 1986. As described in greater detail in Chapter 5, the debt capitalization program gave companies large discounts on their investments if they agreed to convert Mexican debt purchased on the secondary market into equity held in Mexican firms. In 1986, $1.5 billion worth of investment was converted in the program. While this program can and should be considered as indicative of Mexico's more welcoming attitude toward FDI, it should be viewed more as an incentive program rather than a change in investment regulations because it gave investors a discount on capital costs. The distinction between these two sorts of policies is important and is discussed more fully later.

Clearly, changes in the regulation of FDI alone cannot explain changes in investment flows. In fact, one could just as easily describe patterns in FDI according to more general political and economic conditions in Mexico and abroad. For example, the slump in foreign investment in 1976–77 followed one of the most serious economic recessions of the last two decades. The mid-1970s also witnessed widespread social unrest in Mexico, as the controversial president Luis Echeverria clashed with both capital and labor. Numerous strikes and land takeovers by peasants in the mid-1970s contributed to a general ambiance of political instability. Similarly, the dramatic decrease in FDI in 1982 corresponds with Mexico's announcement that it could not make its debt servicing payments, a factor that almost certainly had a deadening effect on FDI flows. In fact, with the exception of the turbulent post-1982 years, there is about a one-year time lag between changes in GDP growth and FDI inflows.

Looking at foreign-investment trends in a single country sidesteps the argument that regulations may create such a negative invest-ment environment that companies do not even consider investing there. Instead, they direct their investments to more welcoming host countries. The data in Table 1 indicate that this was not the case with Mexico. Mexico attracted 25.3 percent of total investment in all developing countries between 1974 and 1976—the period imme-diately following the implementation of harsh regulatory guidelines in 1973. This contrasts with the 9.3 percent of investment to less developed countries that Mexico attracted in the two year-period prior to the implementation of the law.

An examination of Canada shows similar patterns. The most

Table 1. Mexico's share of FDI to developing countries[a]

	Percentage of total to all less developed countries	Percentage of total to all less developed countries except Venezuela and Saudi Arabia	Percentage of total to Latin America
1968–70	8.9	9.3	24.4
1971–73	9.3	9.0	21.4
1974–76	25.3	9.2	24.0
1977–79	8.0	8.7	20.5
1980–82	17.4[b]	17.4[b]	33.1
1983–85	—	—	12.2

Source: José Casar, "An Evaluation of Mexico's Policy on Foreign Direct Investment," in Riordan Roett, ed., Mexico and the United States: Managing the Relationship (Boulder: Westview Press, 1988), p. 44, and United Nations Conference on Trade and Development (UNCTAD).

[a]Investment originating in Japan, Federal Republic of Germany, France, Italy, Netherlands, the United Kingdom, and the United States. Figures correspond to the simple mean of annual shares.

[b]1980–81.

significant change in Canada's FDI regulations occurred in 1974, when the Foreign Investment Review Agency was created. Even after the implementation of this program, FDI levels continued to grow until 1975–76, when, like Mexico, Canada experienced a drop in foreign-investment levels (Figure 2). This outflow was almost certainly the result of the recession following the 1974 oil shocks. The next major change in investment flows did not occur until 1981–82, when Canada experienced a net outflow of foreign direct investment. Almost all the gross outflow of investment during this period occurred in the petroleum and gas industry. The change could be interpreted as a response to foreign-investment regulations because it followed the implementation of Canada's National Energy Program (NEP), a nationalist program designed among other things to increase Canadian ownership of the domestic oil industry.

Still, even this observation must be made with caution. While the NEP undoubtedly created an atmosphere of uncertainty for investors in the oil industry, one of the major downfalls of the program was that it was implemented during a period of falling global demand for oil and gas and general instability in the oil industry. As oil prices fell throughout the early 1980s, there was a corresponding

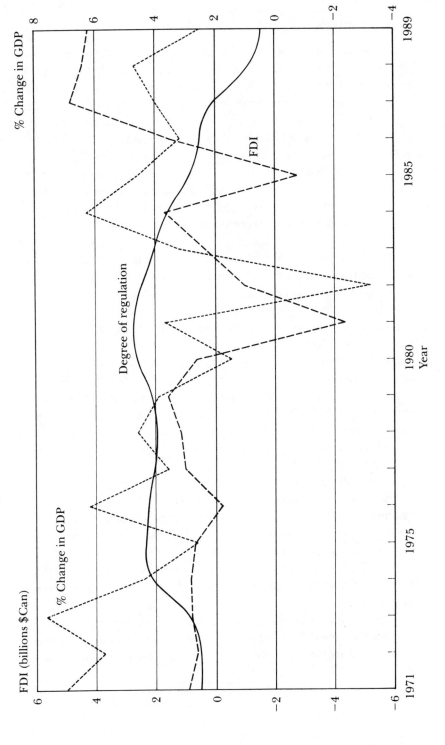

Figure 2. FDI inflows and investment regulation in Canada

Sources: Statistics Canada and OECD Historical Statistics.

decrease in investment levels in the industry. Simultaneously, the market for gas in the United States, Canada's primary export customer, collapsed. The result was a 25 percent overcapacity in the industry. Oil industry executives interviewed shortly after this period listed recession, falling oil prices, and decreased demand as the key reasons for their disinvestment during this period, not the National Energy Program.[28] In any case, the negative net outflow figures are primarily a reflection of the fact that in response to the NEP's incentives to increase Canadian ownership of the industry, Canadian companies began buying foreign firms. Thus net FDI outflows during this time should be interpreted not as capital flight but as divestment that was actively encouraged by government policy.

On a symbolic level, the first significant liberalization of Canada's investment policies occurred in 1985. At this time, the Canadian government announced that it was changing FIRA into Investment Canada, which was to become an investment promoter as well as the regulator of FDI. It also announced more liberal entry requirements, which decreased considerably the number of investments requiring permission from the agency. Actually, a de facto period of liberalization began in 1983 and continued with the election of the conservative government of Brian Mulroney in 1984. After Mulroney's election, few foreign-investment applications were refused. Yet the introduction of Investment Canada and the new liberal investment in the 1983–85 period corresponded with another major outflow of investment.

Admittedly, the Canadian situation is not as easy to interpret as the Mexican one. The Canadian government had the misfortune to implement its two most significant investment policies, FIRA and the NEP, just prior to major economic recessions. The drop in FDI in both 1976 and 1981 were preceded by major slowdowns in GDP growth (Figure 2). Because of this timing, it is difficult to tell whether FDI outflows were primarily the result of state intervention or economic cycles.

A greater understanding of investment flows to Canada and Mexico can be gained by looking at investment flows from the major foreign investor in both countries—the United States. Investment

28. Jenkins, "Re-examining The Obsolescing Bargain," p. 160.

by the United States amounts to approximately 70 percent of foreign investment in Mexico and 75–80 percent of foreign investment in Canada. Changes in FDI patterns in the United States and changes in its GDP growth appear to be closely correlated (Figure 3). Especially in the 1980s, there was a one-year lag time between a fall in GDP and a decline in FDI outflows.

This correlation between trends in the economy and foreign-investment flows has been established elsewhere as well. In a quantitative study examining the relationship between GDP cycles and foreign investment in Mexico, José Casar forecasted foreign-investment rates by using a trend value for GDP between 1950 and 1986. The only investment trend the model failed to predict was the investment upswing in 1986, which was strongly associated with the government's debt capitalization program.[29]

The most pertinent point that arises from this analysis is that overall, FDI flows correspond much more closely to general economic trends than they do to changes in foreign-investment regulations. It is possible to argue that insofar as FDI regulations contribute to general perceptions of the relative economic stability of a country, they must be considered to affect investment flows. As an independent variable, however, FDI regulatory regimes have very little predictive value. In fact, changes in FDI regulations have little impact on investment flows.

FDI Flows Do Have an Impact on Regulatory Policy

Is the converse true, however? Do FDI flows influence the relative liberalism of host country regulations? The answer to this question is yes, although this relationship was much more direct in Canada than it was in Mexico. Returning to Figures 1 and 2, we see that sharp changes in FDI flows elicited changes in government policies in both countries after 1980. In response to sharp declines in FDI in 1981–83, Canada and Mexico both liberalized FDI policies. In Mexico, the de la Madrid government's more flexible attitude toward

29. José Casar, "An Evaluation of Mexico's Policy on Foreign Direct Investment," in Riordan Roett, ed., *Mexico and the United States: Managing the Relationship* (Boulder: Westview Press, 1988).

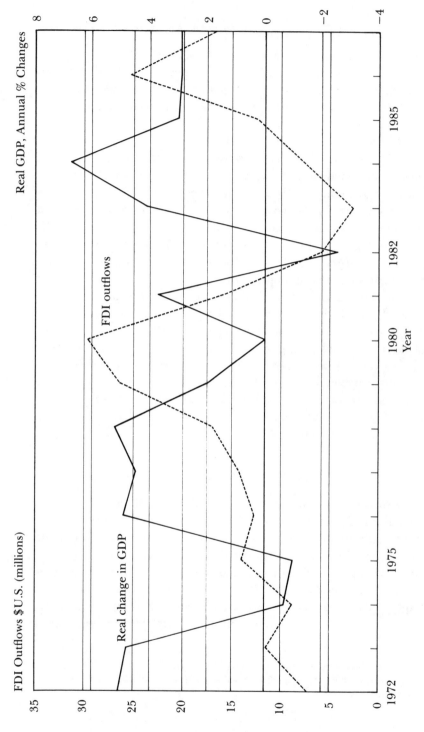

Figure 3. FDI net outflows and real GDP growth in the United States

Sources: FDI outflows: U.S. Department of Commerce: Survey of Current Business (adjusted for borrowing from Netherlands Antilles) (Washington: U.S. Government, 1972–1987); real GDP: OECD Historical Statistics (Paris: OECD, 1972–1987).

foreign investment was clearly a reflection of the economic difficulties the country faced during this period. The same can be said for the even more dramatic changes that began to occur under Carlos Salinas de Gortari. The absence of inflows of foreign capital in the form of loans and FDI greatly exacerbated Mexico's economic problems. In response, both presidents initiated regulatory changes in order to appear more welcoming to investors.

Despite this relative deregulation, however, I show in Chapter 5 that Mexico continues to regulate MNEs to a far greater degree than Canada does. Canada's response to lower investment levels was an immediate de facto liberalization under the liberal government in power in 1983, followed by a more significant de jure opening with the election of the Mulroney government in 1984. This deregulation culminated in the formation of Investment Canada in 1985 and the signing of the Canada–United States Free Trade Agreement in 1988. The FTA significantly reduced investment regulations in all but a few designated areas, such as cultural and communications industries and oil and gas.

Between 1972 and 1980, however, the reaction by the two countries was mixed. Mexico resisted the temptation to deregulate in response to declining FDI levels, while Canada continued to adapt to fluctuations in FDI flows. In a study of FIRA's record of foreign-investment acceptances, Steven Globerman found a close correlation between the number of applications accepted by the agency and general macroeconomic conditions. In general, FIRA's standards tended to be more stringent in times of economic boom than in times of bust. Globerman concluded that variations in the stringency with which FIRA applies its acceptance criteria "appear to be tied at least partially to broad economic conditions. Investors can improve their assessment of FIRA's de facto criteria, therefore, by incorporating current economic information into their analyses."[30] In fact, business in Canada is quite aware of this phenomenon, and business people frequently describe Canadian nationalism as occurring in waves. In commenting on the National Energy Program, one busi-

30. Steven Globerman, "The Consistency of Canada's Foreign Investment Review Process: A Temporal Analysis," *Journal of International Business Studies* 15, no. 1 (Spring/Summer 1984), p. 128.

nessman noted, "Nationalism has a one-to-one correlation with the economy. If you look at the economy over a 25 year period, you'll see nationalism going up and down with the economy."[31]

To summarize, three conclusions can be derived from these data. First, there is no strong, direct relationship between changes in foreign-investment regulations and FDI flows. Strengthening such regulations did not necessarily deter foreign investors, nor did policy liberalization result in a surge of inflows of foreign capital. This conclusion corresponds to the theoretical argument in Chapter 1 that state intervention does not necessarily disrupt the operation of markets, and it indicates that states should not hesitate to make demands of foreign investors if they want to. Yet states are reluctant to do so when confronted with economic downturn.

The second conclusion is that while regulations do not appear to have a significant impact on FDI inflows, the converse is not true. That is, as was shown for both Canada and Mexico in the 1980s and for Canada prior to 1980, foreign-investment regulatory policies are amended in response to changes in FDI flows. Amendments occurred even though there was little or no evidence to indicate that they would lead to greater inflows of FDI. The situation is a familiar one. As Block notes, capital may complain that state regulations are so onerous that it cannot possibly invest, when in truth they have little or no negative effect. In both Canada and Mexico in the 1980s, for example, firms were reacting to broader macroeconomic factors, such as business cycles. Nonetheless, states feel compelled to retreat in such periods, anxious not to be blamed for economic slowdowns. On a practical level, this phenomenon has major implications for state strategies to regulate international firms. Timing is extremely important. In general, states should avoid implementing policies they suspect might not be popular with business if they are in the midst of or due for an economic downturn. Inevitably, any such interventions would be blamed for causing economic stagnation, whether or not they had anything to do with it. Politically, therefore, it is better to wait until the economy begins to slip into a period of growth.

A third conclusion is that Canada is relatively more sensitive than

31. Quoted in Jenkins, "Re-examining The Obsolescing Bargain," p. 160.

Mexico to changes in FDI trends. Although both states deregulated foreign investment in the 1980s, Mexico continues to intervene more extensively than Canada. One of the primary reasons for this difference between the two countries is the existence of a stronger "state tradition" in Mexico than in Canada. Because the Mexican state has historically played a more integral role in the economy, it cannot withdraw as easily from active interventionism. Well-developed social, economic, and institutional ties keep the state bound to an important role in the Mexican economy.

Policy Issues

On a policy level, the evidence shows that states should not be reticent about regulating FDI, since regulations seem to affect investment decisions only on the margin. They should, however, be strategic about the timing of such interventions. But this issue sidesteps the one of whether foreign-investment review in general is a desirable thing.

Reich argues against singling out foreign companies as a focal point for regulation, maintaining that some of the changes in the nature of global production outlined above make it difficult clearly to define "who is us?" or "who is them?"[32] Is a domestically based MNE, he asks, any less likely to move production to a cheap-labor country or diffuse technological advantage than a foreign-owned firm?

While Reich's argument may be valid in an American context, it is less applicable to the other cases examined here. In Canada, for example, many have blamed the country's low innovative capacity on the predominance of MNEs in high-technology industries. And since Mexico relies almost exclusively on foreign firms to bring in new products, technology, and processes, it too must pay particular attention to how such advantages are integrated into its economy. Furthermore, the tendency of MNEs to have larger trade deficits

32. Robert Reich, "Who Is Us?" *Harvard Business Review* 68, no. 1 (January–February 1990), and "Who Is Them?" *Harvard Business Review* 69, no. 3 (May–June 1991).

than domestic firms is of major concern for Mexico, given its continued focus on accumulating foreign exchange to repay its external debts.

Reich's point is important, however, in that it reinforces the notion that the regulation of foreign companies must be integrated into broader industrial policies that also focus on the performance of domestic firms. In Canada it is doubtful that the issue of innovation can be adequately dealt with by focusing on foreign subsidiaries alone. Similarly, in Mexico one of the biggest problems the country faces is getting domestic business to invest, rather than sending its capital abroad. Also, in Mexico, foreign-investment regulations may have benefited foreign firms more than Mexican citizens, given the effect they have had on insulating MNEs from competition. In fact, proponents of foreign-investment review in all three countries have consistently argued that FDI regulations must be entrenched in broader industrial policies, and the verity of this point will be driven home in the case studies.

But what are these industrial policies to look like? Because investment strategies must be tailor-made country by country and even company by company, policy issues specific to each economy are examined in the case studies and in the concluding chapter. But some of the broader issues that appear in the country studies should be discussed here. The first of these issues is the question of investment incentives. An optimal solution for states might be to combine regulations with investment incentives to lure foreign investors into the country. Recall that the sudden burst of FDI flows into Mexico in 1986–87 was the result of a debt-conversion program implemented during this period that provided MNEs with significant reductions in capital costs. By offering investors discounts on the price for which they redeemed debt bought on the secondary market, Mexico attracted $1.5 billion of FDI in 1986. That this was twice the amount that entered the country in 1985 indicates that incentives can be used with considerable effect to attract foreign investors.

Investment incentives are an extremely sticky issue, however, and it is important not to exaggerate their impact. A study by Stephen Guisinger showed that investment incentives do not have an unequivocal positive effect on investment decisions. Also, I do not want to be understood as defending debt conversion policies, since Mexico has had significant problems with this policy. Numerous surveys have found that other factors, such as labor, infrastructure, and proximity to markets are more important than incentives in investment decisions. While two-thirds of the companies surveyed in Guisinger's study indicated that incentives did affect their decision, they also said that in general, incentives were not a major factor in their investment consideration.[33] When asked whether the investment would have been made if the host country had not offered incentives while other countries retained their incentive programs, however, two-thirds of the respondents said no. This response reveals the prisoner's dilemma aspect of incentive programs. Companies may, for example, be willing to make investments without government handouts, but unless all countries agree not to use such enticements, individual abstainers fear they might be deflecting investment elsewhere. The result is self-defeating bidding wars, in which host countries may be forced to make greater concessions than they would like.

This prisoner's dilemma is exacerbated if the three countries in question continue to reduce tariff barriers and concurrently fail to come to an agreement on subsidies. Guisinger's study also found that almost one-half of the respondents who claimed that incentives were important in their investment decisions listed tariff and nontariff barriers as the most significant incentives offered to them.[34] Since the use of tariffs is prohibited in a free trade agreement, states will have to come up with more handouts to increase their attractiveness. This competition between countries and within countries (that is, between provinces in Canada and state governments in the United States) is not healthy and benefits companies who would have made their investments even in the absence of incentives. In addition,

33. Stephen Guisinger, "Host Country Policies to Attract and Control Foreign Investment," in Theodore Moran, ed., *Investing in Development: New Roles for Private Capital?* (New Brunswick, N. J.: Transaction Books, 1986). The author uses a very broad definition of investment incentives, which includes items such as tariffs and quotas. Of fifty companies that indicated that incentives affected their decision to invest, twenty-four indicated that tariff and nontariff barriers were important, while seventeen pointed to fiscal incentives (p. 166). For more detailed industry studies, see Stephen Guisinger and Associates, *Investment Incentives and Performance Requirements* (New York: Praeger, 1985).

34. Guisinger, "Host Country Policies," p. 166.

incentive programs and subsidies are expensive and encourage corporate reliance on government handouts. Federal government transfer payments to business in Canada, for example, amounted to $7.9 billion in 1987, while provinces transferred more than $4 billion.[35] Handouts can also create dependencies. After Mexico suspended its debt conversion program in 1987, some MNEs postponed their investment decisions in anticipation that the program would be reinstated.

Unfortunately, in the absence of international agreements on incentive programs, it is unlikely that states will discontinue to use subsidies. The FTA did not include an agreement on subsidies or on the countervailing duties designed to offset them. Provisions were made in the FTA for further negotiation of such issues, but resolution is not likely to come easily. Even the question of what constitutes an unfair trade subsidy is unclear.[36] Unquestionably, whether such issues are resolved in any NAFTA negotiations will be of major importance in each state's investment strategies.

For the time being, therefore, the challenge for host countries is to use investment incentives strategically by targeting particular sectors and by making the incentives conditional. If host countries could provide a system of incentives that made them attractive as an investment site, then regulate FDI to suit the economic and political interests of the country once it arrived, they would probably incur little risk of deterring foreign investors. This kind of quid pro quo obviously involves performance requirements from both foreign and domestic recipients of incentives. Trade-related requirements, such as local sourcing, export requirements, or taking on local partners, are forbidden in the Canada–United States Free Trade Agreement. Performance requirements related to employment and R&D are permitted under the FTA, however, and for the time being Canada and the United States should make use of such measures to

35. Jean-François Bence, "Analysis of Provincial Transfer Payments to Business in Canada," *International Economic Issues* (Halifax: Institute for Research in Public Policy, April 1990), p. 28.

36. For a discussion of the complexities of these issues, see Murray Smith, "Overview of Provincial and State Subsidies: Their Implications for Canada-U.S. Trade," *International Economic Issues* (Halifax: Institute for Research in Public Policy, April 1990).

ensure some return on their investment incentives. As I will show in greater detail in Chapter 6, subsidies on social payments may also be used without contravening trade obligations. Mexico has continued to stipulate limits on foreign ownership in a number of industries, which has an obvious effect on local sourcing. It has also placed export requirements on foreign firms to ensure that they maintain a positive trade balance. Whether Mexico will be willing to relinquish such measures in the future remains to be seen.

States may worry that such demands will alienate foreign investors, but Guisinger provides evidence to show that MNEs do not strongly object to performance requirements, primarily because such requirements often do not run counter to the company's long-run intentions. Guisinger found that investments made in response to state-mandated performance requirements would have been made elsewhere in only four of the seventy-four cases studied.[37] He concludes, "Performance requirements act as turbochargers for incentive instruments. They magnify and redirect the rents from incentive measures by linking the receipt of incentive benefits to the fulfillment of certain performance criteria."[38]

If incentives and regulations are blended skillfully and on a quid pro quo basis, foreign investors have a vested interest in supporting them. Using a blend of incentives and regulations in this manner more closely resembles an industrial policy than an investment regulatory scheme. Obviously, a state's goal is not to keep MNEs out of the economy but to make them do what the state wants. The aim of FDI regulation should not be to control absolute volumes of foreign investment but rather to decide on the right mixture of incentives and regulations to attract firms to the desired sectors.

Mexico's automobile policy provides an example of how FDI regulation and industrial policy can be successfully mixed. By the late 1970s the Mexican auto industry had become a net importer, accounting for 58 percent of the trade deficit in 1981.[39] Yet as a result of government decrees in the industry in 1977, 1983, and 1989, Mexico became an export platform for automobiles. This auto pol-

37. Guisinger, "Host Country Policies," p. 169.
38. Ibid., pp. 168–69.
39. Casar, "An Evaluation," and Bennett and Sharpe, *Transnational Corporations*, p. 274.

icy is not only an example of skillful quid pro quo bargaining, but it illustrates three other keys to successful bargaining: the use of trade policy to leverage access to the domestic market, the importance of timing, and the need to be aware of corporate strategy.

Helen Shapiro argues that Mexico's adeptness in using trade policy to monitor access to its domestic market was a significant factor in the country's transition from an import substitution industrialization (ISI) strategy to a successful auto exporter.[40] Because of its booming domestic market, Mexico was able to implement an automotive decree in 1977, ordering firms to balance their trade either by increasing domestic content or increasing exports. If firms did not balance their trade, they would be denied various subsidies and tax exemptions. More important, they could risk losing market share in the Mexican domestic market because of reduced access to imports. As a result, all foreign auto firms eventually responded by building new engine capacity and subsequently increasing exports.[41]

The 1983 decree increased local content requirements from 50 percent to 60 percent by 1987, allowing exemptions from this requirement for vehicles destined for export. It also rationalized the number of car makes and models being produced, making the production of additional ones contingent on proof that they would be self-sufficient in foreign exchange. This in itself reduced imports, since firms often imported parts for small-volume models that could not be produced efficiently within Mexico.[42] In return, automobile companies were guaranteed a large market share, since the policy, in effect, restricted the number of automobile producers in the market.

Still, because the 1983 decree was announced during a deep depression, when many firms were reducing domestic production, it met with limited success in terms of exports, and none of the firms balanced its trade. By the late 1980s the situation had changed, however, as the companies accumulated a surplus—a trend that was

40. Helen Shapiro, "The Determinants of Trade and Investment Flows in LDC Auto Industries: The Cases of Brazil and Mexico" (Paper presented at the conference "The Auto Industry: Responding to a Changing North American Trade Environment," Carleton University, Ottawa, October 1991).

41. Ibid., p. 13.

42. Bennett and Sharpe, *Transnational Corporations*, p. 274.

accelerated after Salinas's 1989 automotive decree, which removed the restrictions on production lines mandated in 1983 and allowed foreign auto companies to import fully assembled vehicles for the first time (albeit on a limited scale).[43] The decree also reduced local content requirements to 36 percent for cars and 40 percent for trucks. In return, producers were asked to generate a fixed dollar value of exports for every dollar value of imported vehicles.[44]

Mexico's thriving auto industry is a testimony to the success of these decrees. By using access to imports as leverage to cajole the foreign auto makers and offering increases in production quotas in exchange for increased exports or higher domestic content, Mexico has had considerable success in making foreign firms conform to its desires. This strategy not only underlines the importance of using trade policy as an effective instrument to channel investment, it also illustrates effective quid pro quo bargaining. The Salinas government also agreed to prohibit the import of small cars into the Mexican market until 1993 in exchange for commitments by Nissan and Volkswagen to invest $1 billion each in Mexico. This limit on imports will allow both of these companies sufficient time to bring the output from new plants onto the market to meet competition.[45]

This strategy emphasizes the importance of timing. Mexico's two most successful auto decrees were issued in 1977 and 1989, periods of growth in the Mexican domestic market. The 1977 decree, too, was implemented during a time when the foreign auto companies needed to increase their engine production capacity. Because the decree limited access to the lucrative Mexican market, the auto companies made investments in the Mexican market that may otherwise have been made elsewhere. Shapiro notes, however, that it is not clear that Mexico could have forced these firms to make such investments had they not been considering adding capacity any-

43. The decree allowed firms to import 15 percent of domestic sales in 1991 and 1992 and 20 percent in 1993 and 1994.

44. Companies were asked to export $2.50 for every dollar value of imported vehicles in 1992, $2.00 in the 1992 and 1993 model years, and $1.75 in 1994. See Mark Scheinman, "Corporate Strategy, Globalization, and the FTA: Mexico's New Role" (Paper presented at the conference "The Auto Industry: Responding to a Changing North American Trade Environment," Carleton University, Ottawa, October 1991).

45. Ibid., p. 7.

way.[46] Whether this coordination of government strategy with corporate strategy and the implementation of the decrees during economic upturn was luck or conscious planning we will probably never know. In any case, both of these factors are clearly influential.

The success of Mexico's auto industry reveals the perils of removing trade instruments as leverage for the implementation of state investment strategies. Without the ability to restrict imports, it is doubtful that Mexico could have encouraged companies to increase capacity and relieve the country's trade deficit in autos. Trade restrictions should not be used, however, in the form of a strict ISI strategy focusing on protectionism. On the contrary, Shapiro shows that Brazil's high domestic content regulations effectively limited the use of trade policy as leverage by cutting Brazil off from the global industry. Because 95 percent of the foreign auto companies' components were produced in Brazil, using preferential access to imports as an impetus to export was not a policy option. Without the enforcing stick of limiting imports, Brazil was unable to encourage a thriving export industry.[47] More generally, this example reinforces the argument made above: that without the use of tariffs or quotas as policy instruments, the only carrots left to states to attract new investors may be subsidies and tax write-offs. Not only are such handouts less convincing as investment incentives, they benefit companies while providing few guarantees for states.

Those who charge that state regulations on foreign investors deter FDI are simplifying a highly complex phenomenon. Canada and Mexico definitely felt constrained by market trends in FDI flows, but it was not clear that the policies they adopted had any significant adverse impact on the investment decisions of MNEs. Investment flows are far more affected by business cycles, and states must be cognizant of this when devising investment strategies. In addition, Canada was much more sensitive to shifts in FDI patterns than Mexico was. This conclusion indicates that the logic of investment varies from country to country, and that more case studies are

46. Shapiro, "Determinants of Trade and Investment Flows," p. 14.
47. Ibid., pp. 19–20.

necessary to supplement the macrolevel examination offered in this chapter. In the three case studies to follow, I examine state-specific factors that influence investment policies—for example, the interests of such political actors as capital, labor, and state agencies. In the process, we will gain a greater understanding of the political sources of foreign-investment policies in the United States, Canada, and Mexico.

Chapter Three

The Regulation of Foreign Direct Investment in the United States

In an 1890 address on the new industrial lords of America, the social critic Edward Bellamy proclaimed to the people of Boston, "The British are invading the United States, in these days, with a success brilliantly in contrast with their former failure in that line. Are we going to permit the American people to be rounded up, corralled and branded as the dependents of some hundreds of great American and English families?"[1] Exactly one hundred years later, the Massachusetts governor, Michael Dukakis, declared to the employees of Norton Company that the attempt by the British multinational BTR to take over the firm was yet "another attempt by a foreign power to interfere with our ability to shape our own destiny."[2] Bellamy's statement may be understandable given that a U.S. revolution against Britain was relatively recent history, but Dukakis's statement seems out of place coming from the premier economic and military power of the 1990s. Yet exhortations of this sort can be heard from many contemporary legislators in the United States, at both the federal and the state government levels. More often the adjective is not "British" but "Japanese," yet the message is the same: the United States is being threatened by foreign companies who are acquiring some of America's most prominent firms.

1. Cited in Mira Wilkins, *The History of Foreign Investment in the United States to 1914* (Cambridge: Harvard University Press, 1989), p. 573.
2. *New York Times*, May 27, 1990.

This renewed nationalism toward foreign investors has arisen for complex reasons, and this chapter is dedicated to explaining the politics surrounding the phenomenon. In the process, we will see the implications of changing U.S. attitudes toward FDI not only for domestic policy but for a continental market as well. The growing protectionism of the United States concerned both Canada and Mexico throughout the 1980s, and the evidence suggests this problem is not destined to disappear in the 1990s. Consequently, a full understanding of the political economy of U.S. investment policy is necessary to provide a critical backdrop for the analyses of Canada and Mexico in Chapters 4 and 5. For now, I will focus on the sources of U.S. foreign-investment review and examine some of the policy debates surrounding this issue.

FOREIGN-INVESTMENT REVIEW

Foreign-Investment Legislation

Despite the rhetorical statements noted above, the United States has generally maintained an open attitude toward inward flows of foreign direct investment. Even Alexander Hamilton, famous for his nationalist admonitions to protect American industry, argued that foreign direct investment should be encouraged. Foreign capital, he maintained, "ought to be considered as a most valuable auxiliary, conducing to put in motion a greater quantity of productive labor, and a greater portion of useful enterprise than could exist without it."[3] Notwithstanding this relatively welcoming stance, protectionist reactions against foreign investment have periodically arisen, often in response to major inflows of capital from abroad.

The nascent nation relied heavily on foreign capital for its economic development, although until the late nineteenth century most incoming capital took the form of portfolio investment. Much of the financing for U.S. railways and canal systems came from

3. *Annals of Congress* (1791), p. 994, as cited in Michael Seitzinger, "Foreign Investment in the United States: Major Federal Restrictions," in Subcommittee on Economic Stabilization, *Foreign Direct Investment: Effects on the United States*, report for the U.S. House of Representative Committee on Banking, Finance, and Urban Affairs, 101st Congress, 1st session, July 1989, p. CRS-48.

Europe; indeed, more than half of the Erie Canal bonds were in foreign hands by 1829 and 26 percent of railroad bonds by 1853.[4] It is estimated that by the mid-nineteenth century, foreigners owned half of federal and state debts and one-quarter of municipal debts. During this period, "the United States became the greatest debtor nation ever in history, a magnet attracting unprecedented amounts of both foreign portfolio and direct investments."[5]

Not surprisingly, opposition to such extensive foreign ownership began to emerge, peaking in the 1880s and 1890s. Passionate entreaties to stop the selling of American railroads and land were particularly prominent, as critics accused railway executives of encouraging foreign overinvestment in the U.S. industry and selling valuable public lands to so-called foreign syndicates. Similar attacks were made against absentee foreign landlords.[6] The implications of foreign investment for national security were also a major concern, and the navy complained that the expanding foreign control of strategic industries such as shipping, wireless communication, and fuel oil supplies could compromise U.S. military capacities. In 1898, for example, the U.S. War Department was forced to annul a contract with the subsidiary of the German firm Mannesman after the navy protested.[7]

In addition, numerous federal laws that discriminated against foreign investors on a sectoral basis were enacted in the late nineteenth century. To list but a few examples, an 1872 mining act specified that mineral deposits on public lands were open to exploration and purchase only by U.S. citizens or those declaring their intention to obtain citizenship. In the forestry industry two pieces of legislation were passed in 1878 that restricted foreign ownership of timberland and logging. Foreign ownership of real estate was a particularly sensitive area, and eighteen laws were passed between 1883 and 1886 that prohibited aliens from owning land in the territories or in the United States. In 1887 the Alien Land Act was

---

4. James K. Jackson, "Foreign Ownership of U.S. Assets: Past, Present, and Prospects," in House Committee on Banking, Finance, and Urban Affairs, *Foreign Direct Investment*, p. CRS-21.

5. Wilkins, *The History of Foreign Investment*, p. 144.

6. Ibid., p. 567.

7. Ibid., pp. 576–77.

passed, restricting ownership of real estate in the territories to U.S. citizens. In banking, legislation existing between 1875 and 1913 stipulated that all national bank directors must be U.S. citizens. Finally, the shipping industry was governed by an 1817 statute that banned foreign carriers from shipping in the United States.[8]

Overt hostility to foreign investors was somewhat muted by the diminishing U.S. reliance on foreign capital over time, particularly once the country moved from international debtor to international creditor status after World War I. Nevertheless, numerous information-gathering and disclosure statutes directed specifically toward foreign investors were enacted by Congress throughout the twentieth century. The International Investment Survey Act of 1976 gave the president the authority to collect information on international investment and foreign trade in services. And both the Foreign Corrupt Practices Act of 1977 and the Agricultural Foreign Investment Disclosure Act of 1978 made specific disclosure requirements of foreign investors. Sectoral policies restricting foreign ownership still exist in maritime shipping, aircraft, mining, energy, lands, communications, and banking. Some of these provisions additionally discriminate in favor of U.S. investors.[9]

In response to congressional concern over the political and economic motives of OPEC investments in the United States, President Gerald Ford created an investment review agency known as the Committee on Foreign Investment in the United States, or CFIUS, in 1975. Established through an executive order, CFIUS was given executive-branch responsibility for monitoring foreign investment (both direct and portfolio). It is chaired by the secretary of treasury and is composed of eight representatives from the Departments of State, Treasury, Defense, and Commerce; the U.S. Trade Representative Office (USTR); the Council of Economic Advisors; the office of the attorney general; and the director of the Office of Management and Budget.

Until recently, CFIUS attracted very little attention, primarily be-

---

8. See ibid., pp. 580–84. Numerous state-level measures affecting foreign investment were also enacted; they are discussed in greater detail later in this chapter.

9. For a more detailed analysis of these sectoral policies, see Seitzinger, "Foreign Investment," pp. 59–71.

cause of its low-key approach to investment review. The committee met only ten times from 1975 to 1980, and although it investigated numerous cases throughout the 1980s, only three cases (involving two Japanese companies and one French firm) involved any real controversy. Recently, however, CFIUS has acquired a much higher profile as a result of an amendment, sponsored by Senator James Exon (D-Nebraska) and Representative James Florio (D-New Jersey), to the Omnibus Trade and Competitiveness Act of 1988. The Exon-Florio amendment provided for presidential authority to block foreign mergers or acquisitions of U.S. companies on the basis of "national security." President Reagan delegated responsibility for such investigations to CFIUS, thereby transforming CFIUS "from an obscure, toothless interagency committee into an organization that is capable of recommending that the President block a broad range of foreign acquisitions."[10]

The Exon-Florio amendment is only one of a series of legislation regarding foreign investors that have recently emanated from Congress. As of 1991, there were approximately twenty-four bills related to foreign investment waiting to be passed. What follows is a selective review of some of this legislation to give an overall impression of the direction in which foreign-investment review is headed. One of the most controversial bills was the so-called Bryant Amendment, or Foreign Ownership Disclosure Act, introduced by Representative John Bryant (D-Texas). Had it passed, this bill would have mandated stricter reporting requirements for foreign firms and would have required the systematic disclosure of information by foreign firms meeting two different thresholds.[11] For reasons to be discussed in greater detail later, the Bryant Amendment did not make it through

10. James K. Jackson, *Foreign Investment: The Exon-Florio National Security Test*, Congressional Research Service (CRS) Report for Congress, September 26, 1990, p. 6.

11. Foreign companies holding between 5 and 25 percent interest in a U.S. business or with real estate holdings valued between 5 and 20 million dollars would have been required to file only basic information such as the company name, where they were from, what interest they held in the U.S. company, and the value of the U.S. asset. Those with more than a 25 percent interest in a U.S. firm or investments of a value greater than $20 million would have been asked for basic financial data. After failing to pass as part of the trade bill, this measure was reintroduced as H.R. 5, "The Foreign Ownership Disclosure Act." A companion bill was introduced by Senator Tom Harkin (D-Iowa) as S. 289. Neither of these passed the Senate.

the Senate, although a related provision, known as Sharp-Lent-Exon, for its sponsors, Representative Philip Sharp (D-Indiana), Representative Norman Kent (R-New York), and Senator Exon, passed through both levels of Congress in 1990. Supporters of the Bryant legislation argued that the FDI data collected by the U.S. government was insufficient to assess adequately the impact of foreign investment on the U.S. economy.[12] The Sharp-Lent-Exon provision attempted to remedy this situation by providing for the sharing of foreign-investment data between the Bureau of Census, the Bureau of Economic Analysis (BEA) and the Bureau of Labor Statistics (BLS). It thus allowed the more detailed, firm-level data of the Census Bureau to be combined with the broader, enterprise-level data of BEA. Significantly, however, it did not call for additional reporting requirements for foreign firms, the sticking point that doomed the Bryant legislation.

In 1990, legislation was introduced by Representative Doug Walgren (D-Pennsylvania) that would have significantly increased the ambit of CFIUS's review authority and required the agency to seek performance requirements from foreign firms. This legislation did not make it out of committee, but similar legislation was introduced in the House in May 1991 by Mel Levine (D-California) and Frank Wolf (R-Virginia). The bill attempted to broaden the investment review criteria from national security to economic security and makes specific reference to the growing foreign takeovers of U.S. high technology firms.

Another bill, proposed by Cardiss Collins (D-Illinois) in June 1991, sought to broaden the foreign-investment review process to include assessment of the effect of an investment on the industrial and technology base of the United States. Any transaction involving a technology deemed to be "critical" by the Pentagon and the Commerce Department would be investigated. The legislation would further authorize the attachment of conditions to investment approvals and shift responsibility for CFIUS from the Treasury Department to the Department of Commerce. Although President George Bush threatened to veto the bill, it was significant because of the

12. See the testimony of John Bryant in U.S. Senate, Committee on Commerce, Science, and Transportation, *Foreign Investment in the U.S.*, Hearing, 101st Congress, 1st session, July 11, 1989.

high profile and seniority of those supporting it. Collins was chair-woman of the House Subcommittee on Commerce, Consumer Protection, and Competitiveness and had the backing of the House majority leader, Richard Gephardt (D-Missouri). The bill was also important because it constituted an attempt to wrest CFIUS from the grasp of the Treasury Department, a move that reflects the dissatisfaction of many legislators with the agency's attitude toward investment review. To understand this dissatisfaction, a more in-depth analysis of CFIUS's record to date is necessary.

The Committee on Foreign Investment in the United States

As of May 1991, CFIUS had received more than five hundred registration notifications from foreign investors and taken twelve of them through the extended review process.[13] Of these twelve, in only one case was a foreign investor ordered by the president to divest, although in three other cases the investors in question were asked to make changes (at times substantial) in the nature of their commitments. In some instances, the foreign investor voluntarily withdrew. The single involuntary divestment involved a takeover of the aerospace parts manufacturer MAMCO by the China National Aero-Technology Import and Export Corporation, or CATIC, owned by the People's Republic of China. Because CATIC acted as a purchasing agent for China's Ministry of Defense, there was concern that via the acquisition it might gain access to technology that it would otherwise have to obtain under export license. The acquisition was completed before CFIUS could complete its investigation, but the committee subsequently ordered CATIC to divest.[14]

CFIUS's operations have drawn criticism from both advocates and

13. In what is regarded by many as a "slip" by Congress, the Exon-Florio amendment was allowed to expire in October 1990, temporarily suspending CFIUS's authority to block investments. Although provision for the amendment was made in the Omnibus Trade and Competitiveness Act, its actual parent legislation was the Defense Production Act, certain sections of which expired in fall 1990. It is expected that the Exon-Florio amendment will be renewed and that CFIUS will continue to review new investments.

14. Ibid., p. 8. Since this order followed the Tienanmen Square massacre of June 1989, some argue that the divestment order was a politically motivated measure that at the same time allowed the White House to show that CFIUS did have teeth. See Linda Spencer, *Foreign Investment in the United States: Unencumbered Access* (Washington: Economic Strategy Institute, 1991), p. 12.

opponents of investment review. Although critics do not dispute that the president should have the right to consider national security when it comes to foreign investment, there is concern that the term "national security" has not been defined. The absence of a definition allows considerable discretion over how broadly the notion should be construed, which obviously could vary depending on the political inclinations of the president involved. Another consequence is that almost all investors in the United States feel obliged to register with CFIUS, even though their investment may have little to do with national security. The Treasury Department has resisted defining national security because it believes the current vagueness of the legislation gives it greater flexibility. Since the department leans toward a restrictive interpretation of national security, the result has been a fairly lax implementation of the law. Clearly, however, an agency with more interventionist inclinations or a new administration could use this lack of clarity to expand CFIUS's scope without changing the legislation. Consequently, the undefined nature of "national security" has left many foreign investors and foreign governments uneasy.

In addition, the vagueness of the law means that the review process is not "transparent"—no clear guidelines exist to give foreign firms an indication of what is necessary to pass through the review process. This problem is exacerbated by the fact that investment review in the United States is not necessarily a one-stop process. Although CFIUS is the agency formally in charge of investigating foreign-investment cases, investors frequently meet with individual CFIUS members to okay their investments. Depending on the nature of the investment in question, for example, the Departments of Commerce and Defense may take an interest in particular investments. At present, Exon-Florio regulations allow any individual member of CFIUS to initiate review of any merger, acquisition, or joint venture the foreign investor has failed to report. The committee may also notify other nonmember agencies in the course of its review of any particular foreign investment.[15] Critics complain that these factors make the investment review process opaque.

15. Edward Graham and Michael Ebert, "Foreign Direct Investment and National Security: Fixing the Exon-Florio Process," Manuscript (Washington: Institute for International Economics, 1991), pp. 8–9.

Staffers of CFIUS respond that despite the vagueness of this legislation, the U.S. investment review process remains one of the fastest and most open in the world. Once a party has notified the committee, CFIUS has thirty days to conduct a preliminary review and forty-five days to conduct a more intensive review if it considers it warranted. The president must make a decision within fifteen days of receiving the committee's recommendation. Furthermore, they argue, investigations are always conducted in the context of the international obligations of the United States regarding national treatment and trade-related investment measures, or TRIMS.

This claim is true in the sense that none of the changes to investment plans that CFIUS has requested involve trade-related performance requirements such as export targets, import substitution, local content, or local sourcing. Some of the deals that were restructured following a CFIUS investigation clearly involved imposing other performance requirements on the foreign investor, however. In the Monsanto-Huels case, for example, the German firm Huels AG was required to keep production in the United States for at least five years, maintain its U.S. R&D facilities, and make its products available to U.S. semiconductor companies. Similarly, Asea Brown Boveri was allowed to form a joint venture with Westinghouse Electric in electrical power generation, transmission, and distribution equipment only after it assured the committee that it would continue to service, manufacture, and repair high-voltage products in the United States as well as conduct R&D in this area.[16] Moreover, because of the committee's sensitivity to charges that it may be violating its international investment commitments, negotiations regarding the future obligations of the party involved are kept confidential. This secrecy augments the "opaqueness" of the investment review process.

Proponents of investment review complain that CFIUS is not nearly attentive enough in its duties and that neither the president nor the committee is serious about monitoring the impact of foreign investments on the U.S. economy. Because of the Treasury Department's well-known preference for laissez-faire policies, those who would like to see more extensive FDI review policies argue that CFIUS is

16. Jackson, *Foreign Investment*, pp. 7–8.

unlikely to play any role other than rubber stamp. Instead, they would like to see the agency housed in a more sympathetic department, such as Commerce. Those who propose a broadening of CFIUS's mandate argue further that since the Commerce Department is responsible for overseeing the interests of business, it would also make a more appropriate parent ministry than the Treasury Department.[17] These critics, considerably more vocal than those opposing the concept of investment review in general, represent a broad spectrum, including Congress, organized labor, federal bureaucracies, state governments, and even some sections of business. A growing undercurrent of hostility toward foreign investment from each of these constituencies guarantees that pressures for foreign-investment review in the United States will increase in intensity. The following sections are devoted to explaining the origins of this groundswell of nationalism.

THE UNITED STATES IN THE GLOBAL POLITICAL ECONOMY

Nationalism and protectionism are not alien to the American political economy. Historically, the United States has shown at least as much of an inclination toward nationalism as it has toward internationalism. In fact, U.S. internationalism in its purest form corresponded to a rather brief twenty-five-year-period after World War II when the United States was the undisputed world hegemon and had clear interests in supporting a liberal international system. As David Lake documented, however, the postwar internationalism of the United States was the culmination of a long, nonlinear process. From a position of outright protectionism in the nineteenth century, the United States moved first to a strategy of bilateralism and reci-

17. Spencer argues that the Treasury Department was originally given jurisdiction over CFIUS because the committee was initially concerned with OPEC investments, which were primarily portfolio in nature. The Treasury Department is not well suited to monitor *direct* investments, she maintains, and therefore the Commerce Department secretary should either be made chair or co-chair. She also argues for the addition of the secretary of the Department of Energy, the national security adviser, and the national science adviser to the CFIUS panel, and the removal of the director of the Office of Management and Budget. See Spencer, *Foreign Investment*.

procity as represented in the Dingley Act of 1897 and the Payne-Aldrich Act of 1909, then to a more internationalist position in the 1913 Underwood Act passed under President Woodrow Wilson. It eventually reverted to outright protectionism in the Smoot-Hawley Act of 1930, however, and did not fully embrace the liberal national treatment and most-favored nation principles exemplified by the GATT until after 1945.[18]

These twists and turns in U.S. policy coincided with unique historical configurations of changing ideological interests, novel institutional relationships between Congress and the executive branch, a more global focus by significant factions of U.S. capital, and the changing position of the United States in the international political economy. Each of these factors has an important influence and are discussed in subsequent sections. Here, I will focus on the implications of the last point.

The politics of U.S. trade and investment policies are integrally related. In both issue areas, the declining international hegemony of the United States is a key factor in the growth of nationalist, protectionist policies. While there is some controversy over the extent of U.S. decline, there is no question that other trading partners have increased their economic power since World War II. For the purposes of this argument, the only relevant factor is that many Americans perceive that they are falling behind other countries, partly because of the unfair trade and investment policies of their competitors. While the United States has opened its doors to foreign investors and traders, critics argue, other countries (read *Japan*) have not been so forthcoming. The consequence has been an economic double-whammy for the United States: an unprecedented trade deficit and the transition of the United States from international creditor to international debtor. In 1991 the U.S. trade deficit was $95.6 billion. In Table 2 we can see the sizable increase of foreign investment and the transition from international creditor to debtor status that occurred in 1985.

Although there is considerable evidence that both the trade and investment deficits are at least partly "made in the U.S.A.," most of

18. David Lake, *Power, Protection, and Free Trade: International Sources of U.S. Commercial Strategy, 1887–1939* (Ithaca: Cornell University Press, 1988).

Table 2. International investment position of the United States
(billions of dollars, at year end)

	All investment[a]	Direct investment[a]	Corporate equity[a]	Debt holdings[a]
1975	74	96	−26	−8
1976	84	106	−34	−1
1977	73	111	−30	−21
1978	76	120	−31	−25
1979	95	133	−34	−17
1980	106	132	−45	8
1981	141	120	−47	57
1982	137	83	−47	100
1983	90	70	−70	78
1984	4	46	−68	13
1985	−111	45	−84	−72
1986	−269	40	−116	−193
1987	−378	36	−118	−296
1988	−532	−2	−135	−395

Source: Survey of Current Business, various issues, as cited in the Subcommittee on Economic Stabilization, *Foreign Direct Investment: Effects on the United States,* Report for U.S. House of Representatives, the Committee on Banking, Finance and Urban Affairs, 101st Congress, 1st Session, July 1989.
Note: The figures shown are the balances of assets and liabilities in each category, or the "position." A minus sign indicates a net liability (i.e., more investment by foreigners in the United States than by U.S. citizens outside of the United States); it is considered a liability because it is money owed to foreigners.
[a]Position net of assets and liabilities.

the nationalist reaction against these major inflows of foreign investment has taken the form of Japan-bashing. Numerous analysts have argued that the U.S. trade deficit has resulted from excessive budget deficits, which sucked in imports as demand increased. In addition, the high interest rates designed to attract the foreign capital needed to bridge the gap between savings and investment aggravated this situation by creating an overvalued dollar, which in turn worsened the trade deficit.[19] Nevertheless, most of the trade measures introduced into Congress in the 1980s focused on the "unfair practices" of trading partners, claiming that closed markets abroad provided barriers to U.S. exports.

19. Stephen Marris, *Deficits and the Dollar: The World Economy at Risk* (Washington: Institute for International Economics, 1985).

This argument was not lost on proponents of investment review, who argued that while other countries were restricting U.S. investment in their markets, foreign firms were swooping in to pick off strategically important U.S. firms. Although the Exon-Florio provision was apparently prompted by the perceived arrogance of Sir Oliver Goldsmith's attempt to takeover Goodyear, the real trend toward investment review in the United States began with opposition to the takeover of Fairchild Semiconductor by the Japanese firm Fujitsu. The Fairchild acquisition was opposed by both Secretary of Commerce Malcolm Baldrige and Secretary of Defense Casper Weinberger on national security grounds, because Fairchild was being used by Cray (the U.S. producer of supercomputers) to diversify out of its reliance on foreign (again, read *Japanese*) suppliers. There is a definite irony in these complaints, given that Fairchild was in fact controlled by the French firm Schlumberger. Fujitsu withdrew its offer and Fairchild was later acquired by National Semiconductor at a reduced price. A further irony is that when this issue was on the agenda, Japan was only the third largest investor in the United States, with the United Kingdom investing almost twice as much.[20]

A Polanyian protectionist reaction to the trade deficit and the transition to debtor status in 1985 was somewhat predictable; it has historical precedence in the United States, and as noted in Chapter 1, it is a fairly universal phenomenon. As others have argued, the economic opening of the United States was in large part responsible for this reaction. As a share of total U.S. output, international trade doubled in the postwar period, exposing more workers and firms to the whims of the international market. In the context of growing international vulnerability, the economic policies of the Reagan administration were the coup de grace for protectionist sentiments. As U.S. borrowing burgeoned and interest rates reached historic heights, the value of the dollar increased 70 percent between 1980 and 1985. Among the consequences of this revaluation were the

20. In 1990 the United Kingdom remained the largest foreign investor, contributing 29.7 percent of all FDI in the United States. Japan came second, with 18 percent of the total, followed by the Netherlands (14.3 percent) and Canada (7.4 percent).

swelling U.S. trade deficit and growing U.S. outrage at this turn of events.[21]

Regardless of the trade woes of the United States, it still remains the predominant economic and military power in the world. But the clash between the trend toward nationalism and the internationalist responsibilities that accompany the role of hegemon has created some interesting contradictions. As Evans noted in a study of U.S. trade and investment relations with Brazil, increasing challenges from foreign competitors have instigated domestic pressures for protectionism and mercantilism. Yet these forces clash with prevailing ideological definitions of the national interest that are derived from the hegemonic experience, including a commitment to international openness and the maintenance of international alliances.[22] Combined with the classical liberal anathema of state intervention that prevails in the United States, these factors have resulted in some distinctly American policy permutations. For example, some have characterized the growing U.S. penchant to force open markets abroad, exemplified in the Omnibus Trade and Competitiveness Act of 1988, as an example of the growing attractiveness of strategic trade theory to U.S. firms.[23] If so, it is a rendition of strategic trade policy peculiar to the United States. In its original incarnation the theory of strategic trade, described in greater detail in Chapter 1, embodied the principle that strategically placed state subsidies and tariffs could help national firms gain international market shares in oligopolistic industries. The Super 301 clause, in operation until 1990, involved none of these interventionist tactics in the domestic

21. These factors are explained in greater detail in I. M. Destler, *American Trade Politics: System under Stress* (Washington: Institute for International Economics, 1986). Destler's explanation for growing U.S. protectionism focuses on the opening of Congress to lobbying interests and the consequent influence of special interests on trade policy, a factor that is discussed in greater detail later. He places this institutional explanation in the broader context of the changing U.S. political economy, however.

22. Peter Evans, "Declining Hegemony and Assertive Industrialization: U.S.-Brazil Conflicts in the Computer Industry," *International Organization* 43, no. 2 (Spring 1989), pp. 236–37.

23. Helen Milner and David Yoffie, "Between Protectionism and Free Trade: Strategic Trade Policy and a Theory of Corporate Trade Demands," *International Organization* 43, no. 2 (Spring 1989).

market. Instead, it stipulated that other countries open up their markets to U.S. companies or face retaliation in the American market, and did so with the proviso that this opening-up was not to constitute a policy of sectoral reciprocity. Thus, this thinly veiled mercantilism incorporated the internationalist commitment to open markets abroad with the nationalist, protectionist urge toward retaliation, all the time eschewing state involvement in the economy.

United States investment policy includes these same contradictions with a slight twist. It reconciles the protectionist imperative to regulate foreign investors with the internationalist penchant for rule making by drawing on a principle that is compatible with both: national security. National security constitutes one of the two legitimate ideological rationales for government intervention in the United States, the other being the classical liberal veneration of antitrust. Increasingly, however, another rationale has achieved growing attention—the current U.S. absorption with the idea of competitiveness, particularly as it relates to high-technology industries. Concern with these issues is undoubtedly related to the decline United States as absolute hegemon and the rise of strong foreign competitors.

Not surprisingly, the question of competitiveness as manifested in policy debates is itself a synthesis of nationalist and internationalist viewpoints. On the internationalist side is the argument that declining productivity, ineffective R&D policies, and the dominance of the Department of Defense have reduced American capacities to compete. The solutions prescribed for these problems may differ, but the essence of the argument is that the United States is to blame for its changing trade and investment position.[24] On the nationalist side is the concern that growing foreign investment in the United States may mean that foreign firms are acquiring not only U.S. companies but technologies that are critical for military and economic security.[25] In policy terms, this belief is exemplified by the exclusion of

24. See Bertrand Bellon and Jorge Niosi, *The Decline of the American Economy* (Montreal: Black Rose Books, 1988); Robert Kuttner, "How 'National Security' Hurts National Competitiveness," *Harvard Business Review* 69, no. 1 (January–February 1991); and Michael Porter, *The Competitiveness of Nations* (New York: Free Press, 1990).

25. See Martin Tolchin and Susan Tolchin, *Buying into America: How Foreign Money Is Changing the Face of Our Nation* (New York: Times Books, 1988).

foreigners from R&D consortia such as Sematech. It is also the impetus behind much of the investment review legislation being introduced in Congress.

To date, the most nationalist of these measures have either not made it out of committee or have been blocked by the Senate or executive agencies, but the increasingly defensive orientation of investment legislation is unmistakable. The Collins legislation, for example, was apparently introduced in response to the attempt by the Oki Electric Industry Company to acquire Seattle Silicon Corporation. Legislators were angry that CFIUS approved the acquisition, claiming it involved the transfer of key U.S. technologies. This concern was in part motivated by the fact that more than half of the acquisitions by foreign companies in the United States have been by Japanese firms.[26] In this context, the economic challenge from Japan is as much of an impetus for such legislation as national security is.

Yet fear of rising economic challenges and the desire to protect U.S. technologies do not dominate the legislature unopposed. While these issues may gain a somewhat sympathetic ear in the Department of Commerce, more internationalist actors, such as the Treasury Department and the president himself, are determined to check such trends. As we will see, the Exon-Florio amendment itself was a deliberate compromise between internationalist interests embodied in the executive branch and business and more nationalist pressures emanating from Congress and the American public in general. The battles surrounding foreign-investment review thus deserve further examination.

DOMESTIC POLITICS AND FOREIGN-INVESTMENT REVIEW

Congress

The politicization of investment issues within the Congress parallels a much longer trend toward congressional concern with trade issues. As is true of trade legislation, nationalist investment policies are the result of battles between the executive branch and Congress, and the foreign-investment legislation that has passed, such as the

---

26. *Wall Street Journal,* June 13, 1991.

Exon-Florio and Sharp-Lent-Exon amendments, reflect the compromises between these two factions. In both cases, broader and more stringent congressional proposals were altered after sustained opposition from the executive branch and presidential threats to veto such legislation. While the executive branch is generally more attentive to U.S. international obligations, Congress is responsive to special interests threatened by foreign investment as well as public opinion. With regard to the latter, it has fertile ground to draw on; public opinion surveys reveal widespread support for the monitoring of foreign investors. A *Times Mirror* survey found that 70 percent of those interviewed thought that foreign investment was "a bad thing," with only 18 percent arguing that it was "a good thing." Similarly, 78 percent of those surveyed in an ABC News/Washington Post poll in 1988 favored a law limiting the extent of foreign investment in American business and real estate, with only 18 percent opposed.[27] Consequently, Congress has touched a broad range of enthusiasts with its spree of foreign-investment legislation, much to the dismay of the executive branch.

The perpetual struggle between Congress and the president on trade issues has been discussed in detail elsewhere but is examined briefly here because of its relevance to investment issues.[28] As I. M. Destler shows in *American Trade Politics*, the growing liberalism of U.S. trade policy after World War II was in large part due to the willingness of Congress to delegate its trade negotiating authority to the president. Although Congress has clear constitutional authority for foreign commerce, it passed legislation enabling the president to negotiate tariffs in the Reciprocal Trade Agreements Act of 1934 and the trade acts of 1962 and 1974.

None of these bills passed without controversy, however, and as the nature of trade negotiations changed, Congress began to place

27. Cited by Rosita Thomas, "American Public Opinion towards Foreign Investment," in House Committee on Banking, Finance, and Urban Affairs, *Foreign Direct Investment*.

28. See Destler, *American Trade Politics*; Robert Baldwin, *The Political Economy of U.S. Import Policy* (Cambridge: MIT Press, 1985); and Susan Schwab, "Politics, Economics, and U.S. Trade Policy," *Stanford Journal of International Law* 23, no. 1 (Spring 1987).

greater constraints on the president's negotiating leeway.[29] Once non tariff barriers became the focus of negotiations in the Tokyo round of trade talks, Congress began a cautious retreat from its previous willingness to delegate trade authority. In the trade act of 1974, skittishness over the more politicized issues of nontariff barriers (NTBs) led Congress to modify presidential authority through the adoption of the so-called fast-track procedure. Since NTB negotiations could spread into areas well beyond trade policy, the 1974 act stipulated that the president would give notice of intent at least ninety days before entering into any agreement. Congress would then have to act within sixty days of submission of the implementing bill through an up or down vote (a simple acceptance or rejection with no amendments allowed in committee or on the floor).[30]

Although Congress in effect opted out of trade negotiations by passing the fast-track procedure, it still had to legislate at both ends of the negotiating process. It had to pass a trade act to allow negotiations, then vote again on the implementing legislation. This allowed plenty of space for special deals to be made, and gave USTR an incentive to give in to special interests in order to avoid pressures on Congress that might block the implementing legislation. Congress had established a mechanism for authorizing and implementing trade agreements, but it did nothing to divert the product-specific restructuring proposals that inevitably emerged.[31]

The Omnibus Trade and Competitiveness Act of 1988 further expanded Congress's role in the trade-making process by requiring increased consultation. It requires USTR to make annual reports to both the House and the Senate outlining its trade objectives and to seek advice from the existing congressional advisers on trade policy. The president is also required to report to Congress on the progress made in reducing the trade deficit. Finally, the act allows for "reverse

---

29. For example, in the 1958 extension of the Trade Agreements Act, Congress introduced a provision that allowed it to override presidential decisions by a two-thirds vote. The 1962 and 1974 trade acts reduced the vote necessary to veto to a majority of each house and eventually to a majority of those present and voting in each house. See Baldwin, *The Political Economy of U.S. Import Policy*, pp. 35–36.

30. Destler, *American Trade Politics*, p. 64.

31. Ibid., p. 69.

fast track"—Congress may withdraw fast-track procedures if both the House and Senate separately pass disapproval resolutions condemning the president's trade actions.[32]

This institutional weakness, along with the growing politicization of trade on Capitol Hill, proved to be a lethal combination. The threat by Congress not to renew fast-track authority for the negotiation of a North American Free Trade Agreement with Mexico in 1991 was a predictable outgrowth of Congress's increased susceptibility to special interests. Although authority was eventually granted, it came only after a serious threat to block the legislation if certain special interests were not given consideration. Similarly, USTR's willingness to jeopardize the dispute settlement mechanism of the Canada–United States Free Trade Agreement by making an extraordinary challenge to a panel decision on Canadian pork exports reveals how thoroughly besieged it is by congressional threats. In order to avoid irritating Congress before fast-track authority was granted for the NAFTA negotiations, USTR gave in to complaints by U.S. pork producers and rejected a unanimous ruling of a binational dispute settlement panel that found in favor of Canada. As American capital and labor feel more threatened by foreign competitors, these sorts of pressures are bound to increase.

Similar tensions between Congress and the executive branch are evident in the area of investment review policy. Ever responsive to the rising tide of nationalism, Congress has emitted a seemingly endless stream of foreign-investment legislation. But the executive branch remains opposed to any sort of review process that would discriminate against foreign investors and thereby contravene its commitment to national treatment. The initial version of the Exon-Florio amendment, introduced by Representative James Florio in 1987, proposed that the president be authorized to block any foreign acquisition or merger of a U.S. firm that threatened the national security and essential commerce of the United States and contained

32. Section 301 of the act also transferred major responsibilities from the president to USTR to reduce the influence of presidential advisers. The now-expired Super 301 clause required USTR to identify and eliminate unfair trade practices and to retaliate if progress was not made within a three-year period (*Congress and Foreign Policy*, U.S. House of Representatives, Committee on Foreign Affairs, 101st Congress, 1989).

a checklist of factors the president should consider in evaluating such transactions. The Reagan administration vociferously opposed this language, emphasizing the chilling effect it would have on foreign investment and arguing that "it would put the United States in the company of those countries whose investment climates we are trying to improve."[33]

The bill was passed only after the "essential commerce" clause was dropped and after responsibility for investment review was moved from any Executive agency to the Commerce Department. After intervention by Senator James Exon, the final amendment stated that the president would use his authority to block foreign acquisitions or mergers only if there was "credible evidence" of a threat and only if no other legal remedies were available.[34] It also moved authority for investment review from the Commerce Department to an agency to be designated by the president. The president subsequently chose the Treasury Department and CFIUS to review incoming investment, no doubt because of the Treasury Department's disinclination to intervene in such transactions.

Similarly, the administration opposed the information disclosure requirements of the Bryant Amendment because it claimed they discriminated against foreign investors by allowing access to their identities. This in turn, it argued, would damage the system of statistical reporting by eliminating the anonymity of reporters. The administration reiterated this complaint in its opposition to a measure by Senator Frank Murkowski (D-Alaska) that would have provided for the sharing of data between BEA and the Census Bureau and would have permitted BEA to divulge data about individual foreign investors to CFIUS.[35] It made the same opposition to the related Sharp-Lent-Exon bill.[36]

33. Letter from James Baker, then secretary of the treasury, to John Danforth (June 9, 1987), in U.S. Senate, Committee on Commerce, Science, and Transportation, *Acquisitions by Foreign Companies*, Hearing, 100th Congress, 1st session, June 10, 1987, p. 68.
34. Graham and Ebert, "Foreign Direct Investment," pp. 6–7.
35. Statement of Michael Darby, Under Secretary of Economic Affairs, Department of Commerce, in Senate Committee on Commerce, Science, and Transportation, *Foreign Investment in the U.S.*, July 11, 1989, pp. 55–56.
36. The administration supported measures that would allow the sharing of data between the Census Bureau and BEA but opposed divulging disaggregated informa-

The administration's ability to resist the growing pressure for foreign-investment regulation rests on its ability to maintain ultimate authority over the review process. So long as it can continue to deflect foreign-investment review to internationalist agencies such as the Treasury Department, it will be able to maintain the equivalent of a fast-track procedure in investment issues. This authority is constantly under stress, however. One of the provisions of the 1990 Walgren bill, for example, would have allowed congressional committees to participate in and micromanage the foreign-investment review process. This proposed inclusion would reinvent some of the difficulties reviewed in the earlier discussion of trade politics. Congressional micromanagement of the review process would be a conduit for special interests into CFIUS investigations and create an institutional arrangement matched (at least on a formal level) nowhere else in the world. It is highly unlikely that such a motion could ever pass through both the House and the Senate. Since it appears to violate the separation of power doctrine, it would almost certainly be vetoed by the current president.[37] It is noteworthy, however, because it reveals the growing concern of Congress over investment issues, and the extremity of interventionist pressures.

As mentioned, much of the new legislation also argues that authority for investment decisions be moved from the Treasury Department to the Departments of Commerce and Defense. Because it underlines some of the interbureaucratic rivalries over these issues, this issue deserves description at greater length.

---

tion to CFIUS. See Statement of William E. Barreda, Deputy Assistant Secretary for Trade and Investment Policy, Department of the Treasury, in U.S. Senate Committee on Commerce, Science, and Transportation, *Foreign Investment in the United States*, Hearing before the Subcommittee on Foreign Commerce and Tourism, 101st Congress, 2nd session, July 19, 1990, p. 39.

37. Specifically, the bill proposed to (1) let CFIUS seek assurances or performance requirements in writing and publish these assurances in the *Federal Register*; (2) allow congressional committees to participate in a more formalized investigation and review process; (3) alter the "credible evidence" criteria to allow more subjective findings; (4) integrate the Departments of Defense and Commerce into the review process by putting them in charge of the collection and flow of information to CFIUS; (5) require that each of the eight committee members devise their own lists of "essential technologies" that should be subject to CFIUS investigation; and (6) require de facto mandatory notification. See Graham and Ebert, "Foreign Direct Investment," pp. 11–12.

Institutional Capacity and Interagency Conflicts

Much of the literature on state capacities has portrayed the United States as the quintessential "weak state."[38] Although this conception has been challenged, there is no doubt that the unique institutional and ideological configurations of the United States limit effective state intervention.[39] The American state is fragmented, and its power and authority are widely dispersed. On a political level, its two major parties are decentralized and regionally divided. Institutionally, boundaries between state agencies are blurred, making it difficult to know which of multiple departments has jurisdiction over any single area. In most cases several government departments or agencies have competing jurisdictions, and the eventual resolution of many issues is the result of jousting and fighting between them. Overshadowing all this is the possibility that the courts could intervene and make any hard-earned political compromise invalid.

Outside observers could argue that many of these conditions are replicated elsewhere, and they would be absolutely correct. Even in the strong Japanese and French states, for example, inter bureaucratic brawls and the capture of state agencies by societal groups is common.[40] To a certain extent, therefore, a more accurate explanation for the lack of intervention in the United States is "strategic

38. Stephen Krasner, *Defending the National Interest: Raw Materials Investments and U.S. Foreign Policy* (Princeton: Princeton University Press, 1978).

39. For more recent analysis of the United States in this regard, see Margaret Weir, Ann Shola Orloff, and Theda Skocpol, eds., *The Politics of Social Policy in the United States* (Princeton: Princeton University Press, 1988); John Ikenberry, "The Irony of State Strength: Comparative Responses to the Oil Shocks of the 1970s," *International Organization* 40, no. 1 (Winter 1986); Stephen Skowroneck, *Building a New American State: The Expansion of National Administrative Capacities* (Cambridge: Cambridge University Press, 1982); and Margaret Weir and Theda Skocpol, "State Structures and the Possibilities for 'Keynesian' Responses to the Great Depression in Sweden, Britain, and the United States," in Peter Evans, Dietrich Rueschemeyer, and Theda Skocpol, eds., *Bringing the State Back In* (Cambridge: Cambridge University Press, 1985).

40. For Japan, see Chalmers Johnson, "MITI, MPT, and the Telecoms Wars: How Japan Makes Policy for High Tech," in the Berkeley Roundtable on the International Economy (BRIE), ed., *Creating Advantage: American and Japanese Strategies for Adjusting to Change in a New World Economy* (Berkeley: University of California Press, 1987). For France, see Ezra Suleiman, *Private Power and Centralization in France: The Notaires and the State* (Princeton: Princeton University Press, 1987), and Elie Cohen and Michel Bauer, *Les grandes manoeuvres industrielles* (Paris: Belfond, 1985).

95

abstention"—a resolve on the part of the state not to intervene.[41] This reluctance to intervene is, in turn, a consequence of the ideological affiliations of the president and his advisers, various state agencies, and the kinds of pressures they receive from their constituencies. These factors are particularly relevant in the bureaucratic disputes surrounding investment review policies.

Many critics have accused CFIUS of being a rubber stamp, and the slew of litigation to expand CFIUS's mandate reveals congressional dissatisfaction with its performance to date. But is this dissatisfaction due to a lack of institutional capacity to carry out a thorough investment review process, or is it due to a lack of interest on the part of the Treasury Department, CFIUS's parent department, in implementing such a policy? Both of these factors have an impact on investment review in the United States, but this latter point is of particular importance. In Chapter 2 we saw that the best investment review policies were embedded in larger industrial strategies, and one way to convert CFIUS into a purposive agency would be to use it as an instrument in a broader policy context. Since much of the legislation dealing with investment review concerns technology, for example, it would make sense to use CFIUS as a watchdog and a coordinator of R&D policy, regulating collaboration between foreign and domestic companies.

The Commerce Department has exhibited a willingness to oversee such a strategy. Unlike the Treasury Department, with its open-door strategy, the Commerce Department and the Pentagon have been characterized as having an "institutional suspicion of foreigners."[42] Staff members of the Commerce Department speak openly of the need to protect "economic security," and the department has the technical expertise and the data (housed in the Bureau of Economic Analysis) to handle such issues.

Two possible complications arise, however. First, even though the original Exon-Florio legislation designated the Commerce Department as the lead agency for investment review, attempts to move CFIUS from the Treasury to the Commerce Department have subsequently become highly politicized. Precisely because of the latter's

---

41. This is Ikenberry's argument in "The Irony of State Strength."
42. *Wall Street Journal*, March 8, 1989.

willingness to broaden CFIUS's mandate, moving the agency from the Treasury Department would not meet the approval of the Bush administration without a long-drawn-out battle. Recall that the Exon-Florio amendment was not taken off the presidential veto list until the President was allowed, among other things, to designate the appropriate review agency. He chose the Treasury Department specifically because of its narrow understanding of investment review issues, and he can be expected to agree to a transfer to the Commerce Department only if forced to compromise in some larger policy battle.

The second complication is that even if the Commerce Department won out in such a battle, it is questionable whether it would be able to implement an investment review policy that is embedded in a broader technology strategy. For one, no central agency is responsible for nondefense R&D policy in the United States. Instead, responsibility is spread out over twelve executive branch agencies. The National Institute of Standard Technology (NIST), thought to be the primary government laboratory mandated to support U.S. industry, is housed in the Department of Commerce. Its relatively small budget ($170 million in 1990) severely limits its ability to play any concrete role, however. Compared with other R&D agencies, NIST is a financial midget. The Department of Defense receives the lion's share of R&D spending with a 1990 budget of $37 billion, and the Defense Advanced Research Projects Agency (DARPA), which is most oriented to commercial R&D applications, receives about $1.1 billion of this budget. Similarly, the National Aeronautics and Space Administration's (NASA's) budget of $12 billion and the Department of Energy's $7 billion R&D program dwarf NIST's financial capacity.[43]

This focus on defense-related R&D has impaired U.S. trade and investment competitiveness. Although in the past numerous civilian spin-offs were derived from military technologies, today the situation is reversed. Consumer electronics and high-technology goods with commercial applications in computing and telecommunications are increasingly at the cutting edge of technological innova-

---

43. *Gaining New Ground: Technology Priorities for America's Future* (Washington: Council on Competitiveness, 1991), p. 39.

tion, and defense technologies have fewer commercial applications. In addition, efforts by the Defense Department to protect the R&D they have sponsored often restrict the opportunities for future commercialization.[44] Hence this excessive attention to defense-related R&D can negatively affect the competitiveness of U.S. companies in civilian industries.

The Bush administration sought to remedy this situation by creating a Technology Administration Secretariat within Commerce, designed to target emerging technologies, and by strengthening the Office of Science and Technology Policy (OSTP). Also, the creation of NIST's Advanced Technology Program involved heavy investment by the government (about $45 billion in 1990–91), which reveals a commitment to increase the Commerce Department's R&D focus. Even with such capacity, however, the ability of the Department to encourage technology collaboration between government and business is destined to clash with the priorities of other agencies, such as the Departments of Defense and Justice. Because such collaboration often involves subsidies and explicit cooperation between firms, it is important for American competition policy. The National Cooperative Research Act of 1984 relaxed antitrust strictures on research consortia. But companies are still not immune to antitrust challenges nor is the potential eliminated for interagency wrangles between a Commerce Department anxious to promote R&D collaboration and the Department of Justice's mandate to promote competition.[45]

In addition, the organization of R&D in the United States and the failure to coordinate a broad-based technology policy makes U.S. institutions even more open to congressional interference. No central agency could ever be wholly autonomous, but the experience of the Department of Defense reveals that a centralized agency with its own policy agenda, technical expertise, and ideological legitimacy

---

44. See ibid., pp. 20–21; Robert Kuttner, "How 'National Security' Hurts National Competitiveness," *Harvard Business Review* 69, no. 1 (January–February 1991), and Bertrand Bellon and Jorge Niosi, *The Decline of the American Economy* (Montreal: Black Rose Books, 1988).

45. A parallel dispute is occurring in the European Community between the competition commissioner, Leon Brittan, and the research commissioner, Maria Filippo Pandolfi (*Financial Times*, June 17, 1991).

(not to mention extensive budget) could operate somewhat independently.

Developing such an agency outside of the Department of Defense with a focus on commercial R&D is also important in an international context because it would bring U.S. technological efforts more in line with what is happening abroad. The growth of protectionist trade and investment policies in the United States is in large part a consequence of the conviction that foreign firms are unfairly subsidized and protected by their governments. In fact, U.S. government spending on R&D exceeds the contributions of governments in many other OECD countries, including its major trading partners. The U.S. government financed 48.3 percent of gross domestic expenditure on R&D (GERD) in 1989, in contrast to the 18.7 percent the Japanese government contributed to its GERD. Similarly, the German and Canadian governments contributed 32.8 percent and 44 percent, respectively.[46]

The real problem lies in the allocation of these funds in each country. Germany and Japan, two of the chief trade rivals of the United States, concentrate the bulk of their funds on civilian technologies with commercial applications (Table 3). Hence it is not surprising that U.S. firms focusing on civilian technologies believe they are being treated unfairly. It is not foreign governments that are doling out this injustice, however, but their own. Until this situation is remedied, growing nationalism and pressure for protection in the affected industries can be expected to remain a mainstay in congressional debates.

The difference between U.S. policies and those of other countries points up the relevance of institutional fit in promoting national competitiveness.[47] If domestic institutions are inappropriate in the changing global market competition they can have a negative effect on the competitiveness of individual firms. Moves to improve this situation and make U.S. institutions more appropriate in the international market could alleviate much of the protectionist pressure from special interests described by Destler. Appropriate R&D pol-

46. OECD, *Main Science and Technology Indicators* 1 (Paris: OECD, 1991).
47. The notion of institutional fit is described in greater detail in Fred Block, *Postindustrial Possibilities: A Critique of Economic Discourse* (Berkeley: University of California Press, 1990), chaps. 1 and 2.

Table 3. R&D appropriations by mission, 1988 (% of total federal government R&D budget)

	United States	Japan	Germany
Industrial development	0.2	4.8	14.5
Defense	65.6	4.8	12.5
Health	12.8	2.6	3.6
Energy	3.9	22.3	7.8
Advancement of research	3.8	7.6	13.3
General university funds	—[a]	43.7	30.8
Infrastructure[b]	1.8	1.8	1.8
Agriculture	2.0	3.9	2.1
Civil Space	7.4	6.1	5.4
Environmental protection	0.5	0.5	3.4
Other[c]	1.8	2.0	4.8

Source: *Gaining New Ground: Technology Priorities for America's Future* (Washington: Council on Competitiveness, 1991), based on data from the OECD, the National Science Foundation, and national sources for Japan.

[a]The United States has no equivalent to Europe's and Japan's general university funds.

[b]Includes transport, telecommunications, and rural and urban planning.

[c]Includes social development and services, earth and atmosphere, and R&D that is not elsewhere classified.

icies could help firms who believe they are facing uneven competition and could simultaneously diffuse the kind of protectionist reactions that are currently so widespread in the United States.

The importance of institutional fit extends far beyond the agencies that constitute the state, however. Relations between state agencies and other economic actors, such as business, are also key institutional arrangements.

THE INFLUENCE OF BUSINESS

The traditionally adversarial relations between U.S. government and business may prove to be a major obstruction to achieving the kind of R&D policy I have described. Such a policy would involve extensive coordination between state agencies and business, a relationship with little precedent outside the defense industry. The Bush administration attempted to promote such interaction through the 1986 Technology Transfer Act and Executive Order 12591, which established a system of cooperative agreements designed to increase the transfer of technology from federal research laboratories to private firms.[48] Attempts to encourage private investors to match federal expenditures in this area, however, have been hampered by the perception of many businesses that federal laboratories do not conduct commercially relevant research.[49] But as a major business think tank, the Council on Competitiveness, recently noted:

> In addition to the lack of monetary support for technologies of commercial importance, the U.S. government is unsupportive in other ways. Largely because of the federal government's traditional role as regulator, interactions between the public and private sectors have often been adversarial. Moreover, federal law has frequently discouraged cooperation within the private sector. The challenge is to strengthen support for technologies of commercial importance and to build bridges between industry and government.[50]

Given capital's overall importance in policymaking in the United States, this adversarial relationship with government should not be overemphasized. Little legislation passes through Congress that does not have at least partial approval from business. But there is no question that U.S. business and the state do not have the close working relationship evident in Japan and in many European countries. This situation is not only the fault of government; U.S. business itself is obsessed with quarterly profits, short-term horizons, and the bottom line. Consequently, business generally translates international competitiveness into two strategies. The first is an emphasis on "getting the prices right": controlling wages, avoiding social overhead and taxes, and a devalued currency. In the trade and investment arena, devaluation has become a central focal point of business lobby groups.

Devaluation in itself is unlikely to have little long-term effect on U.S. competitiveness, since any significant trade surplus that might result would simply lead to pressures for revaluation. The importance that business attaches to exchange rates, however, was empha-

48. *Gaining New Ground*, p. 16.
49. Ibid., p. 47.
50. Ibid., p. 41.

sized in a letter sent from the National Association of Manufacturers (NAM) to the Bush administration in 1991 asking that any "new [trade] agreement seek to prevent exchange rate manipulation for a country's competitive advantage." In commenting on this letter, a NAM spokesman said that such assurances did not have to be made in a formal agreement and that informal arrangements would suffice.[51]

The importance of exchange rates for U.S. business is a highly conflictual strategy in a continental context that has significant implications for the Canadian and Mexican trade and investment strategies outlined in Chapters 4 and 5. But it also indicates a bias on the part of U.S. business in its approach to international competitiveness. Rather than attempting to develop some of the coordinating relationships with the state that have increased competitiveness elsewhere, or trying to improve productivity, U.S. business continues to focus on such quantitative issues as exchange rates. The implications of such a strategy are discussed in greater detail in Chapter 6.

The second strategy is asking both state and federal governments for protection. It is a truism that business exerts powerful pressures on U.S. trade and investment policy; the only difficulty lies in establishing the *kind* of influence business may hold, for U.S. capital is far from being a united front. On the one hand, most of the protectionist legislation passed in the United States over the last two centuries was a response to requests by specific, threatened industries for assistance.[52] On the other hand, the growth of American multinationals in the twentieth century was one of the essential preconditions for U.S. internationalism. Firms with globally integrated production systems and foreign subsidiaries that might be subject to retaliation from host governments are naturally loath to encourage interventionist or protectionist actions on the part of the United States.[53]

51. Cited in Bruce Campbell and Maude Barlow, *Take Back the Nation* (Toronto: Key Porter Books, 1991).

52. The most famous study of the influence of "special interests" on U.S. trade policy is E. E. Schattschneider, *Politics, Pressures, and the Tariff* (Englewood Cliffs, N.J.: Prentice-Hall, 1935). See also Destler, *American Trade Politics*, and Timothy McKeown, "Firms and Tariff Regime Change: Explaining the Demand for Protection," *World Politics* 36, no. 2 (January 1984).

53. Helen Milner, *Resisting Protectionism: Global Industries and the Politics of International Trade* (Princeton: Princeton University Press, 1988), and John Odell and I. M.

The changing position of the United States in the international political economy, however, has intertwined these two sets of business interests and created some interesting hybrids of international firms with distinctly interventionist interests. Increasingly, international firms besieged by foreign competitors have asked for government assistance in opening markets abroad, subsidizing them at home, or protecting them from hostile foreign takeovers.[54] With regard to investment policy, companies that were previously unalterably opposed to foreign investment review are now changing their perspectives in an attempt to deal with the growing level of foreign acquisitions in the United States, as well as the growing nationalism and interventionism of Congress.

Consequently, it is impossible to determine the interests of firms solely by looking at their domestic or international orientation, and it underlines the importance of analyzing business in a broader environmental context. A recent *Harvard Business Review* poll revealed that U.S. firms are not the world's most avid free traders. About 78 percent of U.S. companies surveyed thought there should be free trade and the "least possible protection for domestic enterprise," putting the United States in sixth place behind Germany (95 percent), Japan (86 percent), Great Britain (83 percent), Brazil (80 percent) and France (79 percent). With regard to foreign-investment review, 38 percent of U.S. companies believed that government should limit the amount of foreign ownership of corporate assets, as opposed to 20 percent of Mexican firms.[55]

Foreign acquisitions form a major component of foreign direct investment into the United States. Although foreign investors established about as many new businesses as they acquired throughout the 1980s, over 80 percent of the dollar value of foreign direct investments was devoted to acquiring U.S. firms. The number of foreign acquisitions fluctuated throughout the 1980s, declining mid-decade and then picking up again in 1986.[56] As recession began in 1990, foreign acquisitions slowed down once again, but the concept

Destler, *The Politics of Anti-Protection* (Washington: Institute for International Economics, 1987).

54. Milner and Yoffie, "Between Protectionism and Free Trade."

55. Rosabeth Moss Kanter, "Transcending Business Boundaries: 12,000 World Managers View Change," *Harvard Business Review* 69, no. 3 (May–June 1991).

56. Jackson, *Foreign Investment*, p. 1.

of alien companies snapping up American firms remains a politically salient factor.

The U.S. business community naturally stands to benefit from legislation that might enable it to ward off hostile takeovers from foreign predators. Business is thus not completely opposed to investment review as embodied in the Exon-Florio provisions. In October 1987, the Emergency Committee for American Trade (ECAT), the Business Round Table, the U.S. Chamber of Commerce, the National Association of Manufacturers, the U.S. Council for International Business, and the National Foreign Trade Council issued a statement that in general approved of the Exon-Florio amendment, with some provisos. As the ECAT vice-chair, Robert L. McNeill testified at a House hearing on the amendment, Exon-Florio, the business community found it "eminently reasonable that the President and his Cabinet Officers have the authority to prohibit foreign investments in American industries that are essential to the national security."[57]

Business supported the Exon-Florio amendment for two primary reasons. The first involves capital's cognizance of the brewing sentiment in favor of interventionism in investment policy in Congress. Given the myriad pieces of legislation regarding foreign investment that had been presented, an altered version of the Exon-Florio amendment was by far the least objectionable. If the inexorable trend toward investment review could not be halted, support of the amendment provided a politically expedient way of taking the middle ground. The testimony of ECAT was pivotal in achieving wider congressional support for the Exon-Florio provision. Once it was clear that business could give at least conditional support to the bill, opponents such as Senator John Danforth (R-Missouri) reversed their objections to the measure. The amendment was duly altered according to the recommendations of the six business organizations listed above, which involved among other things the exclusion of references to "economic welfare and substantial unemployment," dropping the "essential commerce" clause, and removing all explicit references to joint ventures and licensing agreements. With regard

57. Statement of Robert L. McNeill, in U.S. House of Representatives, Hearing before the Subcommittee on Economic Stabilization, Committee on Banking, Finance, and Urban Affairs, 100th Congress, 1st session, October 1987, p. 21. ECAT first expressed this opinion in hearings in June 1987.

to government remedies, reference to forfeiture or divestiture was dropped and replaced with a reference to "appropriate relief."[58]

In contrast, business opposed the Bryant Amendment to the Omnibus Trade and Competitiveness Act and subsequent related legislation in the form of the Bryant-Harkin bill. Both the Association for International Investment and the National Association of Manufacturers opposed the latter bill on the grounds that it discriminated against foreign investors by requiring them, and not domestic firms, to disclose certain information and that it threatened the confidentiality of reporting firms.[59] This opposition to the Bryant bill combined with the concessions demanded for acceptance of the Exon-Florio amendment indicates that business cannot be expected to support any significant broadening of the foreign-investment review process.

The second reason business opted in favor of the Exon-Florio amendment is that, along with state-level provisions to be examined in the next section, this legislation could be a possible tool in avoiding hostile takeovers by foreign firms. Because of the vagueness of the national security mandate, firms desiring to fend off foreign acquirers can turn to CFIUS or its committee members as the ultimate takeover defense. Indeed, the Pentagon was apparently besieged by investment bankers and corporate lawyers after the legislation was passed. As one corporate lawyer noted, "Since there aren't any clear-cut rules, you can submit whatever information you want to the government and contact anyone at any agency who is willing to listen."[60] Those most persuasive in their entreaties may not ward off

---

58. Additionally, these business organizations successfully requested that a confidentiality clause be added to protect information submitted during the course of an investigation and that the discretion of the investigation lie entirely with the secretary of commerce rather than with any or all of the executive agencies. The new changes also gave both the secretary of commerce and the president full discretion *not* to act in the face of a request for an investigation and gave the secretary of commerce guidelines for the writing of specific investment regulations. Subsequently, business organizations supported the president's choice of the Treasury Department as an appropriate home for CFIUS.

59. Statements by Elliot Richardson, Association for International Investment, and Jerry Jasinowski of the National Association of Manufacturers, in U.S. Senate Committee on Commerce, Science, and Transportation, *Foreign Investment in the U.S.*, July 11, 1989.

60. *Wall Street Journal*, March 8, 1989.

aggressive acquirers, but they may achieve a more attractive restructuring of the takeover offer.

The tendency to use legislation to ward off hostile acquirers is even more pronounced at the state level. To this point, we have focused on national institutions and relationships that affect investment policy in the United States. An analysis of investment policy would not be complete without some mention of state-level efforts to attract and regulate foreign investment.

STATE-LEVEL INITIATIVES TO
REGULATE FOREIGN INVESTMENT

Subnational legislatures, in the United States, and also in Canada, have not hesitated to intervene in both a proactive and a reactive sense in the foreign-investment process. State governments have been highly active in recruiting foreign investors to their territories. By 1989, forty-one states had opened 120 offices in twenty four countries to promote trade, tourism, and investment, and about 15 percent of the time they spend recruiting potential investors is directed at foreign firms.[61] States have become particularly notorious for targeting large foreign investors and assembling lucrative incentive packages for them, including low-interest loans, real estate deals, job training subsidies, and outright grants. Following the path of developing countries, many states have created "enterprise zones." Firms investing in these designated zones are eligible for state tax deductions, partial payments of employee wages, reductions on municipal taxes, and property tax breaks. Approximately 1,500 of these zones had been created by 1990. Foreign firms have benefited handsomely from these arrangements, as states try to out-bid each other by offering increasingly generous deals. Many of these packages involve hundreds of millions of dollars in incentives.[62]

Conversely, since the early 1980s states have increasingly moved to protect local firms from takeovers by foreign companies. States

61. Early Fry, "The Economic Development Policies of U.S. State and Local Governments: Implications for the Canada-U.S. Free Trade Agreement," *International Economic Issues* (Halifax: The Institute for Research on Public Policy, April 1990), pp. 41–43.

62. For a review of some of these packages see ibid.

have historically been active in implementing antitrust legislation (affecting both domestic and foreign firms) as well as laws that discriminate more directly against foreign investors. Most of this legislation was intended to regulate alien land ownership, but between 1880 and the early 1900s states introduced new regulations on foreign banks, insurance companies, and mortgage lenders.[63]

More recently, the most prominent state laws affecting foreign investors have been state-level antitakeover laws. While these laws are not directed specifically at foreign investors, they have had major ramifications for non-U.S. companies seeking to acquire American firms. One of the most widely publicized of these cases was the attempt by the BTR PLC of Britain to acquire the Norton Company of Massachusetts. Concerned that BTR would simply disassemble Norton as it had another Massachusetts firm, Governor Michael Dukakis signed into law a bill designed explicitly to squelch the deal. Specifically, the legislation required staggered terms for company directors, prohibiting incorporated companies from electing more than one-third of their board members each year. This in effect meant that BTR could gain only three of eleven seats on the board, making it impossible to gain control of Norton through a proxy fight. The legislation effectively scuttled the deal, and Norton was eventually acquired by the French firm Compagnie de Saint-Gobain, who topped Norton's offer by $15 per share.

The fact that another foreign company acquired Norton indicates that the law was not explicitly intended to keep the company out of foreign hands; rather, it was designed to prevent a corporate raid. This did not stop Governor Dukakis from capitalizing on nationalist sentiments and making the rather inflammatory statement noted in Chapter 3. A similar law limiting voting shares was implemented in Pennsylvania in response to an attempt by the Canadian Belzberg family to acquire Armstrong World Industries in 1990, and in 1988 Ohio passed a law intended to stop Canadian Robert Campeau's bid for Federated Department Stores by postponing all foreign takeovers until state officials could assess their economic impact. In all, forty-one states had antitakeover laws on their books by 1990.[64]

63. Wilkins, *History of Foreign Investment*, pp. 579–80.
64. For a review of state takeover laws, see Ellen Lieberman and Jeffrey B. Bartell, "The Rise in State Anti-Takeover Laws," *Review of Securities and Commodities Regulation* (September 5, 1990).

These measures technically do not abrogate U.S. national treatment commitments to apply policies equally to both foreign and domestic firms because they do not specifically discriminate against foreign firms and can be tailor-made for individual situations to ensure they do not. It could be argued, however, that these measures are not acceptable because under the principle of national treatment, foreign companies are supposed to be granted treatment equal to the most favorably treated domestic company. Although the federal government acknowledges this point, it has refused to face up to the states, and in recent OECD National Treatment negotiations it declined to put controls on state-level legislation of this nature. To date, little research has been done on the issue of subnational investment policies, yet this could be one of the biggest threats to foreign investors. If states continue to protect local firms in this fashion, investor access to the U.S. market is no longer guaranteed.

Broad changes in global power configurations and the nature of international competition have filtered through the economic and political realities of the United States to result in some unique policy adaptations. These new policies are having a major effect on U.S. trade partners and international competition in general. The predictable protectionist reaction of Congress to significant FDI inflows has interacted with and been diffused by the internationalist tendencies of the executive branch. Thus it is clear that the lack of action in investment review does not necessarily show a lack of institutional capacity but rather reflects the ideological proclivities of the chief executive. United States institutions have proven inadequate in terms of supporting R&D policies in commercially oriented industries, however. The result has been inappropriate institutional relationships in the United States that lead domestic producer groups to charge that they are being treated unfairly in the international market. This issue must be dealt with directly in order to diffuse nationalist sentiments in U.S. trade and investment debates.

United States stances on trade and investment policy have also generated considerable panic and some confusion for trade partners, such as Canada. As an ominous nationalist cloud loomed over Congress, the Canadians scrambled to sign a free-trade agreement in the hope of taking advantage of the remaining internationalist, rule-making leanings of the United States. Whether they succeeded in doing so is dubious: the Omnibus Trade and Competitiveness Act containing the Exon-Florio provision as well as the Super 301 and Special 301 clauses was passed in August 1988, one month before the Canada-U.S. Free Trade Agreement was passed. The act therefore is grandfathered, meaning that it takes precedence over any FTA commitments. Canada hopes that it will be able to negotiate for exceptions ("carve outs") to any future trade or investment policies that would have a significant negative impact on Canadian companies, but to date there have been no examples of such precedents. Whether the U.S. Congress or future presidents will feel constrained by the FTA in regard to investment policy toward Canada, as many analysts have claimed, remains a question of faith, not law.

CHAPTER FOUR

Canada: A Small State with a Hegemon's Mentality

Canada is typically portrayed as a nation of compromise, a country that takes the middle road in all aspects of its internal and external relations. There is one area in which Canada has not exhibited its usual moderation, however, and in which it stands out as a leader among advanced industrial states. Canada has encouraged the flow of foreign direct investment into its economy to such an extent that by the 1970s it had the highest proportion of foreign ownership of any developed market economy. Although the extent of foreign ownership declined over the 1980s, about 46 percent of Canadian manufacturing and 69 percent of mining remain foreign owned. This situation has stimulated endless debate among Canadians as they puzzle over explanations for this uncharacteristic lack of restraint.[1]

Canada's industrialization-by-invitation strategy has significance beyond the country's borders. Canada is interesting from a comparative perspective because it poses something of an anomaly. For example, Canada does not behave like a model "small state."[2] Peter Katzenstein argues that because of their small domestic markets and

---

1. For a thorough examination of these theories see Neil Bradford and Glen Williams, "What Went Wrong? Explaining Canadian Industrialization," in Wallace Clement and Glen Williams, eds., *The New Canadian Political Economy* (Kingston: McGill-Queen's University Press, 1989).

2. The reference here is to Peter Katzenstein, *Small States in World Markets* (Ithaca: Cornell University Press, 1985).

their dependence on world trade, small European states such as Sweden, Belgium, and the Netherlands are generally free traders that avoid measures such as tariffs and import quotas. Instead, while adopting liberal policies internationally, they employ domestic social and economic policies that compensate their citizens for the harsh changes the international market thrusts upon them. In Katzenstein's words they "live with change by compensating for it."[3] In many small European countries, these compensatory policies are the result of corporatist political arrangements based on an ideology of social partnership and the existence of highly centralized producer groups that voluntarily coordinate conflicting goals.[4]

Although Canada fits part of this description, the differences outnumber the similarities. As in other small states, Canadian federal and provincial governments have attempted to reduce external dependence through the ownership of public enterprises or Crown corporations.[5] In an argument very similar to Katzenstein's, Harold Innis illustrated how Canada's "staples-led" growth pattern necessitated more interventionist state policies than those of either the United States or Britain. Heavy reliance on natural resources exposed the Canadian economy to fluctuations in world commodity markets, he argued, tying the country's fate to swings in the prices of natural resources and changes in global demand. Domestic economic crises frequently resulted, striking various regions within the country disproportionately. To maintain national unity, the federal government was forced to intervene with adjustment efforts. Consequently, the state gained a prominent role in organizing the economy, as it underwrote the huge infrastructural investment in transportation necessary to get resources to market, and as it compensated for the economic havoc created by fluctuations in international markets.[6]

But the comparison with small European states cannot be pushed much further. While the Canadian state may be more intervention-

3. Ibid., p. 24.
4. Ibid., chap. 3.
5. See Jeanne Laux and Maureen Appel Molot, *State Capitalism* (Ithaca: Cornell University Press, 1987).
6. Harold Innis, *Problems of Staple Production in Canada* (Toronto: Ryerson Press, 1933).

ist than its laissez-faire neighbor to the south, its involvement in the economy does not compare to that of other small states. It cannot engage in corporatist politics because it lacks the coherent and centralized producer groups necessary to hammer out compromises at the bargaining table.[7] In any case, it is questionable whether its weak and incessantly reorganized state agencies have the capacity to implement many of the policies derived from such compromises. Consequently, Canada does not possess many of the compensatory policies evident in other small states. On the contrary, the Progressive government elected in 1984 conducted a sustained attack on such social policies as unemployment insurance, health insurance, and family allowances.[8]

Finally, despite the recent conclusion of a free trade agreement with the United States, Canada historically has not been a free trader. Instead, it has relied extensively on tariffs as a tool in the industrialization process. Indeed, the first major flow of foreign direct investment into Canadian manufacturing was in part a response to the tariffs imposed under the National Policy of 1879. This policy enabled American firms to jump tariff barriers through subsidiaries designed to service the Canadian market.

Curiously, the Canadian government seems consciously to avoid emulating the adjustment policies adopted by other small states. State officials often note that Canada lacked compensatory policies at home because it was an advanced industrial state and as such had to behave like "one of the big boys." Clearly, the relevant comparison in their minds was not to countries of comparable size, such as Sweden or the Netherlands, but rather to the United States. Given Canada's historical position as a member of first the British and then the American empires, its choice of role model is not surprising. But the choice has led to an interesting anomaly: although Canada has the objective status of a small state, it has the mentality of a hegemon. Its allegiance to the Anglo-American style of state intervention is much more solid than its recognition of its status as a small,

7. See Keith Banting, "The State and Economic Interests: An Introduction," in Banting, ed., *The State and Economic Interests* (Toronto: University of Toronto Press, 1986).

8. Bruce Campbell and Maude Barlow, *Take Back the Nation* (Toronto: Key Porter Books, 1991).

open economy. One consequence has been the predominance of a continentalist political discourse that assumes Canada has no alternative but to behave like the United States.

In this chapter I show how this discourse and its policy aftermath have affected Canadian policy toward foreign direct investment. With regard to the theoretical discussion in Chapters 1 and 2, I outline the prominence of Polanyian "protectionist reactions" in influencing Canadian investment policy and show why Canada is more willing to retreat from the regulation of foreign investors than Mexico is. I also illustrate that the development of a continental market was not inevitable but was in large part due to policy decisions by successive Canadian governments. Finally I consider how the 1989 free trade agreement with the United States affected investment policy.

FOREIGN-INVESTMENT REVIEW: THE RUBBER STAMP

The Foreign Investment Review Act was passed on April 9, 1974, by a Liberal party minority government headed by Pierre Trudeau. Legislation of the act followed several widely publicized reports emphasizing the adverse effects of the predominance of foreign capital in the Canadian economy. Building on the warnings of the Liberal finance minister Walter Gordon in 1957, the authors of the government-commissioned Watkins Report of 1968 argued that the widespread presence of multinational enterprises in Canada's economy had led to an inefficient "branch plant" economy. According to the report the replication of American industrial structures in the smaller Canadian market meant that too many products were produced in too small quantities to reach optimum economies of scale. The authors also warned that large transborder flows of goods and services within private firms increased the potential for transfer-pricing and excessive imports of components, practices that threatened Canadian economic welfare.[9]

---

9. Government of Canada, *Foreign Ownership and the Structure of Canadian Industry: Report of the Task Force on the Structure of Canadian Industry* (Ottawa: Queens Printer, 1968).

The Gray Report of 1972 expanded this analysis by arguing that the large number of branch plants in Canada had led to the "truncation" of the Canadian economy.[10] The authors argued that since these branch plants were only part of the integrated operations of MNEs, they were often bereft of critical parts of the production process, such as R&D, and were left only with assembly and sales operations.[11] For this reason the Gray Report recommended the establishment of a screening process that would monitor the progress of foreign corporations in the Canadian economy and pressure them to increase the benefits they provided to the country. Significantly, it argued that this screening agency should operate in the context of a larger industrial strategy designed to realign the Canadian economy. The government responded with the creation of the Foreign Investment Review Agency, in 1974.

The original legislation placed FIRA under the aegis of the Ministry of Industry, Trade, and Commerce, which in turn reported to the cabinet.[12] This legislation stipulated that takeovers of Canadian companies by non-Canadians (non-eligible persons) required prior review and approval by FIRA if the companies had assets of $250,000 or more or gross revenues of greater than $3 million. In 1975, regulations for new establishments were enacted, requiring that all new investments by non-Canadians be reviewed by the agency to determine whether or not they brought "significant benefit" to the Canadian economy. The determination of significant benefit was derived from five criteria:

1. The effect of the acquisition or establishment on the level and nature of economic activity in Canada, including its impact on employment, resource processing, and manufactured imports produced in Canada and its exports from Canada
2. The degree of participation by Canadians in the new business
3. The effects on productivity, technological development, and product variety

10. Herb Gray, *Foreign Direct Investment in Canada* [The Gray Report] (Ottawa: Information Canada, 1972).
11. Government of Canada, *Foreign Ownership in Canada*.
12. This ministry is now known as Industry, Science, and Technology. Investment Canada is not a part of ISTC, although it reports to ISTC's minister.

4. The effects on competition in Canada

5. Compatibility with national industrial and economic policies at both the federal and the provincial level[13]

Despite the broad scope of FIRA's potential powers, relatively few proposals for new investments or acquisitions by foreigners were refused by the agency. Although many complained that FIRA was arbitrary and deterred potential investment, the agency turned down a relatively small number of foreign requests to invest in Canada.[14] Particularly in the late 1970s, FIRA handled the consideration of foreign-investment applications liberally, approving the vast majority of them (Table 4; see Appendix 1 for the refusal rates by sector). Furthermore, the agency reviewed only those new investments coming into the country, ignoring investments made through reinvested earnings. This was an important omission; given the large stock of investment already in Canada, reinvested earnings provided the bulk of increased FDI flows during this period.[15] For this reason, FIRA was often described by its critics as "toothless."

FIRA's relaxed attitude toward FDI changed in 1980, when a newly elected majority Liberal government regained power after a year on the sidelines. Elected on a nationalistic platform that included calls for increased federal government involvement in the oil and gas sector and more stringent monitoring of foreign capital, the Liberals believed they were in a position to act strongly on their campaign commitments. They engaged upon a course of policymaking symbolized by two major policy changes. The first of these was the establishment of a surprisingly nationalistic and interventionist program in the oil and gas sectors known as the National Energy

13. Paraphrased from Steven Globerman, "Canada's Foreign Investment Review Agency and the Direct Investment Process in Canada," *Canadian Public Administration* 27, no. 3 (Fall 1984), p. 316.

14. For a survey of these complaints, see Christopher Beckman, *The Foreign Investment Review Agency: Images and Realities*, Study no. 84 (Ottawa: Conference Board of Canada, 1984). See also Steven Globerman, "The Consistency of Canada's Foreign Investment Review Process: A Temporal Analysis," *Journal of International Business Studies* 15, no. 1 (Spring/Summer 1984).

15. It is interesting that Canada, along with France and Japan, does not include reinvested earnings in its calculations of FDI flows. Were it to do so, annual flow figures would be considerably higher.

Table 4. Cabinet decisions on foreign-investment applications

	Allowed (%)	Disallowed (%)
1974	81.82	18.18
1975	85.06	14.94
1976	78.47	10.22
1977	94.99	5.01
1978	91.89	8.11
1979	92.69	7.31
1980	89.40	10.60
1981	86.40	13.60

Source: Adapted from Jack Layton, "Capital and the Canadian State: Foreign Investment Policy, 1957–1982" (Ph.D. diss., York University, 1983).

Program (NEP). Part of the NEP's purpose was to increase Canadian ownership in the oil and gas industry (which in 1980 was only 30 percent) by phasing out tax depletion allowances and replacing them with incentive grants based on the percentage of a firm's Canadian ownership. One of the most contentious aspects of this legislation was that it allowed the government-owned oil firm Petro-Canada an automatic 25 percent share of all offshore and Arctic oil ventures.[16] Foreign investors protested the NEP measures strongly, as did the government of the United States.

The Liberal government's second major policy change was to increase the stringency of the review process by appointing Herb Gray (author of the 1972 Gray Report) as the minister responsible for FIRA. In a highly contentious cabinet report, Gray argued that the government would have to monitor the behavior of foreign subsidiaries extensively if it was to overcome Canada's structural impediments to sustained economic development.[17] As we will see, this nationalism was short-lived. But the refusal rate did increase slightly in nonresource sectors in 1980–81 (especially in services),

16. For a more in-depth examination of the NEP, see Department of Energy, Mines, and Resources, *The National Energy Program* (Ottawa: Supply and Services Canada, 1980).

17. Department of Industry, Trade, and Commerce, *Framework for Implementing the Government's New Industrial Development Policy during the Next Four Years and Proposals for Immediate Action* (Ottawa: Government of Canada-Supply and Services, 1980).

and the review process was conducted much more meticulously, with only fifty-four of the average number of sixty-three applications that arrived each month being processed. This slowdown eventually caused a backlog of 400 cases and slowed review considerably.

Domestic and foreign capital as well as the United States government reacted strongly to the "new" FIRA. In combination with the NEP, the increased stringency of FIRA's review process was viewed as intolerably nationalistic. The U.S. government formally challenged FIRA's legality in front of a GATT panel in 1982, and along with U.S. business, strongly protested the NEP.

In response to this vociferous opposition to its policies, the Liberal government backed down on both the NEP and the "tougher" FIRA. The NEP was considerably liberalized (and eventually rescinded by the new Progressive government elected in 1984). Gray's interventionist policies were rejected within the cabinet, and he was replaced by the more probusiness Edward Lumley, who sped up the review process and eased the stringency of the "significant benefit" test. In 1982 the approval process for small business applications was simplified and the administration of FIRA clarified.[18] In addition, an international campaign was launched to proclaim that Canada was once again "open for business."

Legislative changes in FIRA's structure did not occur until the election of Brian Mulroney's Progressive government in 1984, however. Worried by lower foreign-investment levels and the legacy of nationalism left by the Liberals, Mulroney sought to change foreign investors' perceptions that Canada was a hostile site for investment. Thus, the new government enacted legislation that replaced the Foreign Investment Review Act with the Investment Canada Act, creating a new institution to be known as Investment Canada. Created on June 30, 1985, Investment Canada was intended not only to review foreign direct investment (albeit in a much more lenient

18. The government increased the review ceiling for applications falling under the "abbreviated small business procedure" from $2 million in gross assets and 100 employees to $5 million in assets and 200 employees for direct acquisitions. For indirect acquisitions, the ceiling was raised to $15 million in gross assets and 1,000 employees. See Arpad Abonyi, "Government Participation in Investment Development," in Andrew Gollner and Daniel Salée, eds., *Canada under Mulroney: An End-of-Term Report* (Montreal: Véhicule Press, 1988), p. 168.

fashion) but also to encourage both foreign and domestic capital to invest in Canada. Overall, the entire outlook of the agency was to change from a negative, cautious attitude toward foreign investment to a more positive, inviting stance.

The more open attitude of Investment Canada is spelled out clearly in the mandate described in its 1986–87 *Annual Report*:

1. to promote investment in Canada by Canadians and non-Canadians.
2. to undertake research and to provide policy advice on matters relating to investments.
3. to review significant investments by non-Canadians to ensure net benefit to Canada.[19]

The third point marks a major change in the review process. Under FIRA, the standard allowance for incoming foreign investment was that it bring "significant benefit" to Canada. Under the Investment Canada Act's "net benefit" criterion, any investment that brought even the smallest benefit had to be accepted. In addition, the review thresholds were changed. Under the Investment Canada Act, filing was necessary to acquire direct control of a Canadian business if that business was worth $5 million or more or to acquire indirect control if the business was worth $50 million or more.[20] These changes meant that approximately 90 percent of foreign-investment transactions were nonreviewable, although even under these new thresholds 90 percent of the transactional value of foreign investments would still be reviewed.

Under the Investment Canada Act, no "new establishment" investments are reviewable, although special consideration is given to foreign investments and acquisitions in cultural industries and in oil and gas. This is a major change from the Foreign Investment Review Act, under which *all* new establishments were reviewable. The real proof of Investment Canada's new leniency is in its review record, however. Since the election of the Mulroney government in 1984, very few foreign-investment acquisitions or establishments

19. Investment Canada, *Annual Report 1986–87* (Ottawa: Government of Canada, Supply and Services, 1987), p. 12.
20. Indirect control is obtained when a foreign company gains control of a Canadian subsidiary through its acquisition of another firm.

have been denied, a result of the "net benefit" criterion: If there is one iota of benefit in an investment, it must be approved. In only one case, the bid by Aerospatial of France and Alenia of Italy to acquire the Canadian aircraft company de Havilland in June 1991, did Investment Canada decline a foreign-investment application. Clearly, the creation of Investment Canada marked a shift in attitude from the more defensive, watchdog role played by FIRA.

Investment regulations applying to U.S. investors were further liberalized by the Canada–United States Free Trade Agreement implemented in January 1989. Under the FTA, U.S. investors must be provided with "national treatment," meaning that they must be treated in a manner no less favorable than the most favored treatment given to domestic investors. There are numerous exclusions to the national treatment provision, however. First, all existing legislation regarding foreign investment in both countries is grandfathered, although all future legislation must meet the national treatment criteria. Certain sectors are also excluded, including financial services, transportation services, cultural industries, energy and basic telecommunications. Businesses owned by the federal or provincial governments and Crown corporations are exempted with regard to "prospective ownership," which means if they are sold, ownership may be restricted to Canadian citizens only and conditions may be imposed to ensure future control of the business by Canadians. Government-owned or Crown corporations established after the implementation of the FTA may also restrict prospective ownership to Canadians, but only in the initial sale of shares. Subsequent resale of shares may not be restricted.[21] Government procurement is also excluded from the investment chapter.

Although the Investment Canada Act was considered to be existing legislation and therefore was grandfathered, the Canadian government agreed to lift the review of thresholds for direct acquisitions by U.S. firms. Direct acquisitions under $150 million were to be made exempt from the review process by 1992. Review of indirect acquisitions was also completely phased out in 1992. The number of acquisitions subject to review is thus considerably reduced but ac-

21. Jean Raby, "The Investment Provisions of the Canada–United States Free Trade Agreement: A Canadian Perspective," *American Journal of International Law* 22 (April 1990), p. 411.

quisitions of the top 600 firms in Canada will still have to be reviewed. These companies in turn represent two-thirds of the total assets of the Canadian economy and more than three-quarters of the assets that were reviewable under the previous act.[22]

Financial industries were not mentioned in the investment chapter of the agreement; however, the FTA contained a financial services agreement that exempted U.S. banks from many existing restrictions on foreign ownership. Commercial banks of the United States are no longer subject to the 16 percent ceiling on foreign bank share of total domestic assets of banks, and there are no longer restrictions on the establishment of intra-Canada branches by United States–owned Schedule B banks. Those U.S. commercial banks desiring to enter Canada after the implementation of the agreement must be granted national treatment and U.S. firms are no longer restricted to 25 percent foreign ownership of Canadian Schedule A banks. Ownership restrictions were also removed for insurance, trust, and loan companies.[23]

Aside from the raising of Investment Canada's review thresholds and the new provisions for services, many argue that Canada's foreign-investment legislation was left relatively unchanged. Sectoral policies are grandfathered and government-owned and Crown corporations are exempt. Trade-related performance, requirements concerning import substitution, export performance, and local sourcing are prohibited, but Canada can still demand concessions with regard to local employment, R&D, technology transfer, and world product mandates.[24] The FTA does nothing to impede the expansion of Canadian control of an industry through public ownership, its supporters argue, nor does it prohibit influencing investors through tax policies, and competition policy.[25]

22. Ibid., p. 422.

23. Jeffrey J. Schott and Murray G. Smith, "Services and Investment," in Schott and Smith, eds., *The Canada–United States Free Trade Agreement: The Global Impact* (Washington: Institute for International Economics, and Halifax: The Institute for Research on Public Policy, 1988), pp. 143–44.

24. A. E. Safarian, "Direct Investment Strategies and the Canada-U.S. Free Trade Agreement," in Clark W. Reynolds, Leonard Waverman, and Gerardo Bueno, eds., *The Dynamics of North American Trade and Investment: Canada, Mexico, and the United States* (Stanford: Stanford University Press, 1991), p. 151.

25. Raby, "Investment Provisions," pp. 426–29. Raby argues that the FTA actually *encourages* recourse to public ownership because of the provision that Crown corpora-

Critics respond that the concessions on performance require-ments were significant and could have a major impact on local firms that supply U.S. subsidiaries. This situation is exacerbated by the elimination of the right to demand minimum Canadian ownership requirements, which could be used to increase Canadian content in production. More important, they argue, it means that Canadian investment policies are covered and thereby restricted by the FTA. This is not true of the U.S. investment provisions embodied in the Exon-Florio amendment, since they are part of the Omnibus Trade and Competitiveness Act of 1988 and thereby grandfathered.[26] Still, the national treatment and performance requirement provi-sions outlined in the FTA would presumably apply to subsequent U.S. investment regulation. As outlined in Chapter 3, however, many state legislatures in the United States have passed tailor-made legislation that does not explicitly discriminate against foreign firms yet may well affect for Canadian investors.

Canada's position in the international political economy and its unique relationship with the United States partially account for the more extensive deregulation of foreign-investment review in Can-ada than in Mexico. This partnership deserves further examination.

CANADA IN THE INTERNATIONAL POLITICAL ECONOMY

As noted earlier, Canada fits into the category of industrialized states with small, open economies. In fact, Canada has one of the most open economies of all advanced industrial states. Because of its relatively small domestic market, Canada is highly dependent on foreign market access for sales, exporting 30 percent of its gross national product (GNP). As a percentage of GNP, Canada exports twice as much as Japan does. According to the *OECD Economic*

---

tions may restrict the sale of assets to domestic investors. This argument ignores that the compensation provisions of the FTA could make the cost of public ownership prohibitively high if it involved takeovers of already-existing private firms. See also Safarian, "Direct Investment Strategies."

26. Bruce Campbell, *Hard Lessons: Living with Free Trade* (Ottawa: Canadian Centre for Policy Alternatives, 1991). It is important to note that the GATT had already censured Canada's local sourcing practices, although it placed no restrictions on export requirements.

Outlook, Canada was the OECD leader in terms of exports of goods and services as a percentage of gross domestic product (GDP) in 1980. By 1988, Germany had surpassed it and Canada took second place. But even compared to many other open market economies, Canada is distinguished by its high level of foreign ownership. By 1967, 53 percent of Canada's manufactured output was produced by foreign subsidiaries, as opposed to an average of 17 percent in other OECD countries. Given the connections between investment and trade, a distortion in the pattern of foreign investment in Canada would seriously affect trade flows as well.

Canada (like the United States) also relies heavily on foreign-portfolio borrowing to finance increasing levels of government indebtedness.[27] Although Canadian personal savings rates are higher than those in the United States (the American rate is below 7 percent, whereas the Canadian rate has varied between 9 and 15 percent since 1975), they are not especially high by international standards.[28] Despite the major contribution personal savings have made to investment, they have not been sufficient to make up for increased levels of borrowing by business and government. Thus, a downturn or net outflow of nonresident investment would affect the Canadian economy significantly. Portfolio investment has represented a growing proportion of foreign investment flows into Canada (Table 5).

Canada's economy is particularly integrated on a continental scale with the United States. Seventy-five percent of Canada's exports are to the United States, and 70 percent of its imports are from it.[29] In 1987, 71.1 percent of Canada's stock of foreign direct investment was owned by Americans.[30] Because of these close ties, Canada is

27. See Charles A. Barrett, Christopher C. Beckman, and Duncan McDowall, *The Future of Foreign Investment in Canada* (Ottawa: Conference Board, 1985).

28. Savings rates in the United Kingdom, France, and Germany are on average the same as or slightly higher than in Canada while rates in Japan and Italy are considerably higher.

29. Glen Williams, "Regions within Region: Canada in the Continent," in Glen Williams and Michael Whittington, eds., *Canadian Politics in the 1990s*, 3d ed. (Toronto: Nelson Canada, 1990), p. 3.

30. Investment Canada, *International Investment: Canadian Business in a Global Context* (Ottawa: Government of Canada-Supply and Services, January 1991).

Table 5. Portfolio and direct investment in Canada (year-end book value, billions of [Canadian] dollars)

	Portfolio investment as percentage of total	Direct investment as percentage of total
1974	36.4	63.6
1975	43.0	57.0
1976	48.3	51.7
1977	49.9	50.1
1978	54.5	45.5
1979	54.0	46.0
1980	53.0	47.0
1981	55.5	44.5
1982	58.5	41.5
1983	58.4	41.6
1984	59.1	40.9
1985	62.0	38.0
1986	63.8	36.2
1987[a]	63.4	36.6

Source: Canada Facts 1989 (Ottawa: Prospectus Trade and Investment Partners, 1989).
[a]Preliminary figures.

especially sensitive to American political and economic trends. Saying that Canada is sensitive to the United States is not tantamount to arguing that Canada simply does whatever the United States desires (that is, liberalize its foreign-investment regulations). The reality is much more complicated, and country's close relationship with the United States has led to episodes of both nationalism and liberalization. The burst of Canadian economic nationalism that led to the creation of FIRA in the 1970s, for example, was in many ways a response to U.S. actions. Such highly publicized events as the U.S. government's insistence that American automobile companies cancel truck and car shipments to China and Cuba by their Canadian subsidiaries proved particularly galling. Because such shipments contravened the U.S. Trading with the Enemy Act, the American government ordered the parent companies to stop them. Many Canadians found this extraterritorial application of law intolerable.

In addition, the United States implemented various domestic policies in the 1970s that revealed Canada's extreme dependence on U.S. investment flows. Anxious to ameliorate American balance-of-payments problems, President Richard Nixon introduced tax legislation in 1971 that discouraged U.S. investment abroad by providing a 7 percent tax credit for domestic investment and encouraged exports as opposed to FDI through a tax credit on foreign sales.[31] These measures were combined with a 10 percent surcharge on imports to the United States, from which Canada eventually was exempted but which highlighted Canada's fragile economic position. Such U.S. policies increased Canadian determination to reduce reliance on American trade and investment flows.

Throughout the 1980s, however, American pressure was a constant liberalizing force in regard to Canadian investment regulation. This was especially true after the election to the presidency in 1980 of Ronald Reagan, who had little tolerance for the economic nationalism to the north. The Reagan administration was appalled by both the Canadianization strategies of the NEP and the more stringent application of FIRA. The Americans charged that FIRA was distorting trade by placing local sourcing requirements on U.S. companies operating in Canada or by demanding that they export a percentage of their production.[32] While the U.S. government recognized that other countries frequently enacted such measures, Canada was expected "to set a higher standard."[33] More important, it perceived the interventionist policies of the Trudeau government as clashing directly with the long-term interests of the United States in terms of the international free flow of capital. This is evident in the testimony of Assistant Secretary for International Economic Policy Raymond J. Waldmann:

> Canada's growing reliance on government intervention to direct and control national trade and investment patterns conflicts with this Ad-

31. The latter measure was implemented through the DISC program (Domestic International Sales Corporations), which allowed companies to write off 50 percent of the taxes on their foreign sales. See Claire Turenne Sjolander, "Foreign Investment Policy Making: The Canadian State in the Global Economy" (Ph.D. diss., Carleton University, 1989), p. 277.

32. Testimony of the United States, GATT Council Meeting, March 31, 1982.

33. Testimony of Robert Hormats, Assistant Secretary for Economic and Business Affairs, State Department, in U.S. Senate, Committee on Foreign Relations, *U.S. Economic Relations with Canada*, Hearings of the Subcommittee on International Economic Policy, 97th Congress, 2d session, March 10, 1982, p. 4.

ministration's advocacy of free market oriented policies. In the first instance, Canada's growing ardor for pursuing policies and programs of economic nationalism (Canadianization) has resulted in discrimination against U.S. business interests. Secondly, and perhaps more importantly in terms of our long term interest, we believe that the methods used by Canada to enforce economic nationalism pose a threat to the international trading system by erecting barriers to cross-border flows of trade and capital.[34]

The response of the Reagan administration to Canada's "economic nationalism" was threefold. On a national level, the Department of Commerce undertook a survey of U.S. companies with operations in Canada to determine how these companies were affected by FIRA. On a bilateral level, the Reagan administration held extensive consultations with a number of high-level Canadian officials regarding investment policies. It also considered a possible action under the Section 301 clause of the 1974 Trade Act, which allows the president to retaliate against countries using unfair trade practices. On a multilateral level, the U.S. government initiated and held consultations with respect to trade-related performance requirements associated with Canada and prepared a case in which a GATT panel considered whether Canadian investment policies violated its obligations under the GATT. Specifically, the case related to FIRA's export and "buy Canadian" policies. In addition, with specific reference to Canada, it pushed for an investigation by the OECD into government intervention in trade and investment flows by applying discriminatory requirements. The Americans saw the Canadian action as part of a more general trend in this direction and won agreement by the OECD Trade Committee to initiate a study of trade-related performance requirements.

The Reagan administration was further irritated by an apparent flow of Canadian capital into the United States, symbolized by some highly visible takeovers of American firms by Canadian companies, such as Seagram's takeover bids on St. Joe Minerals and the Canadian Pacific Enterprises purchase of the U.S.-owned company Cana-

34. Prepared statement of Raymond J. Waldmann, Assistant Secretary for International Economic Policy, U.S. Department of Commerce, in ibid., pp. 1–2.

dian International Paper Company. American companies resented the ability of Canadians freely to acquire U.S. firms, arguing that they were restricted from doing the same thing in Canada.[35]

The United States eventually won a partial condemnation of FIRA from the GATT. While supporting FIRA's right to exist, the GATT panel said that its "buy Canadian" provisions did break international trade rules, although it had no authority to rule on export performance requirements. Ottawa's greater willingness to appease U.S. dissatisfaction came only after the election of the conservative Mulroney government in 1984, however, when a free trade agreement with the United States became an explicit part of the Progressive Conservative policy agenda. Terrified by the rising protectionist sentiment in the United States, the government was convinced that a free trade agreement was the only way to prevent being victimized by congressional protectionist efforts.

The FTA was designed not only to stave off American protectionism but also to institutionalize the "internationalist view of Canada."[36] More correctly, it formalizes a continentalist perspective on the Canadian economy and a view that further integration with the United States is desirable and inevitable. In this sense, the trade agreement is yet another example of the process of building a continental market. Contrary to those who argue that continentalization is inevitable, evidence indicates that the extensive integration of the U.S. and Canadian markets was not a spontaneous phenomenon. On the contrary, it was the result of a series of policy decisions by the Canadian government that encouraged the inflow of U.S. investment. As noted earlier, the National Policy of 1879 encouraged foreign investment by inviting U.S. firms to jump high tariff walls and produce in Canada. This option was made even more attractive by the system of imperial preferences in place until World War II, which provided foreign investors preferential access to other Commonwealth economies.

Connections between the two economies multiplied during World War II, however, when Canadian exports to the United States tri-

35. Stephen Clarkson, *Canada and the Reagan Challenge* (Toronto: Lorimer, 1982), p. 57.

36. Michael Hart, *A North American Free Trade Agreement: The Strategic Implications for Canada* (Ottawa: Centre for Trade Policy and Law, and Halifax: the Institute for Research on Public Policy, 1990), p. 47.

pled and U.S. exports to Canada doubled owing to joint defense production arrangements. During this period, Canadian industries became highly dependent on the importation of U.S. capital goods, components, and technologies.[37] The postwar policies of C. D. Howe, a cabinet minister, were specifically directed to making Canada an attractive investment environment through such incentives as double depreciation and the privatization of wartime manufacturing establishments at exceptionally low prices. These incentives, combined with the relative unattractiveness of the war-torn European economies, encouraged a massive inflow of investment from the south. Throughout the 1950s, Canada also pursued policies explicitly designed to enhance the North American integration of its resource industries.

Naturally, the closer integration of the two economies was politically significant: the massive flow of U.S. dollars into Canadian raw materials increased the influence of the predominantly foreign-owned resource sector, and extensive U.S. ownership of manufacturing created a series of branch plants that were dependent on continental integration. Sectoral agreements between Canada and the United States in automobiles, defense production, and energy consolidated this trend.[38]

The FTA was the next stage in this process of continentalization, but it is important to emphasize that like other continentalist policies, it was not inevitable. In fact, the FTA was signed because of a historically unique coincidence of party politics, business interests, favorable exchange rates, and a government that endorsed laissez-faire policies.

DOMESTIC POLITICAL INFLUENCES

Economic Nationalism and Party Politics

A clear understanding of the evolution of foreign-investment regulation in Canada is impossible without some consideration of the domestic politics surrounding the debate over the role of FDI in

37. Janine Brodie, *The Political Economy of Canadian Regionalism* (Toronto: Harcourt Brace Jovanovich, 1990).

38. Ibid., pp. 151–55.

the Canadian economy. A key force in the dynamics of this process was the ebb and flow of economic nationalism. Nationalism and the fear of being absorbed by its powerful neighbor to the south has always been a prominent element of Canada's political economy. American direct investment in Canada became a focal point for these nationalist sentiments.

United States investment in Canada began its most rapid period of growth just after World War II. Perceiving it as a quick path to economic development and higher standards of living for all Canadians, Canada participated eagerly in this project, which is often referred to as a "second National Policy." During this period foreign capital, encouraged as part of a more general policy to reinforce Canada's participation in the international economy,[39] flowed into the economy in large quantities (Table 6).

As a result of this openness to foreign capital, non-Canadian ownership of the economy increased rapidly (Table 7). Not surprisingly, a Polanyian protectionist reaction to these huge inflows of FDI began to appear in the late 1950s, its first prominent advocate being the Liberal finance minister Walter Gordon. Gordon's nationalist sympathies found little support within Lester Pearson's internationalist Liberal party of the time. His warnings about the perils of excessive foreign ownership of the economy, however, were eagerly picked up by forces within the social democratic New Democratic party (NDP), in which a nascent stream of economic nationalism began to blossom in the late 1960s. Known as the Waffle, this nationalist faction achieved nationwide attention in the early 1970s. One of the earliest government-commissioned reports on FDI was headed by a Waffle member, Mel Watkins, in 1968. Nonpartisan groups, such as the Committee for an Independent Canada (CIC), also were formed to lobby for government action in response to what was portrayed as a threat to the nation.

Many of the U.S. actions outlined above served to galvanize support for foreign-investment review during this period. Assessments of the economic impact of foreign direct investment varied accord-

39. See François Houle, "L'état canadien et le capitalisme mondial: Stratégies d'insertion," *Canadian Journal of Political Science* 20 (September 1987), p. 485, and Brodie, *The Political Economy of Canadian Regionalism*.

Table 6. Foreign direct investment in Canada (in millions of Canadian dollars)

	1945	1950	1955	1961	1971	1974
United States	2,304	3,426	6,513	11,284	22,443	28,996
United Kingdom	348	468	890	1,613	2,715	3,525
Other	61	81	325	840	2,760	3,716
Total	2,713	3,975	7,728	13,737	27,918	36,237

Source: Steven Globerman, *U.S. Ownership of Firms in Canada* (Montreal: C. D. Howe Institute, 1979), p. 7.

Table 7. Percentage of capital under Canadian and foreign control

	1926	1939	1948	1954	1962	1970	1975	1980	1984
Manufacturing									
Canadian	65	62	57	49	40	39	45	49	51
Foreign	35	38	43	51	60	61	55	51	49
(U.S. share)	30	32	39	41	45	47	42	40	38
Mining and Manufacturing[a]									
Canadian	62	58	60	49	42	30	40	59	62
Foreign	38	42	40	51	58	70	60	41	38
(U.S. share)	32	38	37	49	52	59	46	29	27
Oil and Natural Gas[a]									
Canadian				31	26	24	26	50	56
Foreign				69	74	76	74	50	44
(U.S. share)				67	63	61	38	35	35

Source: François Houle, "L'état canadien et le capitalisme mondial: Stratégies d'insertion," *Canadian Journal of Political Science* 20 (September 1987), p. 486.
[a]For the years 1926, 1939, and 1948, mines, refineries, oil, and gas are calculated together.

ing to the ideological inclinations of the analyst involved, but there was considerable consensus that FDI caused major *political* problems for Canada. Many Canadians viewed the extraterritorial implications of U.S. laws as an intolerable side effect of excessive amounts of foreign investment. Claire Turenne Sjolander argued that this agreement on extraterritoriality provided the common ground necessary for political action to regulate foreign investment.[40]

As the strength of the nationalist current grew, concern about

40. Sjolander, "Foreign Investment Policy Making," chap. 4.

foreign direct investment eventually spread to the Liberal party. By 1975, Gallup polls showed that 71 percent of those interviewed believed that there was "enough" U.S. foreign investment in Canada, and 58 percent thought that Canada should buy back 51 percent ownership in all U.S. companies in Canada.[41] Yet despite the recommendation of the Liberal minister Herb Gray that an investment review agency was necessary, the Liberal party remained divided. It is illustrative that FIRA was created between October 1972 and July 1974, when the Liberal minority government was in power. During that time the NDP held the balance of power in the legislature and, bolstered by public opinion, was able to pressure the Liberals into adopting the FIRA legislation.

But the nationalist cause lost much of its steam as economic conditions worsened during the 1970s, and public attention to the foreign-investment issue began to wane. Party politics reflected this loss of interest; by the federal election of 1978, there was little difference between the internationalist, free market election platform of the Progressive Conservatives and that of the Liberal party. Indeed, Trudeau's loss of this election to the Progressive Conservative leader Joe Clark was a signal to many within the Liberal party that their platform had become indistinguishable from that of the Progressive Conservatives. During his year in the Opposition, Trudeau used two of his oldest political confrères, Herb Gray as shadow finance minister and Marc Lalonde as energy critic, to shape an interventionist and nationalist platform that would differ significantly from that of the Progressive Conservatives.[42] When Clark's minority government was forced to call a new election in 1980, the Liberals were returned to office on the basis of a nationalist, interventionist platform that included a more stringent application of FIRA and a highly interventionist National Energy Program.

As noted in Chapter 2, however, Canadian governments seem to have a very bad sense of timing, and nationalist policies of this sort

41. Gallup poll data cited in Williams, "Regions within Region," p. 15.
42. It is important to note that this was not the only goal of the orientation of Liberal policy. Particularly in the area of energy, these interventionist policies were designed as much to garner revenues for the federal government and bolster federal power in relation to the provinces as they were to separate the Liberals from the Progressive Conservatives.

were economically risky. Real GDP growth slipped to −3.3 percent in 1982 (the lowest growth rate of all OECD countries), and the unemployment rate rose to 11.9 percent in 1983. Interest rates rose from an average of 7.83 percent in 1974 to peak at over 20 percent in 1981.[43] Canada's economic stagnation was mirrored internationally, as all countries slipped into recession in 1980. It is clear that slower economic growth and higher unemployment rates chastened the government's nationalist efforts considerably. Public opinion changed as well: in 1984, 50 percent of Canadians believed Canada had enough foreign investment (down 21 percent from 1975), and only 36 percent thought Canadians should repurchase 51 percent control from U.S. firms (down 22 percent from 1975).

Intracabinet disputes also played a large part in the demise of nationalist policies. To promote an expanded mandate for FIRA, Herb Gray, the minister of what was then Industry, Trade, and Commerce, argued that foreign subsidiaries had to be monitored more closely to ensure they performed to world standards in terms of exports and R&D expenditures, but his views were never well received in the cabinet. In the face of growing U.S. criticism of FIRA's stricter policies and declining public support for them at home, a counter policy document presented by the minister of Economic Development, H. A. Olsen, gained growing credence.

The Olsen document, which was far less interventionist than Gray's, won out in cabinet discussions. An ad hoc committee assigned to reconcile the two perspectives presented a position paper in 1981 that ignored the need for restructuring urged in Gray's report. Instead, it argued that with prices rising for commodities such as oil, emphasis should be placed on natural resources.[44] Of course, the falling commodity prices of the 1980s revealed the shortcomings of this perspective. Still, by 1982 the Liberal government had already begun loosening FIRA's review process and the NEP was in the process of being dismantled. By the time of the Progres-

---

43. GDP and exchange-rate statistics are from OECD, *Main Economic Indicators, Historical Statistics* (Paris: OECD, 1984), and interest rates are from *The Economist, World Business Cycles*.

44. Maureen Appel Molot and Glen Williams, "The Political Economy of Continentalism," in Michael Whittington and Glen Williams, eds., *Canadian Politics in the 1980s*, 2d ed. (Toronto: Methuen, 1984), pp. 90–91.

sive Conservative party victory in the election of 1984, there was little effective political opposition to the deregulation of foreign-investment review.

By the 1990s public opposition to foreign investment had all but disappeared, partly because foreign control of the Canadian economy had declined from its peak of 36 percent in the 1970s to about 27 percent by 1987. But the fading of the opposition was also a consequence of a twist in the nationalist discourse during the debate over the FTA. As falling tariffs became an increasing focus of nationalist and social democratic opponents to the FTA, critics began to usher in arguments regarding the *importance* of foreign investment for the Canadian economy in support of their position. Increased tariffs, they argued, were a major impetus to the growth of foreign investment in Canada. If these tariffs were dropped, why would anyone invest there anymore? Instead, potential U.S. investors would simply manufacture goods locally and export them to Canada. Third Country investors could do the same thing by investing in the larger U.S. market and shipping their goods northward. Many of those propounding this position would likely still be willing to argue for controls on FDI. Nevertheless, in political terms it meant a shift in emphasis from regulating FDI to attracting it.

Domestic and International Capital

A major contrast between Canada and other small states is Canada's lack of highly centralized producer groups. Canadian business, for example, is exceedingly segmented institutionally. Coleman counted 480 nationally relevant business associations.[45] Of these, several major groups represent cross-sectoral business interests: the Business Council on National Issues (BCNI), the Canadian Manufacturers' Association (CMA), the Canadian Chambers of Commerce, the Canadian Federation of Independent Business (CFIB), the Canadian Organization of Small Business (COSB), and the Conseil du patronat du Québec. Each of these groups represents a different constituency, although some overlap exists. For example,

45. William Coleman, "Canadian Business and the State," in Banting, *The State and Economic Interests*.

the CMA, the Chambers of Commerce, and the Conseil du patronat are all members of the BCNI. This organizational pluralism makes the coordination of business interests a complex endeavor. As William Coleman notes,

> There is little doubt that the system of business associations is underdeveloped. It is characterized by congeries of isolated groups: intersectoral associations operate independently of divisional associations, divisional associations of sectoral associations and sectoral associations of subsectoral associations. Regional interests are paid little attention and the representativeness of associations with more general domains is suspect.[46]

To complicate things more, many of these groups contain a mixture of foreign controlled and domestically controlled groups, which "may on occasion reduce the clarity of an association's collective view."[47]

This organizational chaos should not mask essential coincidences of interest among these groups, however. Differences certainly exist, and clashes over policy issues have made the representation of business interests to government difficult in the past. But business interests in the area of foreign-investment regulations have become increasingly coherent during the past decade. While certain businesses have exhibited "nationalist" concerns over time, it is clear that a general trend toward approval of deregulating foreign investment and in favor of freer trade has emerged. Without this trend, neither the FTA nor the development of Investment Canada could have come into being.

One business group appears to have emerged as dominant among this conglomeration and has been a prime supporter of the trend toward freer trade and deregulation. The BCNI was created in 1976, one year after the implementation of mandatory wage and price controls.[48] The group was established specifically to address

46. Ibid., p. 272.

47. Taskforce on Business/Government Interface, quoted in Banting, "The State and Economic Interests," p. 18.

48. David Langille, "The Business Council on National Issues and the Canadian State," *Studies in Political Economy* 24 (Autumn 1987).

the organizational pluralism of business, since events surrounding the institution of wage and price controls in the 1970s made it clear that it was difficult for business to articulate a clear position. The BCNI is an umbrella organization that represents domestic and foreign firms and includes many of the other business organizations listed above. It is a sophisticated, articulate organization based on the Business Roundtable in the United States. As Langille notes, however, the BCNI is not as virulently laissez-faire as its American counterpart. It is not antiunion, and it acknowledges an important role for the state within the national economy. During the two Mulroney governments, this group came to play a key role in policymaking, with direct input into policy initiatives.

The BCNI has consistently opposed foreign-investment regulation, and it applauded Mulroney's decision to reform the Foreign Investment Review Agency in 1985. It opposed FIRA not on the grounds that it deterred investment; in fact, BCNI officials openly acknowledged that FIRA got a "bit of a bum rap" in the past.[49] The group's opposition was based on the position that whether or not FIRA actually had a negative effect on foreign investment, it was perceived negatively by international investors and thus reduced Canada's appeal as an investment site.[50] More fundamentally, the BCNI argues that investment decisions should be made by the firm, not by the government. In this sense, it touches on the very essence of business interests in Canada: that investment decisions are a private, not a public, decision.

This is not to say that business denies the legitimacy of any state involvement in the economy. Many Canadian companies rely on government support in the form of procurement policies, contracts, and protection from foreign competitors. Specific industries have asked the Canadian government to protect them from foreign investors, and they usually have been granted such support. Firms in the transportation, publishing, and communications industries have all received state protection from foreign investors in the past.[51] Even

49. Interview at BCNI, December 1987.
50. Testimony of Thomas Acquino, BCNI President, in *Minutes of Proceedings and Evidence of the Standing Committee on Regional Development*, March 5, 1985 (Ottawa: Government of Canada, 1985), p. 11:27.
51. The Canadian Transport Commission must authorize any foreign investment

financial capital, which is generally characterized as having internationalist interests, has asked for investment protection from the
state. After the takeover of Royal Securities in 1969, the Ontario
government instituted strict regulations on takeovers of securities
firms by foreigners.[52]

There is, however, much less enthusiasm for across-the-board
regulation of FDI in Canada than there is in Mexico. Like Mexican
capital, Canadian companies have supported the implementation of
policies that would enhance their competitiveness, such as procurement contracts, subsidies, and tax write-offs. But few companies
ardently supported the creation of FIRA, and many of those that did
have changed their position over time. Among the strong supporters of the original FIRA legislation were the Canadian publishing
industry and the Canadian Federation of Independent Business,
but even this support was qualified. The CFIB argued that it did
not want to stop U.S. companies from investing in Canada, it just
wanted them to stop taking over Canadian firms. A similar complaint came from Canadian-owned drug companies. Both parties
requested state assistance to help Canadians keep their companies.
This line of argument reveals a parallel to the investment review
debate in the United States: firms who see the potential of investment review as an antitakeover device are not unalterably opposed
to the process. Canadian drug firms also asked for tax benefits and
procurement contracts to help them compete with American subsidiaries.[53]

The Canadian Chambers of Commerce and the Mining Association opposed the FIRA legislation, however, since their membership
was primarily made up of multinationals and Canadian service

in commercial air, water, rail, and motor carriers. In 1964, the government prohibited more than 25 percent foreign ownership of insurance, loan and trust companies. Canada's Bank Act previously stipulated that 75 percent of bank directors
must be Canadian and restricted foreign ownership of banks to 25 percent of shares,
although these rules were changed in the FTA. Similar measures apply in the communications sector. Foreigners can own no more than 25 percent of Canadian televi-
sion companies, and foreign publications distributed in Canada are not allowed to
carry advertisements directed at the Canadian market.

52. Ontario deregulated the securities area in 1987 in response to Quebec's decision to do so.

53. Jack Layton, "Capital and the Canadian State: Foreign Investment Policy,
1957–1982" (Ph.D. diss., York University, 1983).

groups (such as real estate, engineering, architectural, and manage-ment consulting firms) who have foreign companies as clients.[54] The position of the banks was particularly interesting. Bankers opposed the implementation of FIRA. A common criticism of Cana-dian banks has been that they channel their capital to foreign inves-tors, leaving domestic producers to languish.[55] The banks favor large foreign multinationals because their advanced technological and production techniques tend to make them lower risks as bor-rowers than many Canadian companies. Thus, at the same time Canadian banks were benefiting from regulations that restricted foreign investment in the financial sector, a former vice-president of the Bank of Nova Scotia noted, "the nationality of the individuals controlling Canadian industry is an irrelevant factor in the perfor-mance of the Canadian economy."[56]

Certain Canadian business people have been vocal in their sup-port of FDI regulation. An important source of support for the nationalist platform of the Liberal government elected in 1980 was an emerging nationalist strain of Canadian businesses that called for greater government support of domestic firms. Businessmen such as Robert Blair of NOVA, John Shepherd of Leigh Instruments, Jack Gallagher of Dome Petroleum, and Raymond Royer of Bom-bardier began in the 1970s to call for preferential treatment for Canadian capital in government procurement policies and for in-dustrial policies designed to increase Canadian industrial and tech-nological independence.[57] By the 1980s, however, Blair had sold NOVA to a U.S. company and Leigh Instruments was acquired by a British firm. In general, Canadian capital began to move away from nationalist positions and began to champion more internationalist issues.

This trend is reflected not only in the growing approval of business for foreign-investment deregulation but also in the near-unanimous support of business for a free trade deal. Three reasons for this

54. Ibid.
55. Tom Naylor, *The History of Canadian Business, 1867–1914* (Toronto: Lorimer, 1975).
56. Cited in Layton, "Capital," p. 335.
57. Stephen Clarkson, *Canada and the Reagan Challenge* (Toronto: Lorimer, 1982), pp. 18–19.

transition stand out. First, as noted above, the level of foreign owner-ship of Canadian business assets has decreased. Especially for oil and gas companies, nationalist policies such as the NEP allowed domestic capital a chance to catch up with its foreign competitors in the domestic market: the NEP doubled Canadian ownership in this sector. Second, investment abroad by Canadian companies has also grown. Canadian direct investment outflows increased ten times between 1970 and 1980. During this same time period, the book value of Canadian FDI grew at a compound annual rate of 14.3 percent as compared with a rate of 8.3 percent for FDI coming into Canada.[58] The stock of Canadian foreign investment abroad in-creased from $16.4 billion in 1978 to $74 billion in 1989.[59] A large percentage of this investment went to the United States—by the late 1980s, approximately 71 percent of the book value of Canada's FDI was invested in the United States. These trends make Canadian foreign investors particularly sensitive to Canadian relations with the United States, and provide little incentive for them to lobby for investment controls.[60]

But probably the most important reason Canadian manufactur-ing companies supported the FTA was exchange rates. Canadian merchandise exports as a percentage of GDP rose from 15.6 percent in 1965 to 25.6 percent in 1980. This trend was particularly marked in manufacturing, which grew from 15.3 percent of merchandise exports in 1965 to almost 30 percent in 1980, primarily as a result of the signing of the Canada–United States auto pact in 1965.[61] But another significant burst in trade occurred after a major devaluation of the Canadian dollar in 1980. Between 1980 and 1985, Canada's trade surplus with the United States increased from US$1.3 billion to US$15.7 billion.[62] Predictably, Canadian manufacturers were ea-ger to hold on to their expanded share of the U.S. market, confident

58. Arpad Abonyi, "The Business Environment," in Financial Post, *A Business Introduction to Canada-U.S. Free Trade* (Toronto: Financial Post Information Service, 1989), p. 7.

59. Investment Canada, *International Investment*, chart 28.

60. Arpad Abonyi, "Investment," in Financial Post, *A Business Introduction*, p. 52.

61. Jock Finlayson, "Trade Policy and Performance," in Financial Post, *A Business Introduction*, p. 27.

62. Jeffrey Schott, "The Free Trade Agreement: A U.S. Assessment," in Schott and Smith, *The Canada–United States Free Trade Agreement*, p. 9.

in their new-found competitiveness. They therefore opposed measures such as investment review that might alienate the U.S. government or U.S. firms. The subsequent revaluation of the Canadian dollar to its 1991 peak of US$0.87 has somewhat dampened business support for the FTA, however. In the first three years after the agreement was implemented, Canada's merchandise trade surplus with the United States dropped Can$6.1 billion compared to the three years before the FTA.[63]

Foreign investors in Canada have generally opposed investment regulation. While this may not appear surprising, foreign investors in Mexico frequently do support state regulations on FDI because of the benefits they gain from such protection. The position of the Canadian Manufacturing Association toward the FIRA legislation, however, indicates that opposition to foreign-investment review is not absolute. The CMA is primarily composed of foreign companies and it generally opposed the FIRA legislation, although not vociferously. One change it proposed in the legislation was to separate the rules governing established foreign-owned companies from those governing new takeover attempts by foreign investors. Such a measure would have effectively grandfathered established foreign investors, giving them an advantage over newcomers.[64] This is analogous to the position taken by grandfathered MNEs in Mexico, which oppose liberalization because regulations provide barriers to entry to new competitors.

Generally speaking, however, Canada's foreign-investment regulations do not raise high enough barriers to entry to garner support from foreign capital. On the other hand, foreign investors have supported tariffs that *did* play a role in protecting their market position. Harold Innis notes that in 1911, the Canadian Manufacturers' Association, which was composed mainly of foreign firms even then, supported the campaign against "reciprocity" or free trade.[65] Doing away with tariffs on U.S. goods would have exposed them to import competition and negated the original impetus for

63. Statistics Canada, *Balance of International Payments*, 1991 (Ottawa: Government of Canada, 1992).

64. Layton, "Capital," p. 330.

65. Harold Innis, *Essays in Canadian Economic History* (Toronto: University of Toronto Press, 1956), p. 405.

investing in Canada. Williams also emphasizes that foreign capital supported the system of Imperial Preferences developed in the 1930s, even though it involved tariffs on American goods. American producers saw that by jumping the tariff and producing in Canada they could have duty-free access to the rest of the empire (although not all large U.S. firms took advantage of this opportunity).[66] Recently, however, the CMA reversed its traditional position on tariffs and threw its support behind the FTA, since after the major tariff cuts instigated under the GATT, the few tariffs remaining did not provide a significant barrier to foreign competition.

Given their overall lack of support for foreign-investment regulation, foreign companies have acted as a liberalizing force within Canada's business lobby groups. Because the major associations represent both domestic and foreign capital, the preferences of foreign firms dilute potential nationalist or protectionist sentiments. Considering that in industries such as mining and manufacturing foreign firms control almost one-half of sales, the political influence is unquestionable.

Capital's opposition to FDI regulation would be less important if there were strong support of regulation from other producer groups, such as labor or farmers. Gordon Laxer argues that it was the absence of a strong agrarian lobby as a political force that led to Canada's adoption of an "industrialization by invitation" strategy at the turn of the century. He argues that in Sweden, the presence of strong popular-democratic groups like the agrarians made the state less welcoming to foreign investment.[67] These groups had a more national focus and were more concerned with domestic issues. The weakness of Canadian agrarians meant there was no effective opposition to the internationalist interests of financial and commercial capital.

The same can be said of Canadian labor. Although the Canadian Labour Congress (CLC) is in favor of foreign-investment review and has increasingly argued that it should be integrated into broader industrial policies, it has always been too weak to assert its will. Like

66. Glen Williams, *Not for Export*, updated ed. (Toronto: McClelland and Stewart, 1986).

67. Gordon Laxer, *Open for Business: The Roots of Foreign Ownership in Canada* (Toronto: Oxford University Press, 1989).

business organizations, labor organizations are decentralized and are divided on regional and ideological grounds. The CLC is primary among these groups, but in many cases it cannot speak for, nor rely on the support of, all labor groups.[68] In any case, labor's attitude toward FDI regulation has always been ambivalent. Since a large percentage of the work force is employed by foreign firms, worker support for regulation has been hampered by a concern about the effect of regulation on jobs.

Miriam Smith argues that labor's position on foreign investment and industrial policy in general solidified throughout the 1970s and 1980s. Prior to 1975, labor focused primarily on monetary and fiscal policy. This focus changed in 1975, she maintains, when wage and price controls were instituted. Since the imposition of these controls threatened labor's right to collective bargaining, if only temporarily, it resulted in a major reassessment of the CLC's policy platform. The consequence was a growing emphasis on regulating FDI and the need for industrial policies that supported Canadian capital, a trend that was reinforced by the major layoffs resulting from the 1981–82 recession. Since the Canada–United States Free Trade Agreement, the CLC's policy platforms have focused on the rollback of the FTA and on the growing need for tax reform.[69] Given the overall weakness of labor in Canada (there is a 36 percent unionization rate), however, it is questionable how influential the CLC can be.

THE INSTITUTIONAL CAPACITIES OF THE STATE

Many have argued that, in the Anglo-American tradition, Canada does not possess any strong history of state intervention. Michael M. Atkinson and William D. Coleman maintain that this lack is in part a function of the Westminster model of parliamentary government. In such a system, emphasis is placed on Parliament as a source of policy initiatives, led by an executive cabinet that draws on party loyalty

68. Pierre Fournier, "Consensus Building in Canada: Case Studies and Prospects," in Banting, *The State and Economic Interests*.

69. Miriam Smith, "Labour without Allies: The Canadian Labour Congress in Politics, 1956–1988" (Ph.D. diss., Yale University, 1990).

to enforce its platforms. The parliamentary system encourages a devolution of state power by requiring that "political power be exercised through party government premised on single-member constituencies," not through powerful state bureaucracies. This tendency, they argue, is reinforced by the federal structure of the Canadian government, which provides for a number of autonomous decision-making centers and thereby delegates centralized policy-making authority.[70]

In the absence of a strong state tradition, they argue further, state bureaucracies are often simply a reflection of the interests of the most powerful societal actors. Since different social interests influence different bureaucracies, the result can be conflicting and incoherent state initiatives. Without a strong, centralized bureaucratic leadership, policymaking becomes ineffectual and, at times, paralyzed. This policy vacuum is broadened by an ideological proclivity on the part of many state officials toward "firm-centered" industrial strategies. Atkinson and Coleman claim that government officials frequently share the firm-centered industry culture that predominates in business, and are reluctant to institute policies that conflict with the directives of business managers.[71] Consequently, a great deal of emphasis is placed on individual companies.

This latter point is consistent with Rianne Mahon's argument that the lack of state intervention in Canada is not because of the fragmented nature of the state but rather because of the hegemony of state agencies that support laissez-faire policies and eschew state involvement in the economy. She argued that the hegemonic state agency was the Department of Finance, which in turn was a reflection of the dominance of resource or staples companies in the Canadian economy. Resource companies are suspicious of state intervention because they believe it benefits manufacturing capital disproportionately, and they prefer to rely on a liberal trading environment that ensures the export of their goods.[72] Because of the

70. Michael M. Atkinson and William D. Coleman, *The State, Business, and Industrial Change in Canada* (Toronto: University of Toronto Press, 1989), p. 56.

71. Ibid., p. 73.

72. Rianne Mahon, *The Politics of Industrial Restructuring: Canadian Textiles* (Toronto: University of Toronto Press, 1984).

dominance of the Finance Department and its resource clientele, therefore, an emphasis on macrolevel intervention through fiscal and monetary policies prevails.

These factors—the lack of a state tradition, federalism, and a resistance to interventionist strategies—are all relevant in analyzing the evolution of investment policy in Canada. Investment Canada's widespread reputation as a rubber stamp is a function of conflicting and overlapping bureaucratic jurisdictions, an emphasis on firm-level initiatives, and an ideological proclivity to abstain from intervention. These influences come into play both in Investment Canada's investment review and investment promotion strategies.

Investment Canada reports to the Ministry of Industry, Science, and Technology Canada (ISTC), an agency created in 1987 to support the development of strategic technologies, enhance sector competitiveness, and improve business information and the development of services.[73] The agency was constituted through a merger between the Department of Regional Industrial Expansion (DRIE) and the Ministry of State for Science and Technology (MOSST). As Bruce Doern outlines, ISTC is characterized by two institutional capacity gaps that greatly restrict its ability to formulate effective industrial and investment strategies.

The first is the lack of ministerial continuity and influence in the federal cabinet. Nine ministers and seven deputy ministers were appointed to the industry portfolio between 1982 and 1989. Not surprisingly, this "minister-a-year" syndrome did not provide ISTC or its predecessors with an overwhelming sense of continuity. This lack of continuity, a reduced budget, and continuing pressure from regions to deal with local problems ensures that ISTC does not have the clout to enforce any sort of strategic vision. Second, ISTC lacks ongoing relationships with key Canadian firms, which makes business-state policy coordination difficult, if not impossible.[74] Clearly, Investment Canada's parent ministry cannot be expected to provide any coherent vision for the agency.

---

73. Bruce Doern, "The Department of Industry, Science, and Technology: Is There Industrial Policy after Free Trade?" in Katherine Graham, ed., *How Ottawa Spends, 1990–91* (Ottawa: Carleton University Press, 1990), p. 52.

74. Ibid., pp. 66–67.

Bureaucratic overlaps have hampered Investment Canada's efforts as well. In its capacity as an investment promoter, Investment Canada works in cooperation with DRIE (which was subsumed as an agency within ISTC) to coordinate its promotional efforts within Canada and with the Department of External Affairs in promotional efforts abroad. A working committee of DRIE, Investment Canada, and the External Affairs Department meets regularly under the auspices of Investment Canada. In addition, a steering committee of deputy ministers chaired by the deputy minister in charge of Investment Canada and including deputy ministers from International Trade, DRIE, the Finance Department, and the Employment and Immigration Department works to coordinate investment promotion initiatives. In cooperation with DRIE, which fixes priorities for regional and sectoral development, Investment Canada provides sector-by-sector information for prospective investors. It also attempts to target individual companies that appear to be good potential investors, although this sort of activity is still at a nascent stage. Internationally, Investment Canada attends investment fairs abroad and provides an investment counselor for the main Canadian Consulates.

These extensive coordination activities do not always run smoothly. Often, even when provincial and federal governments can agree on investment promotion policies, Investment Canada has proved to be ill-equipped to implement them. For example, at a 1986 meeting in Whitehorse, the provinces agreed to a three-year investment promotion plan presented to them by Investment Canada. The plan was primarily devoted to the promotion of domestic and foreign investment in Canada. It included visits to branch plants to question managers on appropriate investment incentives, programs to promote individual entrepreneurs, and the creation of a National Investment Fund. Based on the EEC's Euroventure Fund, the National Investment Fund was to be financed by donations from large companies (primarily foreign investors) which would be urged to make a contribution.

This investment promotion effort failed for a variety of reasons. First, a lack of direction at Investment Canada's upper-management level severely hampered lower-level initiatives. The staffers who devised the investment promotion plan said that they were con-

143

stantly pulled between pressures to organize expensive, high-profile "events" such as investment fairs and initiating the longer-term measures outlined in the investment promotion plan. Because events like the international investment fair "Opportunities Canada" provided a high profile for Investment Canada's president and the minister, they were instinctively attractive to upper-level decision makers. Yet numerous policy reviews had revealed that such fairs attracted relatively few serious investors and hardly any large multinational investors. As a result, staffers complained that Investment Canada had turned into a "publicity agency," using its resources for short-term, ad hoc "events" rather than for any of the programs mentioned in its long-term plans.

Similarly, the National Investment Fund fell through because it did not receive sufficient attention by the minister or Investment Canada's president to make it work. The majority of companies interviewed for Investment Canada's feasibility study of the fund indicated that although they were not predisposed to donate to such an effort, they would do so if explicitly asked to by upper-level Investment Canada officials. Such donations would obviously involve high-level lobbying efforts between senior company executives and the minister. In the absence of cabinet-level interest, however, this initiative foundered.

Second, because of its small budget and staff, Investment Canada cannot implement investment promotion policies on its own. Instead it must rely on DRIE and its regional offices for domestic promotional efforts, but it is not clear that DRIE has the ability to operationalize such policies. The agency has been commonly described as rudderless, with an unclear mandate and no experience in exercising what little mandate it does have. Five major reorganizations of DRIE in as many years served further to disorient it. Abroad, ISTC's international fair unit was another potential avenue for Investment Canada to promote Canada as an investment site. But the international fair unit was regarded as relatively unimportant within ISTC, and Investment Canada staffers claimed it was difficult to get funding for the fair and information from DRIE.

In 1989, Investment Canada did initiate a more proactive investment program, and it has had considerable success in matching Canadian companies up with foreign joint venture partners. This program has been particularly important in high-technology industries, but it remains very small. Yet such efforts are indicative of the "firm-centered" mentality Atkinson and Coleman found to be widespread among state managers. While these endeavors are important, they can be truly significant only if implemented in the context of a broader strategy that targets industries and technologies and seeks to develop links between carefully selected Canadian and foreign firms.

Investment Canada is also hindered in making the decisions necessary to implement such policies by its legislative mandate. This became evident in late 1989 when a French company, Institut Mérieux, tried to acquire Canada's largest biotechnology company, Connaught Laboratories. The Industry, Science, and Technology minister, Harvie André, turned down Institut Mérieux's first offer, arguing that it did not provide sufficient guarantees that Connaught would retain its R&D facilities in Canada. Institut Mérieux responded by providing some guarantees in this area, but in the meantime another company, J. V. Vax, made a competing offer for the company. The presence of two offers for the company provided a dilemma for Investment Canada: whereas Institut Mérieux was offering seven dollars per share more for the company, Vax, a joint venture between Ciba Geigy of Switzerland and Chiron Corporation of California, had vastly superior technology.

Given that the government had emphasized technology issues and the need to increase research and development as policy priorities, the offer from Vax was far more appealing. Yet opting for this company would have been counter to the wishes of Connaught's board of directors, which was clearly interested in Institut Mérieux's higher financial offer. The issue remained in the cabinet's priorities and planning committee for two months, largely because of the conundrum presented by Investment Canada's mandate. According to the legislation, Investment Canada could evaluate an offer only on the basis of whether or not it provided "net benefit" to the country. It made no provision for a circumstance where two foreign firms were bidding to acquire a Canadian company and one of these companies was preferable to the other. Given that this was the only legislative basis on which the government could intervene in the situation, the minister opted for Institut Mérieux's bid, arguing that he was bound by the decision of the company's board of directors.

Canadian federalism has also affected investment policy, although there is some question as to how constrained the capacities of federal institutions are by provincial governments and regional conflicts. There is no question that federal policies have been influenced by and have contributed to regional divisions.[75] Yet Ottawa still retains considerable clout; Atkinson and Coleman found that only 5 percent of the federal officials they interviewed considered federalism to be a serious obstacle to attaining policy objectives.[76] Provincial support of foreign-investment review has always been divided. For example, highly industrialized Ontario and Quebec gave qualified support to FIRA. Manitoba, Saskatchewan, British Columbia, Alberta, and the Atlantic provinces were far less enthusiastic, however. Some of the Maritime provinces went so far as to refer to it as a "central Canadian plot" that denied them the capacity to industrialize in the manner that Ontario had.[77] Even those who did support the agency insisted that "the federal government not use it as a tool to alleviate regional disparities," because it would diminish their ability to formulate provincial investment and employment policies.[78]

Provincial-federal government disputes apparently have not seriously disrupted the investment review process, however. Investment Canada regularly consults the provinces on investment cases in which they might have an interest. For example, if a company that has a base in one or more provinces is about to be acquired, Investment Canada contacts the provinces involved to allow them to register their approval or disapproval. Investment Canada officials claim that this consultation process rarely proved to be a problem.

Divisions between the provinces have been more problematic in the area of foreign-investment promotion. First, since many sectors are concentrated regionally, targeting a particular sector means attracting investment to one province at the expense of others. The

75. Janine Brodie, *The Political Economy of Canadian Regionalism* (Toronto: Harcourt Brace Jovanovich, 1990).
76. Atkinson and Coleman, *The State, Business, and Industrial Change*, p. 68.
77. Sjolander, "Foreign Investment Policy Making," p. 296.
78. Molot and Williams, "The Political Economy of Continentalism," p. 88.

Department of Regional and Industrial Expansion does offer regional benefits in particularly depressed areas of the country, such as the Maritime Provinces. Still, DRIE is not mandated to direct foreign investors to particular regions, only to "clarify the comparative advantages for them."[79] Second, any attempt to target sectors or regions for investment draws strong protests from the provinces as an encroachment on their jurisdictional powers. Even if the federal government decided it would ignore the protests of the provinces and implement specific investment promotion policies on a regional basis, it would not have complete jurisdiction in many of the areas relevant to such policies (for example, education policy, provincial taxes, or energy costs).

Furthermore, efforts by Investment Canada to attract specific kinds of investment are often thwarted by competing efforts by the Ministry of External Affairs, which does investment promotion through various embassies, and by the individual provinces. Almost all the provinces have investment offices abroad, with active policies to attract foreign investors to their respective areas. In 1988 the provinces combined spent $209.98 million on trade and investment promotion, whereas the federal government spent only $135.46 million. The provinces thus provide 61 percent of all Canadian funds devoted to trade and investment promotion.[80] In addition, the provinces made transfer payments to firms in the form of subsidies and capital assistance, which amounted to $4.176 billion in 1987.[81] Rarely are provincial investment promotion efforts coordinated with Investment Canada, although the agency states it is not opposed to such efforts in principle. The result of all these separate endeavors is a morass of competing promotional packages.

79. Testimony by former Minister Sinclair Stevens, in *Proceedings of the Committee on Banking, Trade, and Commerce*, February 1985 (Ottawa: Government of Canada, 1985).

80. Murray G. Smith, "Muddling Through Is Not Enough: A Survey of Global and Domestic Economic Changes," in Douglas M. Brown and Murray G. Smith eds., *Canadian Federalism: Meeting Global Economic Challenges* (Kingston: Institute of Intergovernmental Relations, and Halifax: Institute for Research on Public Policy, 1991).

81. Jean-François Bence, "Analysis of Provincial Transfer Payments to Business in Canada," *International Economic Issues* (Halifax: Institute for Research on Public Policy, April 1990), p. 27.

An Evaluation of Canada's Investment Policies

It is often argued that Canada's status as a developed country means it need not be as concerned with monitoring foreign direct investment as a less developed country, such as Mexico. Given Canada's advanced infrastructure and high level of economic development, leaving investment planning up to the market is generally considered to be the most efficient approach. This argument fails to take into account that Canada falls behind in many of the indicators that characterize developed market economies. While its extensive supply of natural resources has allowed Canadians to maintain a high per capita income, Canada's manufacturing sector has always been weaker than that of other OECD countries. Thus Canada has a persistent trade deficit in its merchandise account.

More important, Canada exhibits an alarming weakness in high-technology industries, which are among the fastest growing industries in the world. Canada's R&D figures are not impressive: it spent about 0.8 percent of its GDP in 1988 on R&D, as compared with 2.1 percent spent by the United States and Germany, and 2.0 percent by Sweden and Japan.[82] It was ranked ninth out of ten countries in the number of robots per worker and is estimated to be three to four years behind the United States in the adoption of robot technology. In a comparison with Europe, Canada was ranked behind West Germany, Britain, and France in the adoption of microelectronics technologies in process applications.[83]

A report by the government of Ontario concluded that one of the most significant explanations for this relative backwardness in high technology was the high percentage of foreign-owned high-technology industries. The study showed that, on average, Canadian-controlled companies that performed R&D had an R&D intensity of 1.5 percent of sales, as compared with 0.9 percent in foreign-controlled companies.[84] The disparity is larger in technology-

82. Statistics Canada, Science and Technology Division, *Industrial R&D Statistics, 1988* (Ottawa: Government of Canada, 1988).
83. Economic Council of Canada, *Making Technology Work: Innovation and Jobs in Canada* (Ottawa: Supply and Services, 1987), p. 5.
84. Ministry of Industry, Trade, and Technology, *A Commitment to Research and Development: An Action Plan* (Toronto: Government of Ontario, 1988), p. 13.

Table 8. R&D sales for the most R&D intensive industries in Canada, for 1979

	Canadian controlled	Foreign controlled
Business machines	8.0	1.3
Other machinery	1.1	0.7
Aircraft and parts	19.0	5.2
Communications equipment	9.7	5.5
Other electrical	1.0	1.1
Drugs and medicines	7.5	3.5
Other chemicals	2.6	0.7
Scientific equipment	17.7	0.7

Source: Government of Ontario, Ministry of Industry, Trade, and Technology, *A Commitment to Research and Development: An Action Plan,* January 1988, p. 13.

intensive industries, where foreign ownership tends to be higher. There are marked spending differences between domestic and foreign firms in these R&D-intensive industries (Table 8). This disparity in R&D spending between domestic and foreign firms was challenged by Alan Rugman, who found little difference in R&D spending between foreign subsidiaries and Canadian-owned companies.[85] He did find, however, that foreign subsidiaries spent less on R&D than their parent companies did. A statement by the president of the Natural Sciences and Engineering Research Council of Canada neatly sums up the reason: "When you are a branch plant economy, you don't do R&D in the branch, you do it at head office," he explained. The result is a "structural weakness in the private sector" with regard to R&D.[86]

In the past, multinational firms tended to keep their R&D facilities concentrated in the parent company in order to protect the diffusion of their knowledge advantage and to keep a firm hold on the innovation process. Multinational enterprises began to move away from this strategy in the 1980s, however, when it became clear that significant advantages could be gained by drawing on the local scientific expertise surrounding foreign subsidiaries.[87] Recent Ca-

85. Alan Rugman, "The Role Of Multinational Enterprises in U.S.-Canadian Relations," *Columbia Journal of World Business* 21, no. 2 (Summer 1986).

86. *Financial Post* (a Canadian national daily), April 30, 1990.

87. See Lynn Krieger Mytelka, "Crisis, Technological Change, and the Strategic Alliance," in Lynn Krieger Mytelka, ed., *Strategic Partnerships and the World Economy* (London: Pinter Press, 1991).

nadian experience indicates there are limitations to this trend, however, partly because of the extensive foreign ownership of Canada's technology-intensive industries. A highly touted federal effort to improve domestic production capacity in the medical devices sector, for example, met with resounding failure when it became clear that foreign firms had little interest in the program. The government tried to boost the relatively low levels of R&D in the industry by giving $2.6 million to a program designed to match up companies with university researchers. This funding was to be matched by industry members, but the project attracted relatively little attention from the largest industry players, which were foreign owned. Since many of these firms had adequate R&D facilities outside of Canada, they were not as enthusiastic as the small Canadian companies about the project.[88]

This example reveals the catch-22 situation Canada has found itself in with regard to R&D. Naturally, areas with large concentrations of researchers possessing the relevant skills would be more attractive as future R&D outposts. But because manufacturing has for decades been dominated by branch plants with lower levels of R&D spending than their parents, relatively fewer magnets to attract R&D exist in Canada than in the United States, which is a nation of parent companies. Obviously, the country with a large percentage of parent companies has an advantage over the one hosting branch plants. Since these two countries are joined by a free trade agreement, it makes sense for a company to make its R&D-intensive investment in the United States and ship goods to Canada.

A concerted effort to improve the R&D intensity of Canadian firms could remedy the situation. Yet a spate of foreign buyouts of Canadian high-technology firms such as Mitel, Connaught, and Leigh Instruments may threaten such endeavors. The concern in all these acquisitions was similar: once these companies became part of a foreign firm, their incentive to do R&D would diminish. The bankruptcy of Leigh Instruments in 1990 brought considerable publicity to this concern. Critics argued that its parent company, Plessey PLC of Britain, took Leigh's cash reserves and saddled it with $90 million in debt.

88. *Globe and Mail*, May 20, 1991.

There is also evidence that the foreign ownership of manufacturing has led to a weakness in employment structures. In 1981, 19.4 percent of Canada's work force was in manufacturing, as opposed to an average of about 25 percent in other OECD countries. One of the reasons for this is that management and R&D jobs are concentrated in a head office located outside Canada. Hence these positions are staffed by non-Canadians. Since foreign subsidiaries tend to import their machinery and other inputs, supplier networks are not required in Canada, thereby reducing the potential for Canadian job development.[89]

Canada, therefore, cannot be as cavalier about the nationality of its investors as Reich recommends for the United States (see Chapter 3). This is not to argue that foreign firms do not bring benefits in terms of technology but rather that the extensive presence of foreign firms in high-technology industries has resulted in underinvestment in innovative activities. Unless the structural weaknesses that accompany such massive foreign ownership of industry are alleviated, the situation will not improve. I do not mean to imply, however, that Canada should *discriminate* against foreign investors, nor do I mean to suggest that domestic firms are not relevant to such problems. What I do mean is that a broader industrial strategy must be implemented that uses both foreign and domestic firms to remedy this situation. Such a strategy would include ensuring foreign companies of national treatment but not exempting them from performance requirements. Because the federal government has no national industrial priorities, Canadian industries, outside of the automobile sector, have no protection in the form of specific sectoral policies that might address such problems.[90] Instead, they have relied primarily on macrolevel investment promotion schemes and made little or no attempt to mold incoming FDI to fit national industrial priorities. The Tory government of Brian Mulroney was vocal in claiming that free trade was going to be its industrial strategy. In truth, part of Canada's export success and high growth rates in the mid-1980s was due to another prong of the Tory strategy: a

89. Molot and Williams, "The Political Economy of Continentalism," p. 98.

90. Given that after the phase-out of tariffs on U.S. autos under the FTA there will be no "stick" to enforce the auto pact, even this sector is under threat.

devalued Canadian dollar. The politics surrounding the free trade deal in the United States reveal the shortcomings of this tack.

Some regard the revaluation of the Canadian currency from US$0.71 in 1985 to rates hovering around US$0.87 in 1991 as a direct function of the free trade agreement. The former industry minister Sinclair Stevens leaked information to the press (after his resignation from the government) that his counterpart Malcolm Baldrige was under pressure from the National Association of Manufacturers in the United States to do something about the Canadian exchange rate.[91] Whether Stevens's claim that the Canadian government secretly agreed to a revaluation is actually true is irrelevant. There is no question that Canadian exchange rates were a highly politicized issue in the free trade negotiations, and the recognition that a revaluation would make the FTA more politically feasible in the United States put pressure on Canada to raise the value of the Canadian dollar.

The implementation of this revaluation not only decreased the merchandise trade balance with the United States, it threatened the political coalition behind free trade in Canada. Business interests howled in protest as they watched their competitive edge erode with the rising value of their dollar. In 1991 there was general agreement that the Canadian currency would have to come down; provided the U.S. dollar did not follow it, Canadian competitiveness would be restored. But once again, this would put the government in a catch-22 situation: devaluations would help the competitiveness of the Canadian economy, but they would also incur the wrath of the U.S. Congress and American manufacturers. The growth of American economic nationalism indicates that neither U.S. business nor Congress is likely to accept a major devaluation of the Canadian dollar without a fight. Already, the National Association of Manufacturers in the United States has served notice that it will support only those trade agreements that restrict trading partners from "manipulating" their exchange rates, even if these agreements remain "secret."

Supporters of the FTA argued that the rising economic nationalism in the United States was precisely why a free trade agreement was necessary: to provide Canadian producers and foreign investors

---

91. For a more in-depth investigation of this argument, see Canadian Labour Congress, *Free Trade Briefing Document no. 7* (Ottawa: CLC, 1991).

protection from a nationalist backlash. Yet it is difficult to see how the FTA provides any genuine protection for Canada. All the protectionist legislation included in the Omnibus Trade and Competitiveness Bill of 1988 is grandfathered. This bill includes the Exon-Florio amendment, under which the president may review foreign investments (including Canadian investments) that affect U.S. "national security." Canadian negotiators remain unsuccessful in trying to convince the United States to integrate the limited definitions of national security used in the FTA into the Exon-Florio legislation. The FTA also does nothing to protect Canadian firms against anti-takeover legislation implemented by individual state governments, provided they do not abrogate the national treatment principle. Since legislation can be tailor-made to protect individual firms and can pertain to domestic as well as foreign acquirers, it will not necessarily deny national treatment. Also, the Canadian government has not yet been successful in achieving a "carve out" (exceptional status) for Canadian producers in any U.S. legislation that could potentially harm them.

The revaluation of the Canadian dollar and the lack of security offered to Canadian firms by the FTA could lead to a corporate backlash against free trade. Unless the Canadian dollar is devalued, and unless U.S. nationalism subsides, one can expect Canadian business to be among the most vocal in calling for the abrogation of the treaty—a great irony in view of its previous support for the deal.

Critics of Canada's foreign-investment regulation process charge that in an open economy such as Canada's, the state *cannot* afford to regulate MNEs. A better characterization of reality would be to say that Canada *will not* regulate foreign investment. It is true that institutional factors severely restrict the capacity of the Canadian state to implement such policies. History has shown, however, that when the political will exists, these institutional barriers can be overcome. In the case of the National Energy Program, a Liberal government elected on a nationalist platform implemented a far-reaching regulatory policy that significantly changed the ownership of the oil and gas industry, reducing foreign ownership from 70 to 50 percent. While the government was forced to back down on this policy, the NEP left a lasting legacy in the oil and gas industry.

But in the absence of nationalist sentiment or political pressures to regulate foreign direct investment, capital's inclination to oppose this sort of state intervention and the state's institutional capacity to act are likely to prevail. Thus, Canada's ability to intervene in this area is as much a reflection of the balance of political and institutional forces as it is of Canada's constrained position as a continental partner of the United States. Recently, some provinces and communities in Canada have shown a willingness to target and attract industries that would be of particular benefit to regional development schemes. It is at this level of intervention that one should look for future policies to integrate foreign investment into industrial policies in Canada.

CHAPTER FIVE

Mexico's Apertura

Mexico has struggled with the constraints of being a member of the international economy since its economic fortunes took a turn for the worse in the early 1980s. A mere hint of a change in interest rates or economic policy can send capital flooding out of the country to safer havens in the United States; a drop in the price of oil can decimate foreign-exchange reserves earmarked for the payment of Mexico's massive foreign debt. In the context of this constant punishment, it may seem surprising that Mexico seeks to integrate itself further into the world economy by reaching a free trade agreement with its continental partners. This initiative is only part of a general opening, or *apertura*, of the Mexican economy that has been brewing since Mexico signed the GATT in 1986.

An essential element of the *apertura* is the liberalization of foreign-investment regulations. Mexico's significant relaxation of regulations in 1989 indicated a marked change in attitude from the strong nationalist tendencies it exhibited toward foreign investors in the past. While Mexico has always allowed foreign capital into its economy, it has insisted (with varying degrees of conviction) that foreigners be invited only on terms acceptable to Mexico's economic needs. Particularly since 1973, it has monitored foreign capital closely. This intense surveillance of foreign direct investment placed Mexico near the pinnacle of a small group of host countries that strictly regulated multinational enterprises.

In this chapter I seek to explain the reasons behind the Mexican *apertura* by focusing on the political economy of its investment policies. Investment issues were a key impetus for Mexico's liberalization strategy: one of the motivations behind its quest for a NAFTA was a desire to increase Mexico's desirability as an investment site. In this respect, the new investment policies are directed toward both foreign and domestic investors. One of the stickiest dilemmas Mexico faces in repaying its foreign debt obligations is trying to persuade domestic investors to repatriate the billions of dollars in flight capital that left the country throughout the 1970s and 1980s. Insofar as these investors believe that a more open environment for investment is an essential element of reviving the economy, deregulating FDI is a way of increasing their confidence in the domestic economy.

The campaign to attract direct investment also marks a major change in Mexican development strategy. In the face of the controversy surrounding Mexico's external debt and the reluctance of banks to resume loans, there is a new emphasis on acquiring debt through equity financing, rather than through foreign loans. Foreign direct investment as a percentage of GDP peaked in 1982 at about 1.2 percent, and by 1985 it had dropped to around 0.7 percent.[1] In addition, Mexican investment policy is an integral part of the country's move toward export-oriented industrialization, because it encourages the growth of the *maquiladoras*. This change in strategy could have major political and economic implications over the long run because it will hook Mexico more securely into the continental economy. In this respect it parallels Canada's actions to integrate its markets with the United States. With the absence of policies to remedy the unforeseen consequences of a free trade agreement, Mexico could be exposed to some of the same difficulties Canada has faced (perhaps with even more of a vengeance). It could result in the underdevelopment of Mexico's nascent R&D capacities, and it almost certainly will make the country a target for U.S. nationalism.

Conversely, continentalization is also dependent on domestic political trends. One impetus for the *apertura* was the rise of state

1. Fernando Sanchez Ugarte, "Taxation of Foreign Investment in Mexico: The North American Perspective," in Clark Reynolds, Leonard Waverman, and Gerardo Bueno, eds., *The Dynamics of North American Trade and Investment: Canada, Mexico, and the United States* (Stanford: Stanford University Press, 1991).

managers who pushed for liberal economic policies within the state apparatus. The position of these *técnicos* within the state was bolstered by the growing support by Mexican business for more internationalist strategies. Business support for the *apertura* was in part based on a significantly devalued peso, which gave companies more confidence in their ability to compete. The revaluation of the currency or the appearance of vigorous competition to Mexican business in the domestic market would affect capital's attitude toward liberalization and would destabilize the precarious political coalition that is behind the drive toward continentalization.

The recent liberalization of foreign-investment review seems to belie the claim made in chapter 2, that Mexico tends to be more resistant to pressures to deregulate FDI than Canada is. The new regulations, however, do not necessarily reflect significant changes in Mexico's overall approach to FDI. The Mexican state continues to make demands of foreign investors that other countries (such as Canada) would not dare to consider. Unlike Canada's policies, Mexico's investment policies reflect a long history of intervention combined with broad-based political support for the regulation of foreign capital. Understanding the unique nature of Mexico's approach to investment regulation involves not only an examination of economic pressures to deregulate but also the political sources of policy changes.

FOREIGN-INVESTMENT REVIEW

The Apertura

Mexico's *apertura* has both a national and an international orientation: an opening domestically toward the political opposition, and, more important, a liberalization of trade and deregulation of foreign direct investment on the international level. I examine the domestic aspect of these changes only briefly here.

President Carlos Salinas de Gortari's domestic reforms were characterized by attempts to remove corrupt business and labor leaders and less successful efforts to reduce voting irregularities. Salinas made his mark with labor by arresting the head of the powerful and corrupt oil workers' union, Joaquin Hernández Galicia (La Quina) in January 1989. In the first six months of his *sexenio*, Salinas fired or forced to resign the heads of the musicians' and the teachers' unions and pressed charges on the leaders of the automobile and government workers' unions. All these moves were made in response to protests from dissident union members. To even out the attack, Salinas also jailed Eduardo Legorreta Chavet, a member of one of Mexico's wealthiest families, for irregularities surrounding the stock market crash of 1987.

Salinas has been considerably less successful in opening up the political process to opposition policies. Traditionally, the Ruling Institutional Revolution Party (PRI) has intervened in voting procedures to ensure it retained a majority in the legislature. The results of the 1988 presidential election, which brought Salinas to power, indicate that while this practice may be less extensive, it is still a part of the PRI's election-winning strategy. Although the party won with 50.36 percent of the vote, opposition parties complained that the actual PRI vote was closer to 35 percent.

In the international realm, Mexico's changes have been more significant. In August 1986, Mexico joined the GATT after declining to do so in 1980. Until the mid-1980s, Mexican manufacturers were heavily protected by a policy of import substitution begun in the 1940s. During the government of Miguel de la Madrid, a growing belief that import substitution had only encouraged inefficient domestic production and expensive imports resulted in a transition to a more export-oriented economy. By 1986 this transition was complete. The government argued that the "model of import substitution has in large part been overtaken by the onset of a viewpoint that is essentially global, that seeks to take advantage of and develop market niches at the international level. In this global market, newly industrializing countries can take advantage of their comparative advantage in standardized techniques of production."[2]

Since it joined the GATT, Mexico has gone far beyond its commitments to reduce tariffs, partially as a result of a decision in 1987 to reduce inflationary pressures by dropping tariff rates. The maximum tariff, scheduled to drop to 30 percent in October 1988, was lowered in December 1987 to 20 percent, less than one-half of the

2. Comisión Nacional de Inversiones Extranjeras (CNIE), *Informe, 1983–87* (Mexico City: Government of Mexico, 1988), p. 12. My translation.

50 percent rate allowed under entry to the GATT. This reduction was a major change from 1982, when tariffs were as high as 100 percent. In addition, the government eliminated the official-pricing scheme that set the artificial prices on which tariffs were based. Import permits were cut to 329 categories (from 8,008 categories in 1982) and remained only in strategic and priority sectors: agriculture, petrochemicals, chemicals, electronics (mainly computers), automotives, apparel, and pharmaceuticals.

At the same time, major devaluations of the peso made Mexican exports more competitive internationally. Mexican manufacturers adapted well to the challenges of competing abroad, and between 1982 and 1987 manufactured exports more than doubled. Foreign companies increased their exports from 5.7 percent of total exports in 1982 to 33 percent in 1987, largely in response to government demands that they improve their trade balances.[3] Combined with a slight improvement in agricultural exports (primarily due to higher coffee prices), the balance between petroleum and nonpetroleum goods in Mexico's composition of exports changed dramatically.

By 1990, Mexico had moved from a general, internationalist strategy to one that focused on North America. Salinas returned discouraged from a 1990 trip to Europe in which he failed to arouse European interest in Mexico. Consequently, he turned his attention to the United States and began to push for the conclusion of a free trade agreement. Fearing that such an agreement might threaten its own free trade agreement with the United States, Canada decided to join the negotiations as well. But the push for a NAFTA was a Mexican initiative and indicates a renewed commitment to export-led growth for Mexico.

Changes in Foreign-Investment Regulations

Mexico has always stood out among developing countries for its extensive monitoring of foreign investment. Official statements claim that the country has always welcomed FDI; if so, the welcome was a wary one and had an undertone of latent hostility. The new amendments to Mexico's Law to Promote Mexican Investment and Regulate Foreign Investment released in May of 1989 are significant

3. Ibid., p. 8.

in that this underlying hostility seems to have disappeared. In this respect, changes in the spirit of the law may be more important than changes in its actual content. It is important to note that these changes are only amendments to the existing legislation and do not constitute a new law. Since investment regulations are enshrined in the Mexican Constitution, a two-thirds majority in the national assembly is necessary to institute a new law. Since the PRI no longer holds this kind of majority, this option was not possible. As of 1991 Mexico was also holding off on changing the law in order to give it greater bargaining leverage in the NAFTA negotiations.

Since the introduction of the 1917 Constitution following the Mexican Revolution, foreign direct investment in Mexico has been regarded with suspicion, largely because of nationalist sentiments that arose in response to the prominent role foreign capital played in the prerevolutionary dictatorship of Porfirio Díaz. Díaz's development strategy was designed specifically to attract foreign capital, and between 1876 and 1910, FDI flourished in Mexico. Since this investment primarily was directed to railways and minerals, Díaz enacted laws allowing subsoil rights to surface owners. By 1917, foreign investors owned the majority of the Mexican mining and petroleum industries.

In the aftermath of the Revolution this open attitude toward foreign capital changed dramatically. The new constitution transferred subsoil rights to the state and allowed for the expropriation of foreign private property. At this time Mexico also adopted the Calvo clause, which made foreigners subject to the same laws as national citizens. This move was directed toward the United States, whose past military incursions into Mexico were particularly resented. In the Mexican-American war of 1846, the United States stormed and captured Chapultepec castle, a battle in which thousands of Mexicans were killed. And in 1916 the U.S. army went deep into Mexican territory in pursuit of Pancho Villa. This foreign intervention was considered an affront to Mexican sovereignty, and the postrevolutionary government was determined to discourage such interference in the future, whether it was in the form of economic or military influences.[4]

4. Dale Story, *Industry, the State, and Public Policy in Mexico* (Austin: University of Texas Press, 1986), p. 49.

International oil companies were regarded with particular suspicion, and in 1938 the government of General Lázaro Cárdenas expropriated all foreign oil interests, nationalizing the entire sector. This act, which was greeted with high levels of popular support, is still celebrated as a national holiday in Mexico.[5] In general the 1930s represented a period of highly nationalist sentiments: during this period the railways were nationalized and foreign ownership in electrical industries was limited to fifty years.

In the following decades, foreign investment was treated in a more conciliatory manner, although restrictions on foreign investment continued to grow.[6] The most important challenges to foreign investment came in the 1970s during the *sexenio* of Luis Echeverria, who introduced two major pieces of legislation concerning foreign investors. The most important of these was the 1973 Law to Promote Mexican Investment and Regulate Foreign Investment. This law established 51 percent Mexican ownership as a general rule for new foreign investments and created the National Commission on Foreign Investment (NCFI) to monitor foreign investors. In effect the ruling meant that foreign investors had to take on local partners. Second, in 1973 the Registry on Technology Transfer was created to review all new foreign contracts in order to avoid excessive royalty payments on technology licenses.

Despite these nationalistic laws, the attitude toward foreign investment in the period following the Echeverria *sexenio* generally was pragmatic and flexible. Even in the automobile industry, where local content requirements were strict, foreign firms were allowed 100 percent ownership of their subsidiaries provided they incorpo-

5. This appropriation act also marks the date when Mexico refused to sign the GATT in 1980.

6. Attempts were made to "Mexicanize" industries with high degrees of foreign ownership by requiring majority Mexican ownership in selected investments. Legislation covering the petrochemical industry was introduced in 1958–59, reserving the production of "basic" petrochemicals for the state and restricting foreign participation in the production of secondary chemicals to 40 percent. In the 1960s the government nationalized the electrical and sulfur industries and limited foreign ownership in mining to 34 percent. In 1962, Mexico introduced a policy requiring that automobile components manufactured in Mexico comprise 60 percent of a car's production costs. See Peter Evans and Gary Gereffi, "Foreign-Investment and Dependent Development: Comparing Brazil and Mexico," in Sylvia Ann Hewlett and Richard S. Weinert, eds., *Brazil and Mexico: Patterns in Late Development* (Philadelphia: Institute for the Study of Human Issues, 1982), p. 133.

rated local suppliers or increased their exports. The government always reserved its right to negotiate on specific foreign transactions, allowing such concessions as 100 percent ownership for increased foreign exchange or employment benefits. This flexibility in itself created problems, however. Each request for new investments or enlargement of existing investments required dealing with several bureaucracies—a slow and laborious process that often took up to eighteen months. More important, investors claimed that the process lacked "transparency," in other words, it was difficult to know what criteria a foreign firm had to fulfill in order to be granted permission to invest.

In the face of its serious economic woes and a near halt of foreign income coming into the country in the form of loans, the de la Madrid government consciously set about to improve the investment environment. In 1984 the government issued a list of sectors that would be highlighted for investment promotion.[7] In these sectors, the government would be willing to grant concessions, such as 100 percent ownership, in return for benefits in technology and increased exports.[8] This policy marked a transition from a broader, macro approach to FDI regulation to a more sectorally targeted strategy, where regulations were relaxed in exchange for concessions by foreign firms.

The de la Madrid government also made attempts to increase the transparency of the authorization process while simultaneously re-

7. These sectors included nonelectric machinery and equipment, electric machinery and apparatus, metal mechanics, electronic equipment and accessories, transportation equipment, chemicals, and "other," primarily high-technology industries but also including construction and hotel management.

8. In 1985–86, changes in the NCFI regulations eliminated the need for NCFI authorization for enlargement in the service, storage, or maintenance aspects of established businesses (resolution 9). Automatic authorization was also granted for increases in foreign participation in the capital stock of a company up to 49 percent if the foreign investor previously held a minority share, or up to 100 percent if the investor previously held a majority share. The government also declared that the transfer of shares between foreign investors could be automatically approved (resolution 5). In addition, funds from foreign multilateral sources or government development bank sources were to be considered "neutral," or national (resolution 14). Finally, no authorization from the NCFI was necessary for new foreign investments in small and medium-sized companies provided the investor did not have more than $8 million in sales and invested in a manufacturing firm employing not more than 250 Mexicans.

ducing bureaucratic red tape. In 1985 it introduced the System of the Coordination of Commitments and Goals, which centralized the coordination and monitoring of foreign companies in the office of the executive secretary of the NCFI. Previously, several government departments had been involved in the coordination of the obligations of foreign capital in terms of foreign exchange, employment, exports, and technology transfer. The 1985 law meant that foreign companies needed only a single authorization, that of the NCFI. It also clarified the government's sectoral targeting strategy by providing a clear list of objectives and priorities that the NCFI had for new investments. Finally, it stipulated that programs be negotiated and authorized in sixty days.

Overall, the attitude of the NCFI toward foreign investment changed from a more cautious, nationalist, defensive stance to a more open and internationalist one desiring to integrate Mexico into the global economy. The 1988 report of the NCFI urged an "opening of the economy and a search for a more efficient insertion of Mexican goods and services into the international flow of goods and services." It argued, "This effort to seek out foreign investment, besides bringing in new economic resources, will bring in cutting-edge technology and high organizational capability and in some cases an international distribution network to promote the increase of exports."[9] This was a considerable change from past attitudes toward foreign investment; as late as 1985, Miguel de la Madrid proclaimed on the eve of congressional elections, "If we allow full and open access to foreign investment, we run the risk of losing control over our economy."[10]

Salinas followed the trend set under the de la Madrid administration. The most significant changes in the foreign-investment rules were released in May 1989. According to the new outline, investments will be approved automatically provided they are in "unclassified areas and fulfill the following seven requirements:

1. The investment must not exceed $100 million

9. CNIE, *Informe, 1983–87*, pp. 18–19. My translation.
10. Quoted in Jorge Dominquez, "Revolution and Flexibility in Mexico," in George Lodge and Ezra Vogel, eds., *Ideology and National Competitiveness* (Boston: HBS Press, 1987), p. 294.

2. Financing of the project must be wholly external. Investors already established in Mexico may use funds they already possess in Mexico

3. The initial investment must be worth at least 20 percent of the total investment

4. The investment must be made outside of certain geographical zones where industrial activity is currently concentrated (including Mexico City, Monterrey, and Guadalajara)

5. The new entity must achieve a positive balance of payments during the first three years in operation

6. The investment must generate new jobs and set up training programs

7. Appropriate technology must be used, with attention to Mexico's environmental needs.[11]

Investors complying with these conditions may own up to 100 percent of the new investment. In addition, the legislation stipulates that the executive secretary of the NCFI must make a recommendation within forty-five days of receiving the application. Investments do not qualify for automatic approval if they do not meet the above criteria or are in certain restricted areas. The list of restricted areas is long and is divided into activities reserved for the Mexican state; activities reserved to Mexican nationals; activities that allow up to 34 percent foreign ownership; activities that allow up to 40 percent ownership; activities that allow up to 49 percent foreign ownership; and activities that require prior authorization but where majority foreign ownership is allowed. For a list of these categories, see Appendix 2.

In some industries, these new rules mark significant changes in foreign ownership restrictions. The telecommunications industry, which was formerly reserved for the state, is now open to 49 percent foreign ownership.[12] Regulations regarding foreign ownership in petrochemicals, insurance, banking, and mining have been considerably liberalized. Also, foreigners may acquire up to 100 percent of an existing corporation without authorization, provided it is in an

11. Secretaría de Comercio y Fomento Industrial, "Reglamento de la Ley para Promover la Inversión Mexicana y Regular la Inversión Extranjera," *Diario Oficial de la Federación* (Mexico City: Government of Mexico, May 16, 1989) (my translation).

12. The phone company Telmex was sold to a consortium comprised of France Telecom, Southwestern Bell, and Grupo Carso SA in December 1990.

unclassified activity. Foreigners may acquire temporary majority ownership in restricted areas where the percentage of foreign ownership is limited through a trust fund, or *fidiecomiso*. By using these trust funds, foreign investors may have majority control of companies in restricted areas for twenty years, after which time they must reduce their participation to a minority share. These trusts are intended to help struggling Mexican firms that cannot find Mexican investors, and will be approved only under such circumstances. The NCFI monitors foreign investors by requiring them to file annual financial statements. If a foreign firm is not living up to the conditions under which the investment was approved, either the terms are renegotiated or the firm is fined.

Finally, Mexico altered the 1973 Technology Transfer Law in January 1990 to allow for the free negotiation of royalties, quicken approval rates, and give greater guarantees of confidentiality. In 1991 it passed intellectual property legislation that effectively harmonized Mexican patent protection laws with those of the United States. This is a significant change from past policies, which provided relatively weak patent protection and ordered MNEs to license technologies in areas such as the drug industry.

One of the biggest drawing cards for foreign investment has been the special program for the *maquiladora* sector, created in the 1960s. Primarily set up in U.S. border areas, the *maquiladoras* are assembly operations designed to take advantage of cheap Mexican labor. Under sections 806.30 and 807 of the United States Tariff Schedule, goods assembled in Mexico and shipped back to the United States for sale are taxed only on the value added in Mexico. For this reason many plants were set up on the United States–Mexico border that temporarily import components, assemble them using Mexican labor, then export their entire product line to the United States. In order to attract investment in these firms, the Mexican government allowed automatic authorization of 100 percent foreign ownership of all *maquila* plants. No prior authorization was necessary for transferring stock, fixed assets, or partner interests; for opening new establishments or relocating, or for manufacturing new product lines.[13]

13. For a more detailed analysis of the *maquiladoras*, see Ellwyn Stoddard, *Maquila:*

After 1983 the Mexican government made a special effort to attract investment in the *maquiladoras*. It guaranteed permission within thirty to sixty days, permitted unlimited imports of necessary materials for a period of six months, let exports be exchanged in the open market (unlike other kinds of exports), and set up special industrial parks to provide infrastructure. Under certain circumstances *maquiladoras* could sell up to 20 percent of their products domestically. *Maquiladoras* in the interior could sell up to 40 percent of their products domestically, if they met certain local sourcing criteria. Boosted by Mexico's low real wages and the devalued peso, the *maquiladora* program has grown rapidly. By 1986 it was the second largest source of foreign exchange in Mexico after oil.

In December 1989 the government further liberalized laws regarding *maquiladora* operations. As always, operations are automatically approved and 100 percent ownership is allowed. The Secretariat of Commerce and Industrial Development (SECOFI) now undertakes to process applications in three days, however, and allows *maquiladoras* to be set up in any area zoned for industrial development rather than encouraging them in border areas. Previously, *maquiladora* sales to the domestic Mexican market were restricted to 20 percent of export sales. Now, they may sell the equivalent of 50 percent of export sales in Mexico and may enter subcontracting arrangements with domestic companies. *Maquiladoras* are also exempted from paying value-added taxes on inputs provided they meet a 20 percent local content requirement.[14]

Another key tool for encouraging foreign capital was Mexico's debt conversion program. Mexico has engaged in a variety of debt-to-equity swap plans to reduce its external debt. The best known of these was its debt-bond swap of December 1987 with the U.S. bank Morgan Guaranty. The Morgan Guaranty swap attracted only moderate interest, with only $2.6 billion in bonds sold. Better results were achieved with attempts to swap debt into equity ownership. In

---

Assembly Plants in Northern Mexico (El Paso: Texas Western Press, 1987), and David Ehrenthal and Joseph Newman, "Explaining Mexico's Maquila Boom," *SAIS Review*, Winter–Spring 1988.

14. For a more detailed review of Mexican regulations, see Investment Canada, "The Opportunities and Challenges of North American Free Trade: A Canadian Perspective," Investment Canada Working Paper Series, April 1991, Appendix C.

April 1986 the government initiated a debt-capitalization program under which creditors could swap debt they believed to be unpayable for equity ownership in Mexican companies.[15]

In theory, everyone benefited from such swaps. The bank or company selling the debt got some return from debt it had probably already written off. The investment banker acting as go-between received a commission, and the Mexican government reduced its debt and, consequently, its debt servicing payments. In practice, debt-to-equity swaps reduced only a small proportion of debt. In 1986, $1.5 billion of Mexican debt was converted in the Mexican program, a tiny part of Mexico's overall $103 billion debt. From this perspective, the debt-to-equity program has been more successful as a conduit for foreign investment into the economy. The $1.5 billion swapped in 1986 represented twice the amount of foreign direct investment that flowed into the country in 1985. The NCFI monitored the investment that entered Mexico through swaps in a very liberal manner. Adopting what officials described as a "pragmatic" approach, the NCFI generally allowed swap participants to hold 100 percent of the equity in subsidiaries created under the program. The debt capitalization scheme was suspended in November 1987, however, for reasons that will be discussed in greater detail later.

15. These operations took two major forms. In the first of these, a third party desiring to invest in Mexico approached an investment bank, which in turn bought Mexican sovereign debt on the secondary market. Since banks selling on the secondary market were eager to wipe this debt paper off their books, they were often willing to sell it for fifty to sixty cents on the dollar. The investment bank then bought the debt for the prospective investor (garnering for itself a commission), who in turn sold it to the Mexican government. Mexico repurchased the debt in pesos at a discount ranging from 75 to 100 percent of its face value. The second type of swap was known as a direct capitalization, where a company or bank wiped its debt (or that of a subsidiary or a client) off the books and converted it into an equity share in the Mexican company. Variations on this form of swap also existed. For example, a foreign bank might convert its debt into shares in a sort of "holding company" for equity involving other foreign or Mexican investors, which in turn would hold equity in one or more Mexican companies. These "equity syndicates" were appealing in that they spread risk among the various investors involved; several of them were set up in the Grand Cayman Islands. There are dozens of different ways to convert debt to equity, and numerous variants of the basic models presented here exist. Mexico's official manual on debt capitalizations listed at least seven official mechanisms for swaps. See Comisión Nacional de Inversiones Extranjeras, *Manual Operativo para la Capitalización de Pasivos y Sustitución de Deuda Publica por Inversión* (Mexico City: Government of Mexico, 1986).

Some debt swaps continue to be allowed under the aegis of the Brady Plan agreement Mexico finalized with its foreign creditors in 1990.

In sum, Mexico has engaged in a continual effort to liberalize its investment environment over the past decade. A closer look reveals that this liberalization does not mark a wholesale retreat on the part of the state, however. It is limited to the extent that Mexico continues to extract concessions from foreign investors rather than welcoming them unconditionally. While Mexico has consistently loosened official regulation of foreign investors, the government still channels investment to particular sectors and geographic regions. It ensures that foreign investors maintain balance-of-payment surpluses, restricts foreign ownership in a number of industries, and stipulates that investment be financed by new capital inflows. As mentioned in Chapter 2, it also maintains export requirements for foreign companies in the automobile sector. This blend of liberalization and state intervention is the result of the interaction of Mexico's economic predicament with unique domestic political configurations. A look at economic and political conditions in Mexico throughout the 1980s will illustrate this point more clearly.

MEXICO IN THE INTERNATIONAL POLITICAL ECONOMY

Since 1982, Mexico's position in the international political economy can be summarized in one word: debt. When Miguel de la Madrid took power that year, he inherited responsibility for one of the gravest economic crises Mexico had ever faced. With a shortfall of approximately $14 billion in foreign reserves, Mexico was forced to announce that it could not pay its obligations to foreign creditors. As Mexico's debt of $88 billion was renegotiated, the economy slumped into recession and GDP growth dropped to −0.2 percent. The situation worsened in 1983 as the austerity program implemented after the 1982 crisis took effect, and growth sank to −5.3 percent. Throughout his *sexenio* de la Madrid presided over the lowest average growth rates in Mexican history.

Mexico's economic picture began to brighten in 1984. Old debts were renegotiated on terms that reduced interest payments,

Table 9. Mexico's foreign debt (balance at year end in billions of U.S. dollars)

	1983	1984	1985	1986	1987	1988	1989	1990
Total debt	92.1	96.7	97.7	102.6	108.3	100.4	95.6	93.0
Debt service ratio[a]	—	55%	56%	61%	48%	—	—	—

Sources: Compiled from CEPAL and Mexican Ministry of Finance sources.
[a]Interest from public and private sector borrowing plus amortization of public debt, divided by exports of goods.

stretched out amortization periods, and provided new external financing. As the peso was devalued and domestic interest rates were raised, capital that had fled the country in 1982 slowly began to return. Inflation decreased from 101.8 percent in 1983 to 65.5 percent in 1984. Despite a catastrophic earthquake in 1985, economic performance remained stable, and a growing confidence in the economy was maintained. Crisis struck again in 1986, however, as the price of oil plummeted from an average of $25.30 per barrel in 1985 to its nadir of $8.54 per barrel in July 1986. As Mexico's revenues from oil fell, so did its trade surplus. Unable to meet its foreign debt obligations and bereft of capital due to the loss of oil revenues, Mexico once again turned to its creditors to renegotiate its debt (Table 9).

Mexico's external debt was accompanied by a massive internal debt. By the mid-1980s, it was clear that the expected resumption of foreign loans from foreign private lenders was not going to materialize. The government made up for lost sources of international revenue by increased domestic borrowing, primarily by issuing government treasury bonds, or CETES. This expansion of domestic debt helped to fuel an annual inflation rate that by 1987 had reached 180 percent. The high interest rates thus necessary to attract savings meant, in turn, higher payments on the government-issued CETES and a resultant increase of the government deficit. By 1987 the government deficit reached 17.8 percent of GDP, and service payments on domestic debt were approximately $3.4 billion per month, as opposed to $625 million per month for foreign debt.[16] Furthermore, the high interest rates attracted money into unproductive

16. *Business Mexico*, March 1988, p. 12.

investment. In 1986 only 42 percent of the total credit approvals issued by banks were for productive purposes, as opposed to 85 percent in 1985.

The government faced a difficult dilemma: lowering interest rates would reduce the deficit and inflation and redirect investment into more profitable venues, but it could also trigger the flight of capital. Tight credit conditions, high interest rates, and a devalued peso had achieved some success in pulling capital back into the country. A change in these policies could lead to an outflow of funds. This problem dogged the government throughout the 1980s: in 1989, real interest rates of 35 percent were necessary to persuade domestic capital to keep its money in Mexico as opposed to the United States. In addition, the government feared that lower interest rates could convert savings into consumption, exacerbating inflation.

In December 1987 the de la Madrid government introduced a new austerity program, containing urgent measures to control inflation. The package held the minimum wage stable, decreased subsidies for public sector services, and announced budget cuts that were to be achieved through the sale of state-owned enterprises. Private producers were urged to restrain prices voluntarily. In addition, tariffs were cut drastically to reduce import prices, and the peso was devalued 22 percent.

After his election as president in July 1988, Salinas made the conquering of inflation a primary goal of his administration.[17] By December 1988 the monthly inflation rate was down to 2.1 percent (51.7 percent per annum), and by mid-1989 annual inflation was estimated at 18 percent. Growth increased marginally to 1.5 percent in 1988 from about 1.1 percent in 1987.

In July 1989, Salinas negotiated a new debt-relief package under the aegis of the American treasury secretary, Nicholas Brady. The plan was designed to cut Mexico's medium and long-term debt by 17 percent through a debt forgiveness scheme. Unfortunately, the banks' response to this plan made it less of a relief than was originally figured. Under this proposal banks had three options to choose

17. Salinas's "Pact for Stability and Economic Growth" was an economic strategy that adopted as its goals the reduction of the public deficit, holding prices constant, holding wages constant, and a further devaluation of the peso.

from: they could forgive 35 percent of the principal of old loans in exchange for new Mexican bonds; they could cut interest rates on Mexican loans to 6.25 percent; or they could extend new loans. Success depended on at least 20 percent of the banks choosing the third option—new loans. Only a few of Mexico's five hundred creditor banks were willing to take this option.

Obviously, attracting new foreign investment would go a long way to ameliorating Mexico's perilous economic situation. Although both private and public investment improved after 1982, growth rates remained negative until 1986. By 1987 they approached zero, but the accumulated decline in investment took a serious toll on the investment stock. By 1986, gross fixed investment as a percentage of GDP was the equivalent of 1962 levels. Some catching up was necessary, but with national savings down 5 percent from 1982, it was clear that this catching up could not be based solely on domestic funds. Given the dearth of foreign financing in the form of loans, the only alternative was to attract more foreign investment.

Under these conditions, it would seem that Mexico had little choice but to relax its FDI regulations. The situation is more complex, however, and a review of the economic incentives to change foreign-investment policy reveals only half of the story. The debt crisis changed the interests of various domestic political actors, and the real question is precisely how permanent these changes will be.

DOMESTIC POLITICAL INFLUENCES

In the past, Mexico was often portrayed in the political economy literature as an authoritarian state.[18] Given the dominance of the country's single ruling party, the PRI, this observation was not totally unwarranted. The PRI maintains its own unique form of corporatism through direct links with labor, peasants, and domestic bour-

18. See Susan Kaufman Purcell, *The Mexican Profit-Sharing Decision: Politics in an Authoritarian Regime* (Berkeley: University of California Press, 1975). See also Merilee Grindle, "Policy Change in an Authoritarian Regime: Mexico under Echeverria," *Journal of Interamerican Studies and World Affairs* 19, no. 4 (November 1977), and Evelyn Stevens, "Protest Movements in an Authoritarian Regime: The Mexican Case," *Comparative Politics* 17, no. 3 (April 1975).

geois groups, all of which are incorporated institutionally into the party. The CNC (National Confederation of Peasants) and the CTM (Confederation of Mexican Workers) were both established during the presidency of Lázaro Cárdenas (1934–40) as integrated parts of the PRI. While the incorporation of these groups into the party provided them with some representation, it was primarily instituted as a means of social control. The PRI's tight grasp on social groups is one of the reasons for Mexico's remarkable political stability, despite the prevalence of major social inequities.

The state also has exercised considerable control in economic affairs. Following the model of many late-industrializing countries, the Mexican state intervened extensively in the domestic economy. One of the ways it did so was through state-owned enterprises. Consequently, Mexico has one of the highest rates of government ownership in the world. At one point, the state owned all the communications, electricity, natural gas, railroad, shipbuilding, petroleum, coal production, and banking sectors, and partially owned the steel, airline, and automobile manufacturing industries. In 1982, Mexico had approximately 1,133 state-owned enterprises, accounting for 14 percent of GDP and 30 percent of gross fixed capital formation. Between 1982 and 1990 the government sold or closed 37 percent of these enterprises as part of its economic liberalization strategy.[19] The state still plays a significant role in the economy, however, retaining ownership in more than 700 firms.

Despite the obvious predominance of the Mexican state, a body of work has arisen to challenge the notion that it is a powerful, autonomous entity. While not denying its important political and economic role, these studies argue that the state is in fact highly constrained by societal forces, particularly by the influence of domestic and foreign capital.[20] Some have gone so far as to characterize the state as

19. These figures are drawn from the report of a World Bank Divestiture Mission to Mexico, October 1990.

20. See Nora Hamilton, "Mexico: The Limits of State Autonomy," in Nora Hamilton and Timothy F. Harding, eds., *Modern Mexico: State, Economy, and Social Conflict* (Beverley Hills: Sage, 1986); James Cockcroft, *Mexico: Class Formation, Capital Accumulation, and the State* (New York: Monthly Review Press, 1983); Dale Story, *Industry, the State, and Public Policy in Mexico* (Austin: University of Texas Press, 1986); and Judith A. Teichman, *Policymaking in Mexico: From Boom to Crisis* (Boston: Allen and Unwin, 1988).

"weak" and divided because of its need to satisfy both its private and bureaucratic clienteles.[21]

The deregulation of FDI indicates that capital does have considerable influence on state policies. The interests of foreign and domestic capital were critical in shaping state policy in this area. Whether this proves that the Mexican state is weak is contentious, but the evolution of investment review cannot be understood without an examination of capital's changing interests.

Domestic Capital

As noted above, arguments about the relative autonomy of the Mexican state usually center on the way in which state behavior is constrained by domestic and foreign capital. James Cockcroft argues that while the bureaucratic bourgeoisie (often referred to as the *clase política*) is frequently portrayed as *the* ruling class in Mexico, it is only one part of it. Mexican bureaucratic elites often have strong ties with domestic capital, and many former presidents or other prominent party figures have gone on to successful careers in the private sector.[22] But even without these direct ties, domestic capital plays a significant consultative role in the policymaking process. The PRI has made efforts to ensure the representation of business interests in policymaking, although business is not officially integrated into the party the way workers, peasants, and the popular sector are. While all companies must be affiliated with a business organization, these organizations are considered to be "autonomous public institutions" that act as "consulting organs for the state."[23]

Until the mid-1970s, this consultative relationship between the state and business took the form of an informal pact: as long as the PRI provided an appropriate investment environment, business agreed to stay out of politics.[24] In its attempts to provide such an

21. See Teichman, *Policymaking in Mexico.*

22. Cockcroft, *Mexico,* p. 217.

23. Matilde Luna, Ricardo Tirado, and Francisco Valdes, "Businessmen and Politics in Mexico, 1982–1986," in Sylvia Maxfield and Ricardo Anzaldúa Montaya, eds., *Government and Private Sector in Contemporary Mexico,* Monograph Series 20 (San Diego: Center for U.S.-Mexican Studies, 1987), p. 16.

24. Sylvia Maxfield, "National Business, Debt-Led Growth, and Political Transition in Latin America," in Barbara Stallings and Robert Kaufman, eds., *Debt and Democracy* (Boulder: Westview Press, 1989).

investment environment, the state instituted numerous probusiness policies: it subsidized many businesses through their links with state-owned enterprises; it did not raise taxes despite its huge internal debt; it provided aid for private firms to pay off their foreign debt through loans or by granting them preferential exchange rates; and perhaps most important, it did not place exchange controls on capital leaving the country, other than to exert some control over the exchange rate. It is important to emphasize the state's probusiness stance because the PRI's regulation of FDI is often interpreted as reflecting an antibusiness perspective. In fact, although FDI controls may reflect a hostility toward foreign capital, they are designed specifically to aid and protect domestic capital.

Still, the Mexican state does not simply respond to domestic capital's every whim. Especially since the mid-1970s when Echeverria instituted a controversial series of land reforms, business-state relations have been characterized by rising levels of tension. At times this tension has taken the form of outright conflict. Business considered the Echeverria land reforms as an outright abrogation of their informal pact with the state. In response, it no longer hesitated to turn its grievances with the state into political battles. One reflection of this hostility was a growing business affiliation to the right-wing National Action Party (PAN). A more direct indicator of its anger was the series of business strikes that took place throughout the late 1970s. Mexico is one of the few countries in the world where capital literally goes on strike, setting up picket lines and calling for closures.[25]

Most observers agree that the fundamental blow to the pact between business and the state came in 1982, with the bank nationalizations undertaken by López Portillo in September of that year.[26] These nationalizations represented the culmination of one of the longest and most deep-seated battles between the state and business:

25. In 1976 a business strike was organized to protest the expropriating of 100,000 hectares of land in the Yaqui Valley by President Echeverria. Another strike evolved out of a conflict with labor in the city of Puebla in 1979. In 1982, capital strikes in response to the imposition of exchange controls and bank nationalizations were called for but were unsuccessful.

26. Maxfield, "National Business," and Robert Kaufman, "Economic Orthodoxy and Political Change in Mexico: The Stabilization and Adjustment Policies of the de la Madrid Administrations," in Stallings and Kaufman, *Debt and Democracy*.

the issue of capital flight. Capital flight is not a new problem for Mexico—major outflows occurred in 1960–61 and 1976. But as noted, the most significant outflow of capital began with the economic crisis of 1982. In the first three months after the announcement of the nationalization of the banks, $1 billion left the country in the form of repatriated profits and an additional $7 billion in capital flight.[27] Scandalized by this capital flight, López Portillo nationalized private sector national banks. This action in itself was not enough to stem the outflow of money, however. One estimate claimed that $16 billion left Mexico between 1983 and 1985, while new net borrowing amounted to $9 billion during the same period.[28] A more detailed assessment estimated a cumulative total of $26.29 billion between 1977 and 1985, noting that almost one-third of the increase in total gross debt was attributed to capital flight.[29]

Business did not take kindly to the bank nationalizations of 1982, and subsequently certain factions of domestic capital have become more and more vocal in their opposition to the PRI. This is particularly true of businesses from the north, where a growing group of hardliners have affiliated themselves with the right-wing PAN. The hardliners primarily represent northern business interests in the city of Monterrey, but are also powerful in the areas of Puebla, Jalisco, and in some areas of the Federal District of Mexico City. They constitute a major faction within the PAN known as the *neopanistas*. The former leader of the PAN, Manuel Clouthier, was a prominent businessman from the north.

Domestic capital has not converted en masse to PAN affiliation— several prominent business people remain affiliated with the PRI and even have run for public office as PRI candidates. These "moderates," mainly centered in Mexico City, have also called for reforms, advocating a greater opening of the Mexican economy and arguing that foreign investors should be treated the same as domestic investors. In contrast to northern interests, they believe that such reforms

27. Nora Hamilton, "State-Class Alliances," in Hamilton and Harding, eds., *Modern Mexico*, p. 155.

28. Susan George, *A Fate Worse than Debt* (London: Penguin, 1988), p. 20.

29. Edward Buffie and Allen Sanguines Krause, "Mexico 1958–86: From Stabilizing Development to the Debt Crisis," in Jeffrey D. Sachs, ed., *Developing Country Debt and the World Economy* (Chicago: University of Chicago Press, 1990), p. 152.

can be undertaken within the PRI and maintain their allegiance to the party. In addition, a group of small and medium sized businesses remain firmly tied to the PRI. These companies are much more hesitant about liberalizing trade and controls on FDI.

These political divisions within the business community are mirrored in the organizations that represent them. Numerous business organizations exist in Mexico, although compared with the situation in Canada, business is relatively centralized. The Chambers Law of 1941 divided the single largest business group into three smaller ones: CONCAMIN (for industry) CONCANACO (for commerce) and CANACINTRA (for small and mid-sized businesses). Other important groups include COPARMEX (a voluntary organization created by Monterrey business interests), ABM (the bankers' association) and the CCE (the Coordinating Council for Business, another northern group). While these lobby groups share many general interests, such as an aversion to extensive state intervention in the economy, they often hold different opinions. On some occasions, such as the 1982 bank nationalizations, these differences have blunted the impact of business protests.

Politically moderate business interests are particularly prominent in organizations such as CONCANACO, CONCAMIN, and CANACINTRA. The strongholds of the radical faction are COPARMEX, and the CCE.[30] Groups such as the CCE have harshly criticized the PRI—the former CCE leader Manuel Clouthier once referred to the López Portillo regime as "corrupt and inefficient" and criticized it for its "almost totalitarian 'statization' of the economy."[31] In contrast, the more moderate CONCAMIN, CONCANACO, and CANACINTRA usually support PRI policy.

An examination of the evolution of these groups' policy positions toward FDI regulation reveals that their changing viewpoints are linked to their material positions in the economy at any particular point in time. Jorge Dominguez showed that in the 1940s and 1950s, for example, CONCANACO the commercial group, resisted state intervention in the economy and had a positive attitude toward foreign investment. Conversely, CANACINTRA (small and medium-sized

30. For a more in-depth analysis of these factions, see Luna, Tirado, and Valdes, "Businessmen and Politics."
31. Quoted in Story, *Industry*, p. 102.

firms) supported protectionist policies and had a more cautious attitude toward foreign investment. The industrial group, CON-CAMIN, wavered between protectionist and laissez-faire positions.[32]

As competition from foreign companies heated up throughout the 1950s and 1960s, CONCAMIN and CONCANACO moved to qualify their acceptance of FDI, and both supported policies that discriminated in favor of domestic firms. This convergence of views in opposition to foreign investment was a reflection of the challenges these companies were confronting: 22 percent of Mexican companies had no competition at all when they were founded, but by 1969 only 3 percent of them had none. Similarly, 31 percent of Mexican companies had foreign competition at founding, as opposed to 50 percent at the end of the 1960s. These percentages were higher in more advanced manufacturing sectors, where increased foreign competition had an impact on 54 to 63 percent of Mexican firms.[33]

Domestic capital began to support the regulation of FDI because it provided protection from foreign competition and guaranteed lucrative partnerships with MNEs through the "Mexicanization" provisions. As Jacobo Zaidenweber, former president of CONCAMIN, noted, "It's okay to say welcome to foreign investors, but when the product coming in is one competing against yours, that's something else."[34] Therefore, while domestic business continued to emphasize the importance of FDI to the economy, it simultaneously insisted that FDI must enter the economy on Mexican terms. A survey in 1973 showed that 80 percent of executives of large Mexican firms agreed that more than 50 percent of all foreign operations in Mexico should be in Mexican hands.[35] Dominguez argued that by the early 1970s, "the convergence of attitudes toward foreign investment within the Mexican business community . . . had been completed. There were no longer any statistically significant differences

32. Jorge Dominguez, "Business Nationalism: Latin American National Business Attitudes and Behavior toward Multinational Enterprises," in Jorge Dominguez, ed., *Economic Issues and Political Conflict: U.S.-Latin American Relations* (Boston: Butterworth Scientific, 1982), p. 47.

33. Ibid., p. 48.

34. Quoted in *Forbes*, March 25, 1985.

35. U.S. Information Agency, Office of Research, "Mexican Elite Attitudes toward Foreign Investment" (Washington: U.S.I.A., May 1974).

between the views of executives of large or medium Mexican companies."[36] This convergence of attitudes extended to broader Mexican society, although (significantly) labor leaders and media leaders generally favored the admittance of more foreign firms into the economy.

By the early 1980s, however, major divisions between business interests on the issue of FDI regulation began to reappear. Groups representing radical business interests such as the CCE and COPARMEX and increasingly the more moderate CONCANACO began to look favorably on such internationalist views as opening up Mexico to the world economy through entrance to the GATT and the deregulation of FDI. Conversely, CONCAMIN and CANACINTRA generally continued to support protectionist measures. The conflict between these business interests crystallized around the debate to enter the GATT in 1978–80. While the CCE and COPARMEX pushed for trade liberalization, CANACINTRA in particular strongly opposed it. The debate over this issue was heated, but it was eventually muted by the general economic prosperity surrounding the oil boom, and in the end Mexico declined to enter the GATT.[37]

By the mid-1980s, internationalist views had gained wider acceptance in the business community. The inability of Mexico to repay its foreign debts and the atmosphere of austerity that characterized most of this period convinced many business people that the old import substitution industrialization strategy of economic development was exhausted and that new directions must be pursued. Negative growth rates hurt domestic capital and brought on the realization that a new, more stable source of financing was necessary to fuel economic growth. In addition, businesses associated with groups like the CCE and COPARMEX had less of a stake in supporting state policy. With the sell-off of many state enterprises and the austerity program implemented in the 1980s, the state was less able to subsidize large business through contracts or through outright grants. In response, the larger business interests of the north developed strong financial links with foreign financial markets (especially

36. Dominguez, "Business Nationalism," p. 49.
37. Saúl Escobar Toledo, "Rifts in the Mexican Power Elite, 1976–1986," in Maxfield and Anzaldúa Montaya, *Government and Private Sector*.

in the United States), and their commercial welfare lay less and less within Mexico.[38]

Another and perhaps more significant reason for the change in business attitudes was the devaluation of the peso between 1985 and 1988. The peso dropped from 447 pesos to the U.S. dollar in 1985 to 915 pesos to the dollar in December 1986. By the end of 1987, pesos were being exchanged on the market at a rate of 2,379 to the dollar. Although these devaluations were devastating in terms of paying off external debt, they encouraged more Mexican entrepreneurs to sell in external markets and gave them confidence in their ability to compete. They also brought recognition that access to markets abroad was going to dictate less protectionism at home and more secure access to U.S. markets.

As Mexican companies expanded their U.S. market share, they increasingly confronted growing protectionism. Between 1980 and 1986, Mexico faced twenty-six U.S. countervailing duty actions, nineteen of which led to restrictive actions.[39] In 1987, Mexico lost $200 million in GSP (Generalized Special Preferences) benefits because of a USTR finding that it was not providing adequate protection for intellectual property. The U.S. trade bill passed in 1988 threatened an even more ominous challenge to Mexico's plans of export-led growth, as did the AFL-CIO's growing antagonism toward the *maquiladoras*. As the *Wall Street Journal* noted, "The bitter irony for Mexican industrialists is that their herculean efforts to become competitive in international markets have left them more than ever at the mercy of economic forces beyond their control."[40]

In response to these pressures, Mexico announced limited improvements in its intellectual property laws and entered the GATT in 1986. Even CANACINTRA reluctantly supported the accession to the GATT. An official statement noted, "We are ready to compete provided there is realism in the economy."[41] Changes in the foreign-investment laws are part of this liberalizing trend. As late as 1985,

38. Kaufman, "Economic Orthodoxy," p. 123.
39. Michael Hart, *A North American Free Trade Agreement: The Strategic Implications for Canada* (Ottawa: Centre for Trade Policy and Law, and Halifax: Institute for Research on Public Policy, 1990), p. 38.
40. *Wall Street Journal*, November 23, 1987.
41. Quoted in *Business Mexico*, March 1988.

CANACINTRA had refused to recognize the internationalist business organization CEMAI as representative of business in talks on Mexico's Export Incentive Program.[42] Yet in 1988, CANACINTRA signed a statement on FDI authored by CEMAI that called for revision of the laws concerning foreign investment and a simplification of the regulatory process. As the president of CEMAI, Enrique Madero Bracho, noted, "This is the first time we have had a unanimous vote by the private sector groups on foreign investment. CANACINTRA is simply realizing that it cannot continue to swim against the flow. Many medium-sized companies are now very competitive."[43] Support for NAFTA was an outgrowth both of capital's growing confidence and its fear that its U.S. market shares were under threat. Like Canada, Mexico sought a formal agreement not only to attract new investment but to deflect U.S. nationalism.

The growing support of Mexican private capital for the deregulation of FDI is a critical element in the state's overall internationalization program. The vocal opposition of the hardline business groups to the PRI's nationalist policies is evidence of a growing tension between the state and domestic capital. Since this group of hardliners is one of the primary sources of capital flight, their demands for change cannot be ignored. Indeed, the PRI has taken a very conciliatory stance toward business, reversing the nationalizations of the banks in 1990 and integrating business closely into the NAFTA negotiating process.

In the context of the increasing political and economic threats from the hardliners, the calls for change on the part of moderate business groups within the PRI have gained growing credence. The new FDI regulations adopted in Mexico essentially represent the moderates' line. This is not to downplay the changes the moderates have proposed, some of which are quite radical for Mexico. A recent PRI working group composed of some of Mexico's most prominent business people recommended measures such as dropping subsidies or tax policies that discriminated against foreign capital, aligning tax rates on profits and dividends with those in the home countries of

42. CEMAI (Consejo Empresarial Mexicano para Asuntos Internacionales) is a coordinating group that represents ten of the major business organizations in international affairs.

43. Interview, with author, Mexico City, March 1988.

the MNEs, improving intellectual property laws, and modifying and updating the legal framework to make it more open to foreign investment.[44]

One important caveat to this assessment of the new internationalism of Mexican business is necessary. Domestic capital is making the transition to more internationalist ideas because it is in its interests to do so. Should conditions change in a manner that affects domestic capital adversely, such as a major revaluation of the peso, the closing off of markets in the United States, or heated competition from foreign capital in the domestic market, capital's position on these policies can be expected to change. To a large extent, the continued predominance of internationalist ideals within Mexican capital depends on how well Mexican business fares in the continental economy. The CANACINTRA and CONCAMIN groups in particular are still extremely wary of the changes in regulation.

Moreover, a careful reading of the position papers solicited from business groups during the debate on foreign-investment review shows that domestic capital's acceptance of deregulation comes highly qualified. Even the most ardent advocates of internationalization note that although it is important to welcome FDI into the economy, the state should also "preserve the means to channel and determine the areas and conditions in order to ensure benefits to the national economy."[45] Mexican business is accustomed to operating in an environment where high levels of government intervention exist, and despite its distaste for government initiatives that adversely affect it (such as nationalizations and exchange controls), it accepts intervention as a political and economic reality. Furthermore, many domestic businesses continue to rely on the state for their economic welfare. Not only do they depend on state contracts and subsidies, they will not hesitate to call for state protection if competition from foreign companies becomes too fierce. State involvement in FDI policy thus remains legitimate in the eyes of many domestic business people. For somewhat different reasons, it also remains legitimate in the eyes of many foreign MNEs.

44. These suggestions (among others) were made in Comisiónes de trabajo del PRI, "Programa Gobierno, 1988–1994" (Mexico City: Comisión de Inversiones Extranjeras, 1989).
45. Ibid., p. 11.

International Capital

In theory, international investors have the strongest bargaining position relative to the state. If they decide that Mexico is not a hospitable investment environment, they can simply stop investing there and move somewhere else. After all, Mexico is just another "export platform" in the eyes of the global investor. All the studies of bargaining relations between MNEs and the Mexican state emphasize the important role foreign capital plays in the Mexican economy, and the complex interactions between MNEs, local capital, and the state in a country at a stage of "dependent development."[46] Naturally, foreign capital leans to an internationalist interpretation of the need for investment regulations, and on the whole MNEs would prefer not to have them at all. In this sense, foreign capital is a constant liberalizing force in the Mexican economy.

A less emphasized aspect of the MNEs' role in the Mexican economy is how they *benefit* from foreign investment regulations. Foreign investors may support FDI regulations for several reasons. First, if they are large enough to be able to afford significant concessions they can gain large, guaranteed market shares by outbidding their competitors. Second, those who invested before the investment regulations instituted in the 1960s and 1970s are grandfathered and therefore are allowed concessions that newer investors are not. Third, they may simply wish to avoid antagonizing their host government. And fourth, those who learn how to work the system successfully consider this to be a major competitive advantage relative to newer or less savvy investors. In all these cases, MNEs support regulations because they protect their market shares.

IBM's experience in Mexico reveals a tangled web of political interests which illustrates some of these points. In 1985 after extended and fractious negotiations IBM established a wholly owned subsidiary to manufacture microcomputers in Mexico. The company insisted on 100 percent ownership of its subsidiary, and Mexico agreed, provided IBM increase its intended investment, create a

46. See, for example, Douglas Bennett and Kenneth Sharpe, *Transnational Corporations versus the State: The Political Economy of the Mexican Auto Industry* (Princeton: Princeton University Press, 1985); Gary Gereffi, *The Pharmaceutical Industry and Dependency in the Third World* (Princeton: Princeton University Press, 1983); and Gereffi and Evans, "Transnational Corporations," *Latin American Research Review* 16 (1981).

fund to develop local suppliers, and set up a software development center as well as a semiconductor research center. Foreign computer producers that were in the Mexican microcomputer market prior to IBM's entry (including Apple, Hewlett-Packard, Burroughs, and Honeywell) strongly protested IBM's entry. They were furious that IBM received 100 percent ownership in return for giving concessions they claimed they could not afford to give. In addition, they feared that if IBM were allowed to produce the quantities of computers it proposed, it would flood the market and crowd out existing producers.[47] By agreeing to Mexican demands, IBM was in fact pushing its strongest competitors out of the market.

Although IBM entered the Mexican market on conditions largely dictated by the Mexican state, the company did not support the U.S. Department of Commerce when it issued a protest to Mexico's restrictions in the electronics sector, partly because IBM was hesitant to disrupt relations with the Mexican government. But it also stood to lose a great deal if restrictions in the Mexican electronics sector were lifted. As an Apple Computer executive noted, "Imagine IBM's reaction when it realized that after having made major concessions to the Mexican government, the dropping of restrictions in the sector would mean that Apple California could essentially just ship computers from the United States to Mexico."[48]

While IBM was lobbying to retain restrictions in Mexico, its home government was pressuring the Mexicans to open up their investment environment. The Department of Commerce has been one of the loudest and most persistent critics of Mexico's FDI regulation. It has constantly leaned on Mexico to reduce such restrictions. Much to the chagrin of the Department of Commerce, IBM did not support its efforts to liberalize this sector. Department of Commerce officials were already unhappy with IBM. They argued that in giving concessions that it could afford because of its large size, IBM was setting precedents with which other U.S. companies could not comply.[49] By August 1989, however, the Department of Commerce reported that IBM seemed to have "come around" on this issue.[50]

---

47. Allen Sanguines Krause, "Mexico and the Microcomputers" (A), Harvard Business School Case 0–386–182.

48. Confidential interview with Apple Computer executive, August 1989.

49. Interview, U.S. Department of Commerce, August 1988.

50. Interview, U.S. Department of Commerce, August 1989.

The reasons for this are unclear, but as one Department of Commerce staffer noted, "It just became obvious to IBM that its position was no longer tenable given the general position of the Department of Commerce and the Administration in general." The situation in Mexico parallels IBM's experience in Brazil, where fear of alienating the Brazilians muted its support for efforts by the U.S. government to press Brazil to change its electronics policies.[51] More recent interviews with U.S. Treasury Department officials indicate that they have encountered this attitude among a broad array of U.S. investors in Mexico. Many firms are worried that new market entrants not subject to regulation will have an unfair advantage.[52] These situations reveal the complicated nature of the triangular relationship between home governments, host governments, and MNEs.

Those covered by grandfather clauses because they invested prior to the Mexicanization decree also oppose complete liberalization of FDI regulations. Grandfathered companies were often excluded from some of the more onerous restrictions, such as the need for a majority Mexican investor. Citibank, for example, was allowed to perform many financial services that other foreign banks were not because it entered the Mexican market so early. For this reason, it is likely Citibank would resist any major opening of the Mexican financial sector to foreign investors, since it would place competitors on a more equal footing.

Similarly, General Motors has always owned 100 percent of its Mexican operations. In 1989, Mexico was considering making major changes to its automobile industrial policy that would result in a considerable opening of the Mexican industry. When asked what GM thought about this, an executive at GM's Mexican subsidiary replied, "If they do that, we will oppose it."[53]

Mexico's auto policies, described in greater detail in Chapter 2, require investors to make concessions, such as increasing local content, and adding new engine production capacity. Auto companies who make these concessions are naturally not keen to see new

51. Peter Evans, "Declining Hegemony and Assertive Industrialization: U.S.-Brazil Conflicts in the Computer Industry," *International Organization* 43, no. 2 (Spring 1989).

52. Interview at U.S. Department of the Treasury, April 1991.

53. Interview at General Motors, Mexico City, May 1989.

competitors come into the market who would not be subject to the same regulations. The big three American producers have therefore asked that newcomers face a fifteen-year transition period for performance requirements and tariff reductions. The transition period for companies already in the market would be over a shorter time period. They have also asked that zero tariffs be granted only in exchange for a North American rule of origin requirement of 60 to 70 percent, which would seriously reduce the capacity of non–North American firms for extraregional outsourcing.[54]

These examples indicate that investment regulations do not always work against the interests of MNEs and often can work in their favor by defending market share. From this perspective, host countries may question whether they wish to retain laws that enhance the market power of international investors, perhaps to the detriment of domestic consumers. This question is discussed in greater detail below. Here, it merely serves to illustrate the point that MNEs do not always oppose investment regulations.

Party Politics

The most outstanding feature of Mexico's political environment is that until recently it was virtually a one-party state, run by the PRI. The supremacy of the PRI has been severely curtailed by the emergence in the 1980s of parties on both the Left and Right with strong electoral followings. But even within the PRI, major factional differences have prevented full party unity. As mentioned earlier, the predominance of the PRI in the Mexican political landscape led many to characterize Mexico as an authoritarian state. While this may have been true in the past, the divisions that have erupted within and around the PRI have made this label less apt today. The limited, or exclusionary, pluralism of the past is being overcome by the growing appearance of new political interests and divisions among existing ones. It is impossible to understand the unique

---

54. Miguel Angel Olea, "The Mexican Automotive Industry in the NAFTA Negotiations" (Paper presented at the conference "The Auto Industry: Responding to a Changing North American Environment at Carleton University, Ottawa, October 1991).

nature of Mexico's *apertura* or the future of investment review without some knowledge of what these divisions are and what their impact has been.

Unlike the other cases examined in this book, outright battles between ministries or secretariats appeared to play a relatively minor role in the formulation of foreign-investment policy. Sill, intra-cabinet disputes have erupted numerous times, the most serious occurring over López Portillo's nationalization of the banks in 1982. Also, differences of opinion exist within the bureaucracy: internationalist factions tend to be housed in the Banco de México, the Finance Secretariat (SHCP, or Hacienda), and the Secretariat of Planning and Budget (Salinas's former stronghold). The Secretariat of Energy, Mines, and Parastatal (state-owned) Enterprise has a less probusiness attitude. The Secretariat of Commerce and Industrial Development and the Secretariat of Agriculture and Water Resources traditionally lay somewhere in between, although more recently SECOFI seems to have moved firmly into the internationalist camp.[55] These divisions tend to be fluid and change over time, however, and in the case of foreign-investment regulation there seemed to be relative unanimity in the direction change should take. The ministry responsible for FDI regulation, SECOFI, was headed in 1989 by Jaime Serra Puche, a Yale-educated technocrat who supported increased internationalization.

A more fundamental cleavage within the PRI is the battle between *políticos* (or politicians) and *técnicos* (or technocrats) that began to emerge during the 1970s, a battle that the *técnicos* appear to have won. *Políticos* are those who have made their way up through the labyrinthine PRI hierarchy through elected office positions or on the basis of "social skills and accumulated contacts."[56] Their legitimacy derives from their skills at political bargaining and networking, and their ability to gain or maintain the political support of the party's main constituencies—labor, peasants, and government employees. In contrast, *técnicos* gain their legitimacy from skills or expertise in special areas (such as economics and law) attained after

55. John Bailey, "The Impact of Major Groups on Policy-Making: Trends in Government-Business Relations in Mexico," in Roderic Camp, ed., *Mexico's Political Stability: The Next Five Years* (Boulder: Westview Press, 1986), p. 127.

56. Peter Smith, "Leadership and Change: Intellectuals and Technocrats in Mexico," in Camp, *Mexico's Political Stability*, p. 103.

years of education. Typically, *técnicos* have a degree from the National Autonomous University of Mexico or the Colegio de México and a postgraduate degree from a prestigious foreign university such as Yale, Harvard, Stanford, or Cambridge.

Técnicos are often portrayed as apolitical characters, "more comfortable in the presence of IMF [International Monetary Fund] functionaries than Tlaxaclan peasants."[57] Their purported lack of communication and political skills has led some to argue that the rise of the *técnicos* could have negative implications for the political stability of the country.[58] This view exaggerates the *técnicos'* lack of political skills; the last four PRI presidents have been classified as *técnicos*: Echeverria, López Portillo, de la Madrid, and Salinas de Gortari. While the political prowess of these presidents varied, all managed to maintain political stability. Salinas has surprised many with his political management skills.

The very fact that *técnicos* received presidential nominations reveals their growing prominence within the PRI. Under de la Madrid, two-thirds of the cabinet secretaries and more than one-half of the cabinet under secretaries had postgraduate degrees.[59] The growing predominance of technically trained politicians represents a significant departure in Mexican politics.

This departure was not achieved without friction—controversy surrounded the presidential nominations of both de la Madrid and Salinas de Gortari because of their obvious *técnico* credentials. Salinas was nominated over one of the most prominent of the PRI *políticos*, Secretary of the Interior Manuel Bartlett Díaz. Salinas purportedly fought a losing battle with party officials such as Bartlett over the rigging of the 1988 presidential elections, which the PRI won with a highly suspect bare majority. On policy issues the *técnicos* have been more successful, however. Since the de la Madrid presidency, orthodox, internationalist interests have become increasingly prominent within the majority of state agencies.

The prominence of internationalist views, seen in such policy

57. Ibid., p. 110. Smith is describing others' portrayals of the *técnicos* in this quotation, not necessarily his own.

58. Daniel Levy, "The Political Consequences of Changing Socialization Patterns," in Camp, *Mexico's Political Stability*.

59. Kevin Middlebrook, "Dilemmas of Change in Mexican Politics," *World Politics* 41, no. 1 (October 1988), p. 126.

changes as the new FDI regulations, is a reflection of the technocratic interests of these actors. There is no doubt that *apertura* policies are directly linked to the rise of the *técnicos* within the party. On policy issues, *técnicos* have consistently pushed for less interventionist policies that enhance Mexico's role in the global economy. In contrast, *políticos* tend to favor more nationalist policies.

The conflict between internationalist and nationalist interests has taken a toll on party unity. Insofar as nationalist policies formed a critical part of the platform of leftist factions within the PRI, debates over these policies contributed to the split between left and right that resulted in the formation of the *corriente democrática*, or democratic current, within the PRI in 1986. Led by Cuauhtémoc Cárdenas (the son of Lázaro Cárdenas, the president who nationalized foreign oil companies in 1938), the *corriente democrática* pushed for more equitable economic policies and greater democratization within the party. Several prominent party members participated in its formation; in addition to Cárdenas (who was governor of Michoacán state from 1980 to 1986), adherents included the former minister of labor Porfirio Muñoz Ledo.

Between 1986 and 1988, the *corriente democrática* operated within the PRI, claiming that it still strongly supported the party. Its policy platform brought it into direct conflict with the *técnicos*, however. Cárdenas openly challenged the *apertura* policies, calling for a moratorium on debt and a reversal of Mexico's policy of trade liberalizations. He also opposed the party's welcoming attitude to foreign investment, regarding it as a threat to the PRI's revolutionary obligation to maintaining Mexico's independence. In his words, "I believe Mexico will at some point have to establish controls on foreign investment. Existing patterns of investment have not only failed to provide us with modern technology or to integrate our economy, but have resulted in decapitalization."[60]

In response to Cárdenas's opposition, de la Madrid in 1987 called for "all those who, from now on, do not wish to respect the will of the immense majority of the PRI members to renounce our party."[61]

60. Interview by Andrew Reding with Cuauhtémoc Cárdenas, in Reding, "The Democratic Current: A New Era in Mexican Politics," *World Policy Journal* (Spring 1988), p. 340.
61. Economist Intelligence Unit, *Mexico Country Report*, 2d quarter (London: Economist, 1987), p. 5.

When Cárdenas responded by charging the party with "anti-democratic authoritarianism and intolerance," he was considered to have resigned. He then formed the Authentic Party of the Revolution (PARM). In 1988 PARM joined with other parties of the Left to form an anti-PRI coalition known as the PRD.[62] Cárdenas built a formidable opposition in the 1988 presidential election, defeating Salinas in Mexico City and in the states of Michoacán, Morelos, and Baja California. Opposition parties challenged the election results, with Cárdenas claiming he received 39 percent of the vote and that Salinas received 33 percent. Despite the party's relative lack of success in 1991 congressional and gubernatorial elections, the growing presence of the Left is relevant to an understanding of FDI policies in Mexico.

Given the genuine threat the *corriente democrática* poses at the polls, Salinas must be careful not to alienate constituencies within the PRI (such as labor and peasants) who are potential *corriente* supporters. Labor support is particularly important, since the government relies heavily on its participation in the corporatist economic pact (Pacto) to control inflation. Led by the most prominent labor union, the CTM, labor is tightly integrated into the PRI, and worker unrest is unlikely in the short term. The CTM leader Fidel Velazquez is solidly behind the NAFTA initiative, and historically the CTM has acted only to control labor demands and keep wage increases below productivity growth.[63] Whether it can maintain this control in the face of growing disaffection in the *maquiladoras* remains to be seen, but labor groups could hold a future swing vote if extensive deregulation results in the elimination of Mexican firms and the jobs they generate. With his more nationalist policies, Cárdenas could easily capitalize on such dissatisfaction in an election campaign.

The nationalism Cárdenas builds on is an important consideration for the government as it moves to internationalize the economy. While the PRI is pushing for deregulation in many areas, it must constantly reassure its citizens that it will continue to monitor economic activity closely to ensure the prosperity of Mexicans. This

62. Reding, "The Democratic Current," p. 324.

63. Ian Roxborough, *Organized Labor: A Major Victim of the Crisis*, in Stallings and Kaufman, *Debt and Democracy*, p. 102.

scrutiny places continuous political pressure on the state to maintain an interventionist role in areas such as FDI regulation, where it must be careful not to alienate potential swing voters, and reveals the fragile political base of Mexico's *apertura*; if the *técnicos*' policies do not achieve results, a nationalist backlash can be expected to result, and Cárdenas will surely capitalize on it. Even in the absence of a political challenge from the PRD, there may be a renaissance of factions within the PRI that support less internationalist policies.

Pressures from the PAN must also be considered, given its growing electoral prominence. In the 1988 presidential elections, the PAN received about 14 percent of the vote. The PAN also won two gubernatorial elections in 1991. The disaffection of business with PRI policies and its growing affiliation with the PAN increased the influence of business factions within the PRI that pushed for an *apertura*. The PRI thus faces the challenge of balancing pressure from the Right to liberalize, with the nationalist rumblings of Cárdenas on the Left. Salinas's FDI policies reflect this tension: on the one hand, they constitute a significant trend toward liberalization. On the other hand, they reserve an interventionist role for the state in directing where investment goes.

Unlike the United States and Canada, Mexico has a long history of state intervention. Ben Ross Schneider argues that Mexico constitutes a hybrid form of a "bureaucratic political economy," in which legislatures and judiciaries are weak and subordinate.[64] In fact, the Mexican bureaucracy is so influential that it is frequently designated as a social group unto itself, known as the *clase política*. Because such an influential bureaucracy means that representation is often via the administration, state managers frequently control and manipulate critical aspects of the economy to favor the social interests they represent. One way they do this is through state-owned enterprises. Another way is through foreign-investment controls.

Foreign-investment review is much more entrenched in Mexico than it is in either Canada or the United States because it is an

---

64. Ben Ross Schneider, "Partly for Sale: Privatization and State Strength in Brazil and Mexico," *Journal of Interamerican Studies and World Affairs* 30, no. 4 (Winter 1988–89). Note that this argument is precisely the opposite of Atkinson and Coleman's argument concerning Canada, where the Westminster parliamentary system designated Parliament as predominant.

integral part of the political economy. Domestic and international capital rely extensively on investment regulation, but the state relies on such regulation as well. Opening up many of the sectors restricted entirely or partially for the state would "transfer the bureaucratic political economy and, hence, is not merely another policy option."[65] Salinas instituted the deregulation of the investment review process in response to pressure from the United States, international banks, hardline business interests within the PAN, and the growing predominance of *técnicos* within the PRI. But these regulations ensured a continued role for the state in monitoring trade and capital flows and in regulating access to more than 100 restricted sectors. To demolish these regulations would fundamentally challenge the way the Mexican economy is run.

Mexico has made major changes in its foreign-investment regulations over the past decade. Through a variety of amendments and reorganizations, it has simplified and liberalized its foreign-investment rules. This trend toward liberalization, however, is mixed with a strong element of state intervention. The reasons lie in the political, social, and economic configurations of the Mexican political economy. It is these factors that have allowed Mexico to regulate FDI so persistently over the past two decades despite constant economic pressures not to do so.

Pressure for change has come from internationalist interests such as northern business and the growing faction of *técnicos* within the PRI. But at the same time, latent nationalist interests remain important. While the majority of domestic and foreign capital advocate foreign-investment deregulation, all business benefits to some degree from rules that keep competitors out of the market. Therefore, capital generally has withheld unqualified support for a complete deregulation of foreign investment. Instead, it has advocated a more cautious approach, which includes a prominent role for the state.

Finally, political divisions within the PRI and the growing strength of political challenges on both the Left and the Right dictate that the ruling party is somewhat limited in what it can do in terms of changing investment policies. Dramatic deregulation could alienate

65. Ibid., pp. 110–11.

certain PRI constituencies that could defect to the left-wing PRD. On the other hand, complete inaction could strengthen the position of the right-wing PAN. It will be interesting to follow the interaction between nationalist and internationalist factions as Mexico's participation in the international economy grows over time. Mexico's obligations under the GATT and a future NAFTA could easily clash with the welfare of labor and small and medium-sized businesses. If adequate economic growth does not ensue, a strong nationalist reaction can be expected.

CHAPTER SIX

Policy Alternatives

This book began with a paradox: despite rapid and extensive continentalization, markets remain fundamentally nationally based. The evidence presented here indicates that state intervention in international markets is not only feasible but in many cases necessary to enhance the global competitiveness of both firms and the domestic economy. In three case studies, we have seen how states play a critical role in determining the contours of competition in the market.

On a more basic level, these cases show that political interventions are not an external corrupting force that distorts the smooth functioning of the market. Rather, they form an integral part of standard market operations. This point is important on a political as well as a theoretical level. Not only does it reinforce the notion that politics are part of the market, it demystifies the neo-classical conception of the market as a structural constraint on policy initiatives. Decision makers are not constrained by an anonymous institution that punishes them when they transgress market imperatives. They are constrained by the actors who comprise the market—individual firms, classes, or state managers who engage in political battles to get their way.

It is possible to argue that by emphasizing these political factors I have simply replaced the notion of the "market as prison" with that of "politics as prison." This criticism is somewhat justified—the Canadian and U.S. case studies showed that calls for industrial policies will be made in vain without the institutional capacity or the political will to implement them. Similarly, the Mexican state is constrained from withdrawing from interventionist positions in the market by economic and social interests that benefit from such intervention.

The politics-as-prison argument brings a fundamentally different perspective to the state's relationship with the market, however. Political interests and coalitions change over time, and as they do, so will the pressures and constraints weighing on the state. Therefore, bringing politics into an interpretation of the market provides for the possibility of policy change, as well as new opportunities for state action. Market actors base their actions on interests that are derived from their relations with other classes, groups, or state institutions, and in recognition of the challenges and opportunities they face in the international economy. The interests of given actors cannot always be understood from their objective situations in the market. As circumstances change, so do interests—and astute policymakers must be aware of these changes in order to devise effective bargaining strategies that are viable for all parties involved.

That interests change was repeatedly shown to be true with regard to capital throughout the case studies. The functional role capital plays in the market gives it very strong bargaining power, but it is not the only source of power, and it does not dictate a unilateral response by either the state or capital. International capital, which should in theory oppose state intervention, frequently did not because it did not want to jeopardize its relationship with the state or because it derived benefits from such measures. Conversely, elements of domestic capital that objectively should have supported state intervention in the market often did not because to do so would have clashed with other items on their agenda. The assumption that state regulations on capital will bring one reaction—retaliation—is therefore rather questionable.

The cases did show that the market-as-prison argument outlined in Chapter 1 was correct in focusing on capital as a key actor influencing state intervention. Although capital did not always react the way these theorists predicted, its views frequently prevailed. But even when capital opposed state regulations, it did not always get its way. In both Mexico and Canada, highly interventionist measures were employed successfully (although in Canada not for any considerable length of time) owing to strong support from voters and, in Mexico, the key economic role of the state. Once again, political struggles inherent in the question of state intervention are prominent.

Focusing purely on the reduction of trade barriers to increase competitiveness ignores both the economic and political realities of the continental economy and reveals an obsession with delegating the responsibility for economic planning to the market. This kind of policy position is enticing for states who feel their economic control threatened by the internationalization of markets. Since interventionist states may be held responsible for economic outcomes over which they have declining influence, the temptation is to shove this responsibility onto the more anonymous shoulders of the market. But giving over authority to the market essentially means handing the reins of power over to those actors who hold most power in the market. The market is far from being an anonymous institution. In all three countries (although to a lesser extent in Mexico), letting the market prevail means giving control over economic planning to business and other special interests.

Yet there is no guarantee that giving private groups power over public decisions is rational or efficient economically or politically. From an economic perspective, allowing business to drive down input costs such as labor, or social overhead is ultimately self-defeating if it leads to reduced consumption, untrained labor, or reduced education expenditures. What may be efficient in the eyes of the individual investor is not necessarily optimal for the broader economic community. Similarly, failing to take care of national constituents, whether they be firms or individuals, invites a Polanyian protectionist reaction that can scuttle promising international efforts aimed at increasing cooperation between states.

In all three case studies, we saw the fertile ground for nationalist backlashes. These backlashes are hardly desirable, but particularly in Canada and the United States, they seem to be the only way for constituents, including business, to get the kind of protection or adjustment efforts they seek. This is another interesting paradox: the quest for free trade is nearly a mirror reflection of corporate interests, yet businesses threatened by continental competition will probably be among the first to call for abrogation. More proactive state strategies could diffuse pressures for economic nationalism by cushioning people and companies from the extremes of the international market.

Despite the growing continentalization of the economies of the United States, Canada, and Mexico, it is clear that new economic conditions do not dictate withdrawal on the part of the state. On the contrary, reliance on "getting the prices right" in terms of lowering labor costs, reducing social overhead, and devaluing exchange rates has set all three countries on a collision course. Because each state is relying on its costs being cheaper than its trading partners', it is obvious that either a downward bidding cycle or a huge political clash is destined to result. This situation could be alleviated through adjustment policies such as labor retraining programs, R&D policies coordinated by the state, and a social charter that guarantees minimum wages and basic social protection.

State-led social and economic programs are an essential element of a comprehensive free trade strategy. Rather than disrupting market logic by imposing "social overhead" on private investors, these programs would not only make trade more politically viable by diffusing protectionist reactions, they would also increase corporate competitiveness by reducing health-care costs, providing more productive labor, and rationalizing and subsidizing R&D.

There is, of course, the question of how these programs would be paid for. One solution is to replace investment incentives in the form of tax holidays, grants, or real estate deals with the subsidization of firms' social payments. Obviously, this would not create new income, but it would redirect the handouts states are prone to give toward more productive uses. Another solution is for the United States to raise corporate income taxes. Companies may complain that raising taxes will harm their international competitiveness, but North American taxes are low in an international context. Data from the OECD show that the percentage of tax revenues contributed by corporations was 16.9 percent in Canada and 18.3 percent in the United States, as opposed to 28.6 percent in the United Kingdom and 48.4 percent in Japan.[1]

---

1. Cited in Mel Hurtig, *The Betrayal of Canada* (Toronto: Stoddart Publishing, 1991), p. 154. In Canada, personal income tax contributions are already seven times greater than corporate contributions to government tax revenue.

Any initiative to raise corporate taxes would have to come from the United States. Because U.S. taxes are among the lowest of all OECD countries, they are a downward drag on tax rates in its two continental trading partners. Low taxes, in turn, increase budget deficits. This tendency would be heightened should a continental free trade zone be negotiated. A tariff-free zone without a subsidy agreement would encourage states to lure companies into their jurisdictions via incentives such as tax handouts, which would reduce tax revenues even further. If the desirability of not increasing tariffs is generally accepted, the only way out of this dilemma is to disallow such incentive programs and increase corporate tax rates in all three countries in tandem. Such a tax hike instituted by the United States would allow Canada and Mexico greater taxation latitude.

It is apparent, then, that the current conception of a North American Free Trade Agreement leaves out important areas of mutual concern, such as social policy and taxation. Another area that was of central interest in the European Community's 1992 negotiations, yet which is explicitly omitted from the NAFTA agenda, is that of currency and exchange rates. I am not suggesting that Canada, the United States, and Mexico would or should be prepared to enter into a single-currency agreement similar to that in the European Community, or even an exchange-rate pact. I am merely pointing to a problem in the free trade agenda. Omitting an exchange-rate agreement encourages beggar-thy-neighbor devaluations that alienate trade partners and enable companies to put off essential productivity improvements. Minus such an agreement, political battles over exchange-rate issues are sure to ensue.

Still, the drive for a continental free trade agreement may not be successful, and even if it is, these coordinating issues are unlikely to be addressed. In this context, national investment policies are of greater relevance.

THE UNITED STATES

United States investment policy has been a cause for concern for both advocates and opponents of foreign-investment review. Those

opposed to investment review are worried about the rising nationalism in the United States and the growing pressures to expand CFIUS's
mandate from national security issues to questions of essential commerce or economic security. Many proponents of investment review
are concerned as well; some argue that there are no clear guidelines
for investment review and that the system is not institutionally coherent. Others are more concerned with the growing competition
between states and municipalities over investment incentives and
the growing trend toward state regulation of foreign investment.
Still others complain that CFIUS is ineffective as an investment review
agency. Not surprisingly, a policy debate has sprung up around
these issues. In this section, I review some of the most prominent
contributions to this debate in an attempt to elucidate some of the
major policy issues.

International Negotiations on Investment Regulations

On this point, there is near-unanimous agreement on the necessity of international negotiations to set some ground rules for national investment policies. Where commentators vary is in their
relative optimism about the possibility of success. Robert Reich
argues for the necessity of a GATT for FDI, focusing primarily on
establishing rules by which nations seek to attract investment. Reich
also calls for multilateral talks to deter countries from closing off
their markets to certain investors.[2]

Edward M. Graham and Paul R. Krugman argue for multilateral
talks, but they suggest that such negotiations should be restricted to
like-minded developed countries that face similar investment issues.
These talks would devise a set of relatively simple rules and regulations for their signatories. For host countries, they would guarantee
the right of establishment and reinforce the principle of national
treatment for foreign firms. For home countries, they would allow
governments to protect the offshore assets of national firms but
would restrict attempts by governments to extend home legislation
abroad. According to Graham and Krugman, an international treaty

2. Robert Reich, "Who Is Them?" *Harvard Business Review* 69, no. 2 (March–April
1991), pp. 87–88.

should also enforce disclosure requirements on foreign investors but ensure that foreign firms are not required to reveal more information than domestic companies. The authors argue that the free trade agreement between Canada and the United States provides a model for future restrictions on performance requirements and incentives. New performance requirements should be prohibited, they maintain, and already existing ones should be grandfathered, as in the FTA. In their view, the FTA also provides a model for a potential dispute settlement mechanism over the issue of subsidies and incentives. They add that the federal government would have to ensure that individual state governments complied with this legislation.[3]

Clyde V. Prestowitz, Jr. is less optimistic about the potential of multilateral talks and has advocated bilateral negotiations based on reciprocal market access as the only effective way of dealing with countries like Japan. According to this proposal, foreign firms would be granted open access to the U.S. market only if they allow U.S. investors similar access to their markets.[4] In an article that focuses primarily on trade issues, Clyde V. Prestowitz Jr., Alan Tonelson, and Robert W. Jerome make policy arguments that have major relevance for the investment debate. Decrying the doctrinaire "GATTism" of the U.S. government, the authors maintain that excessive focus on the development of detailed international rules has drawn attention away from the real problem facing the United States: national economic strength. International agreements, they argue, do not set up neutral laws that signatory states agree to abide by. Rather, they simply codify international power realities. The GATT worked in the past because the United States was powerful enough to enforce a set of rules on its trading partners and was rich enough to absorb the cost of others' abrogations of the treaty. When U.S. hegemony began to decline, the pitfalls of this approach became evident, and the system started to fall apart. Detailed agreements, they argue further, may satisfy negotiators, but they do not work in practice. Such rule-setting exercises are doomed to failure because they ignore that many trade barriers reflect legitimate and long-standing political

3. Edward M. Graham and Paul R. Krugman, *Foreign Direct Investment in the United States* (Washington: Institute for International Economics, 1989), chap. 7.

4. Clyde V. Prestowitz, Jr., *Trading Places: How We Allowed the Japanese to Take the Lead* (New York: Basic Books, 1988).

and economic arrangements between firms, labor, and government—arrangements that will not be swept away because new
guidelines are devised. Consequently, they believe that the United
States must come to understand that many GATT signatories do not
accept the laissez-faire principles the agreement embodies.[5]

Although the authors make recommendations specifically directed toward trade negotiations, their arguments are also relevant
to investment issues. Those opposed to Prestowitz's policy views
argue that if sectoral reciprocity is applied literally and consistently,
certain types of foreign investors would receive more favorable
treatment than domestic firms. For example, U.S. restrictions on
interstate banking are more stringent than regulations imposed on
U.S. firms investing in Europe. Using the principle of sectoral reciprocity, the United States would have to grant European banks
privileges not given to domestic banks in order to match the regulations governing U.S. bankers in Europe.[6] Obviously, they argue,
advocates of sectoral reciprocity are concerned only when U.S. firms
are more regulated than foreign firms are in the U.S. market.

There is no question that there are problems with the notion of
sectoral reciprocity, and across-the-board sectoral agreements simply
would not be feasible. But the political realism inherent in Prestowitz's argument is valid with regard to excessive reliance on rule
making. It is not realistic to think that making international rules will
obliterate pressure from special interests to contravene such measures in the signatory countries. A perfect example is the Canada–
United States Free Trade Agreement, which has not inhibited numerous bitter and protracted trade disputes in a wide variety of
sectors. In addition, Canadian firms are subject to both the Exon-
Florio amendment and state-level antitakeover legislation. The
guidelines so meticulously negotiated in the FTA simply do not
guarantee Canadian investors access to the U.S. market. Obviously,
rules are not enough.

This is not to say that multilateral negotiations should not be
continued, only that they should not be regarded as a panacea for

5. Clyde V. Prestowitz, Jr., Alan Tonelson, and Robert W. Jerome, "The Last Gasp
of GATTism," *Harvard Business Review* 69, no. 2 (March–April 1991).
6. Graham and Krugman, *Foreign Direct Investment*, p. 117.

investment issues. Two other feasible alternatives could complement multilateral talks. One is bilateral or multilateral sectoral agreements in selected industries. In some particularly contentious industries, sectoral agreements that allocate production may be the only resolution to long-standing political animosities. The North American automobile industry is a case in point. United States labor opposed even the short-term renewal of the 1965 auto pact signed between Canada and the United States in the FTA, arguing that the agreement diverted investment northward, while automobile companies cut back on production in the United States. The growing threat from the Mexican auto industry puts a new twist on this argument, however. As U.S. workers become more and more threatened by cheap labor from the south, some sort of continental agreement may be the only way to ensure some minimal level of job security in all three countries. Preferably, a continental sectoral agreement would also deal with Japanese automakers.[7]

A second possibility is to aid firms and workers in the quest for international competitiveness through government policies designed to coordinate investment efforts with measures that enhance adjustment. The institutional considerations surrounding R&D policies discussed in Chapter 3 are relevant in this regard. Measures to centralize nondefense R&D in agencies such as the National Institute of Standard Technology in the Department of Commerce will help, but they must be combined with efforts to focus more on generic and precompetitive technologies and a greater emphasis on the commercialization of civilian technologies. This latter point has gained growing attention recently because of the changing relationship between civilian and military technologies. By encouraging greater ties between government research agencies, federal laboratories, and business and by increasing its funding for commercial technologies, the federal government could improve the current situation.

Such policies have relevance for investment review in two re-

7. Stephen Herzenberg presents an interesting outline of a continental auto agreement that includes non-North American producers in Herzenberg, "Continental Integration and the Future of the North American Auto Sector" (Paper presented at the conference "The Auto Industry: Responding to a Changing North American Trade Environment," October 1991, Carleton University, Ottawa).

spects. First, as I argue in Chapter 2, any effective investment policies must be embedded in larger industrial strategies and should involve a prominent state role in coordinating and enticing both foreign and domestic firms to join R&D efforts. Second, insofar as such policies are successful in increasing the competitiveness of U.S. firms, they will go a long way to diffusing the nationalist sentiments brewing in both trade and investment debates. Changes in domestic U.S. institutional arrangements could alleviate many of the charges of unfair trade practices that so alienate trading partners.

In addition, the United States must work to standardize and improve its social programs. Workers who are assured that they will be adequately compensated and retrained in the event of a job loss are likely to have more flexible attitudes toward new technologies in the workplace and toward free trade. Yet the United States, along with Mexico, exerts a powerful downward drag on the kinds of expenditures necessary for these programs. Not only are U.S. social expenditures low by international standards, they are unequally distributed among states. Thus while certain states provide extensive social assistance, and thereby attract those in need, many southern states are vocal in advertising the advantages of their low social overhead and lack of protection for workers. Therefore, any charter designed to promote continental social equality must also address disparities *within* the member states.

Screening Agencies and the Regulation of FDI

Robert Reich has most eloquently challenged investment review by asking a question that cuts to the heart of the screening issue: why should one consider globally integrated U.S. firms to be any more responsive to national needs than globally integrated foreign companies? Multinational U.S. companies have been vocal not only in arguing that they must locate where production is most profitable in order to satisfy their shareholders but also in maintaining that they must adapt to the rules set by foreign host governments. Hence, he argues, "global managers at U.S.-owned companies are no more 'us' than are the global managers of non-U.S. companies. And it is in our interests to attract investment from global managers all over the world, rather than raising investment barriers on the faulty basis of national identity."[8] Graham and Krugman also oppose investment review, arguing that the difficulty of devising review criteria means that any screening agency would either be highly politicized or a rubber stamp.[9]

Neither of these arguments addresses the political feasibility of ignoring pressures for review. As in the brewing sectoral fracases, ignoring pressures for investment review could simply result in an explosion of nationalist sentiment. There is considerable truth in the arguments of both Reich and Graham and Krugman that in the United States, differentiating between national and foreign investors is meaningless. And, there are vastly superior ways of dealing with some of the perceived problems associated with foreign investment. Nonetheless, as foreign-investment review is not nearly so bad as its opponents make it out to be in terms of having a "chilling effect" on foreign investment. Recent Treasury Department statements that the debate surrounding FDI in the United States resulted in a 64 percent slump in investment inflows between 1989 and 1990 should be disregarded as propaganda.[10] This slump was unquestionably the result of the slowing down of the economy during this period. Because U.S. firms might be valued less during recession than they were before, many investors stopped takeovers in progress to reassess their offering price.

To make foreign-investment review less offensive, it simply must be more directed. For one thing, a clearer definition of "national security" would give the review process more transparency and reduce the potential misuse of the law. Another suggestion is to integrate antitrust law and foreign-investment screening into a single process, as advocated by Graham and Ebert. These authors use the United Kingdom's Monopolies and Mergers Commission as an example of how antitrust and national security concerns can be integrated into a single screening process that applies to domestic and foreign firms alike. They argue that the actual list of vital

8. Reich, "Who Is Them?" p. 87. This is one of the central premises of Reich's book *The Work of Nations* (New York: Knopf, 1991). Marxist analysts have long made this argument in response to what they regard as "nationalist mythologies." See Bill Warren, *Imperialism: Pioneer of Capitalism* (London: Verso, 1979).

9. Graham and Krugman, *Foreign Direct Investment*, p. 117.

10. *Wall Street Journal*, June 13, 1991.

technologies that should not be exposed to trade or foreign investors is so small that regulating purely on the basis of national security concerns is unnecessary. Instead, authorities should pay more attention to ensuring that the United States is not reliant on a monopoly supplier for critical technologies. The obvious relation of this concern to antitrust issues suggests that the Federal Trade Commission, the Antitrust Division of the Department of Justice, and the Department of Defense should work together in the screening process.[11] It is also an effective way to deal with the potential clashes between the Departments of Commerce and Justice predicted in Chapter 3.

Reich goes farther than this to propose a "United States Investment Representative" who would perform a role in negotiating investment agreements similar to that of the U.S. trade representative. Rather than screening investments, however, the representative would centralize the use of incentives, such as subsidies, tax abatements, and the use of public lands, that have previously been used by states to attract foreign investors. The federal government would thereby preempt state attempts to use incentive programs and bargain on behalf of states and municipalities.[12] This suggestion brings us to the complex issue of subsidies and incentives.

Incentive Programs

There is widespread agreement that the competition between states at both an international and a subnational level over incentive programs may be great for firms, but it is bad for states. States and municipalities may be pushing themselves into bankruptcy by giving away so much potential income: in 1957, corporations accounted for 45 percent of local revenues in the United States. By 1987, they

11. Specifically, they propose combining the British approach with a modification of the Hart-Scott-Rodino premerger statute that would provide a global "reach" in terms of notification thresholds and mandatory information requirements. For more details, see Edward Graham and Michael Ebert, "Foreign Direct-Investment and National Security: Fixing the Exon-Florio Process," manuscript, Washington Institute for International Economics, 1991.

12. Graham and Krugman note that these state programs may be in violation of constitutional prohibition against state regulation of interstate commerce if they involve performance requirements.

contributed only 16 percent.[13] Reich's suggestion of a completely centralized investment representative to deal with this issue is probably not realistic, however, since states are not likely willingly to relinquish their control over incentive programs. At the same time, they should be able to see that this beggar-thy-neighbor strategy is benefiting no one but the firms involved. Incidents such as Volkswagen's flight from Pennsylvania after the state committed millions of dollars in incentives (which it is still paying for) should drive home this point.

Another solution is subsidy negotiations between states that would be conducted at a national level. This is probably a more realistic possibility than Reich's suggestion if it is directed at the gubernatorial level (where there tends to be more restraint toward screening and incentive issues) and involves joint state and federal government coordination of subsidy programs. Since complete abstention from giving incentives is unlikely, part of these negotiations should involve a thorough study of what is an acceptable subsidy and what is not. Robert Baldwin argues that wage subsidies and R&D subsidies are "good" and should not be prohibited, whereas production subsidies or "strategic" subsidies designed to shift income from one state or one country to another by driving competitors out of the market should not be tolerated. These latter subsidies either reduce the incentive for unproductive firms to get out of the market or can lead to subsidy "wars."[14]

In contrast, R&D subsidies may be necessary to encourage adequate investment when there are knowledge spill-overs to other industries or firms. The firm or firms undertaking the R&D gauge their expenditures only on the direct benefits they can capture from their outlays, not on the basis of the broader, secondary effects it may have on the whole industry or sector. Thus, government aid may be necessary to ensure appropriate R&D investment levels.[15] Wage subsidies to workers can also be important tools in the struc-

13. Reich, "Who Is Them?" p. 86.
14. Robert Baldwin, "Assessing the Fair Trade and Safeguard Laws in Terms of Modern Trade and Political Economy Analysis" (Paper presented at the Carleton University–University of Wisconsin conference on trade policy, Carleton University, Ottawa, May 1991).
15. Ibid.

tural adjustment process, but they should be tailored to ensure that they do not discourage workers from moving to other sectors in the belief that such aid is not temporary. Therefore, Baldwin suggests that wage subsidies should be given in the form of wage vouchers that can be used in any industry. He also advocates combining wage vouchers with retraining and mobility grants and direct income payments to those who will find it difficult to find a new job (such as older workers).[16]

One problem with wage vouchers is that workers who have lost a job in one sector cannot easily be moved to another, either because they are not adequately trained or because there is simply no other industry in the region that could employ them. Another pitfall is that vouchers often subsidize low-wage industries that are eager to take advantage of such low-cost labor. These problems could be avoided by integrating wage subsidy plans into strategies designed to attract both foreign and domestic investors. Federal or state agencies could target potential investors that would make commitments to hire or retrain displaced workers and in return offer the benefits of the wage vouchers or training grants given to local workers. Although they may be conducted in cooperation with the federal government, these efforts can realistically be carried out only by state or local authorities for two reasons. The first is that the federal government has shown little inclination to get extensively involved in the retraining or adjustment process. Second, to be effective, structural adjustment policies must sometimes be carried out at a fairly micro level. Government must not only be involved in terms of giving out money but must also coordinate efforts to draw appropriate new investment into the area and set up related training programs. This kind of effort is best delegated to the regional or local level, although it can and should be part of a larger, nationally coordinated project.

Negotiations at the national and international level can help ensure that subsidy wars or flurries of countervailing suits do not ensue and that structural adjustment actually takes place. The Brussels Subsidies draft negotiated under the GATT Uruguay round goes some distance in this regard but has been criticized for allowing retaliation if any industry can prove it has been materially injured by

16. Ibid., pp. 5–6.

foreign R&D subsidies or structural adjustment grants. One solution is to put a cap on R&D subsidies (such as a certain percentage of expenditures) and make structural adjustment subsidies temporary. For example, recipients could receive assistance for a limited time period and would not be eligible for more assistance for five years or more.[17]

Another way to deal with the subsidy issue is to replace the kinds of incentives and subsidies typically given to foreign investors (tax exemptions, grants, and real estate deals) with reductions in their social expenditures. Instead of giving a company a cut on its electricity bill, for example, states could offer to pay for health care, worker retraining, or part of the firm's contribution to unemployment insurance. These kinds of incentives could go a long way to reducing subsidy disputes at an international level, because it is arguable that they cannot be challenged legally by countervailing subsidies. As noted in Chapter 4, Canadian economists have argued that subsidies available to all sectors of the economy, such as social payments, should not be countervailed because they will be compensated for by changes in exchange rates.[18] To be noncountervailable, however, they must be "generally available" on a cross-sectoral and cross-national basis. This is another incentive for the United States to standardize its social programs. In a continental context, social subsidies could initiate an "upward" bidding cycle that would increase the provision of social services in all three countries. Such subsidies would also ensure that the handouts being offered to firms benefit the citizens of the region or country.

States should not hesitate to request performance requirements

17. Ibid.

18. For a more detailed account of this argument, see Richard Lipsey and Murray Smith, "An Overview of Harmonization Issues," in Lipsey and Smith, eds., *Policy Harmonization: The Effects of a Canadian-American Free Trade Area* (Toronto: C. D. Howe Institute, 1986). The authors argue, for example, that U.S. producers could maintain that Canada's national health system reduced the costs of Canadian producers, thereby giving them an unfair advantage. In a system of flexible exchange rates, however, such advantages should be temporary. If a country starts with a balanced current account, any surplus resulting from this "advantage" would be counteracted by the rising value of the country's currency. In response to claims that Canada's higher social overhead would make Canadian firms less competitive, economists responded that these costs would also be reflected in the exchange rate. If Canadian goods were uncompetitive, the resulting trade deficit would bring the value of the Canadian dollar down.

in exchange for such policies, and engage in active quid pro quo bargaining with investors. Stephen Guisinger's study, outlined in Chapter 2, showed that firms frequently do not object to performance requirements. The United States probably can avoid making trade-related requirements such as export quotas or local content rules. But it should not hesitate to make demands on the basis of employment commitments and R&D contributions and to push for guarantees on the length of time the investors will remain in the country.

Critics may argue that policies such as this involve excessive government tampering in the market and impede its efficient functioning. Furthermore, the United States spent years negotiating away performance requirements under the GATT talks on trade-related investment measures (TRIMs). Provided that such requirements apply to both foreign and domestic investors, however, they at least will not abrogate national treatment commitments. Those who decry the spiraling economic nationalism of the United States must realize that the only way to deflect this trend is to cushion and protect those who are hardest hit by their integration into the world economy. Rather than responding to demands for tariffs on the part of special interests, it is preferable to coordinate this protection in an organized manner and try to preempt jingoism. To eliminate subsidies completely is difficult, but states should not give out such incentives without some assurance of benefits for themselves.

The United States is far less constrained in its policy options than its continental partners, Canada and Mexico. Because of their strategies of industrialization by invitation, these two countries are far more dependent on FDI than is the United States. Both countries also face the challenge of adapting traditional notions of how their economies fit into the global operations of the MNEs. At some point in their respective economic histories, Canada and Mexico pursued an import substitution industrialization strategy. Generally speaking, the strategy involved the adoption of tariff barriers to encourage the local production of manufactured goods and licensing technology from foreign firms.[19] Each country had slightly different

19. For a review of the effect of this strategy in Canada, see Williams, *Not for Export.* For Mexico, see Douglas Bennett and Kenneth Sharpe, *Transnational Corporations*

approaches to ISI: while Canada used it to encourage foreign companies to manufacture goods domestically, Mexico focused more on developing the capacities of local producers and integrating them into the production strategies of the MNEs.

Both have found that ISI is no longer appropriate in the face of the MNEs' global rationalization techniques. The Mexican response was to promote the country's abundant supply of cheap labor through the development of its border industry program, known as the *maquiladoras* and to enter the GATT. This marked a transition to a more export-oriented development strategy. In Canada, an increasing number of MNEs have "rationalized" their Canadian subsidiaries, using them to specialize in a particular product or component that is sold worldwide. This trend is likely to continue under the free trade agreement, since the elimination of tariffs will make market access increasingly irrelevant as a motive for foreign investment.[20] Canada has tried to take advantage of this trend by encouraging world product mandates, where all stages of the production process (including R&D) are concentrated in the Canadian subsidiary. Regardless, both of these countries are now faced with the challenge of adapting their investment strategies to new economic realities while at the same time ensuring benefit for their domestic economies. Therefore, their strategies must be somewhat different from those recommended for the United States.

CANADA

Evidence in the Canadian case showed that the country's dependence on FDI flows from the United States at times did operate as a restrictive influence on investment policy. But Canada's high level of dependence on the United States has proved to be a double-edged sword. In the 1970s this dependent relationship led to the rise of nationalist sentiments, and as a result, legislation was enacted to regulate investment flows. In contrast, U.S. pressures in the 1980s

---

versus the State: The Political Economy of the Mexican Automobile Industry (Princeton: Princeton University Press, 1985).

20. Harold Crookell, "Managing Canadian Subsidiaries in a Free Trade Environment," *Sloane Management Review* 29, no. 1 (Fall 1987).

for investment deregulation had a liberalizing effect. The critical intervening barrier in both of these periods was domestic politics: in the 1970s both the Liberals and the NDP were willing to profit from nationalist sentiments and introduce policies to control MNEs. In the 1980s the more laissez-faire Progressive Conservative party was not responsive to such appeals. More generally, the relative unwillingness of domestic capital to support FDI regulations and the lack of political power on the part of labor and agricultural interests meant that there were no solid political coalitions behind such regulatory policies.

But what options remain for Canada in the future? Given the highly politicized trade environment in the United States, including the excessive reliance on exchange-rate manipulations that is evident in both countries, Canada's current industrial strategy of free trade is exceptionally high risk. It ties the Canadian economy even more closely to a United States that is becoming increasingly hostile to foreigners without providing any real protection for Canadian producers. Canadian firms are not exempt from the Exon-Florio amendment, nor are they exempt from state-level antitakeover legislation that does not specifically discriminate against foreign firms. In addition, a key motivation for Canada's pursuit of a free trade agreement was a currency devaluation that would have created nationalist havoc in the United States had it persisted.

One way Canada could mitigate this risk is to diversify its trade and investment partners. Canada has attempted to do this without success ever since Trudeau's "Third Option" of the 1970s, but the stakes are now higher than ever. As Smith pointed out, Canada has invested little in the dynamic economies of the Pacific, and these countries have shown relatively little interest in investing in Canada.[21] Canada may find it difficult to attract further foreign invest-

21. Canada's European investments are concentrated in the United Kingdom, and in the Pacific only Indonesia and Australia have attracted more than 1 percent of Canadian foreign investment. The stock of Japanese investment in Canada is increasing but remains about one-third of its investment in Australia and one-twentieth of its investment in the United States. Murray Smith, "Muddling Through Is Not Enough: A Survey of Global and Domestic Economic Challenges," in Douglas Brown and Murray Smith, eds., *Canadian Federalism: Meeting Global Economic Challenges?* (Kingston: Institute of Intergovernmental Relations, and Halifax: Institute for Research on Public Policy, 1991), p. 203.

ment given that the "rule of origin" provisions of the FTA restrict the amount of foreign content in products eligible for duty-free treatment. In the automobile industry, Canada may no longer provide duty remission schemes to non-U.S. foreign investors as it has in the past, nor will foreign producers be allowed to join the auto pact.[22] Duty remission schemes in general are bound to trigger U.S. countervailing actions.

The importance of geographical and cultural proximity in trade and investment relations also makes it unlikely that Canada will have any major success in diversifying its trade links. A different tack would be to try to reduce Canada's reliance on foreign direct investment. The debate over the FTA changed the nationalist discourse in Canada away from "we have too much foreign investment" to "how will we attract foreign investment without tariffs?" Yet it is not clear that large inflows of FDI are critical to Canada's economic welfare. Advocates of FDI argue that it needs foreign capital to finance its indebtedness. While this may be true in the case of portfolio investment, it is not so in the case of direct investment. On the contrary, about 80 percent of foreign direct investment in Canada is from funds raised domestically.

What Canada needs, then, is not fresh inflows of foreign direct investment but a domestically generated locus for investment funds. Both the federal and provincial governments could contribute significantly in this endeavor. One of the most important problems growing Canadian firms face is acquiring the necessary capital to expand past critical stages in their development. It is at this stage that foreign companies frequently step in to offer capital via acquisition. Federal and provincial governments in Canada could remedy the situation either by creating venture capital funds that could provide these firms with their capital needs or by allying private venture capitalists with particular firms. Alternatively, the state itself could acquire shares in such companies, taking a minority stake that would also provide it with some say over future corporate strategy.

Another option is the Workers Ownership Program under de-

22. The General Motors–Suzuki plant in Ingersoll, Ontario, was allowed to join the auto pact, but all other Japanese or Korean car manufacturers were excluded. The duty remission scheme must be phased out by 1995.

velopment in Ontario. Under the plan, labor unions could set up venture capital corporations that would invest contributions from their members. Individual investors would receive a tax credit of up to $700 on their provincial income taxes (about a 20 percent deduction).[23] Both state ownership and workers ownership plans have the added benefit of making international firms (whether they are based domestically or abroad) less footloose and less likely to leave the country.

The state could also play a critical role in attracting investment through an activist strategic partnering program. Such a program would involve the targeting of both domestic and foreign firms possessing critical product or process technologies and matching them with Canadian business partners. By seeking out such investors, the state could help to shape the kinds of investment deals it wanted, as well as to attract the kinds of investment it needed. Such firm-centered strategies, however, constitute only one aspect of a successful investment policy. Another strategy that must complement this one is a regional development strategy focused on attracting particular industries to certain geographical areas. Organized by subnational governments, these strategies could be used to aid smaller domestic firms desiring to internationalize their production. In Europe, for example, regional development programs run by regional or municipal governments have provided international marketing services and R&D financing for firms and have even devised local zoning laws that reduce speculation and thereby keep the price of local real estate down.[24]

Like the United States, Canada must come to terms with the issue of subsidies, even though this issue is so sensitive that no agreement was reached on it in the FTA negotiations. Subsidies are a questionable means of attracting foreign investment to Canada for two reasons. First, Canada is under severe pressure from the United States government and from U.S. companies to reduce what they refer to as "unfair subsidies." Consequently, even if both parties do come to a subsidies agreement as stipulated in the FTA, the high profile of this

23. *Globe and Mail*, October 7, 1991.
24. Robin Murray, "Regional Economic Policy in Europe in the 1990s, in the Light of the Experience of the 1980s," Mimeo, March 1990.

issue in U.S. trade circles is likely to draw continued fire. Second, subsidies are a contentious means of attracting FDI, and it is questionable whether governments want to give companies such large sums of money when they are restricted by the FTA in demanding many of the performance requirements they may desire. When subsidies are given, they should be handed out in the form of "social subsidies." Instead of cash handouts or real estate deals, this money should be redirected to help firms reduce their health care payments for a limited period of time or to create workers' training programs.

Part of Canada's strategy in addressing the issues of chronic deficits in manufacturing, a dearth of high-technology industries, low R&D spending, and the threat of U.S. nationalism must be to create the kind of investment environment that attracts productive investment on the part of *both* foreign and domestic investors. Critics of investment review may not be correct in arguing that Investment Canada has had a chilling effect on foreign investment, but there is no question that the agency has not been effective. Canada must make a broader, more concerted effort to build a conducive investment environment.

This does not mean giving more handouts in the form of subsidies or attempting to lower production costs by reducing social overhead or putting pressure on Canadian wages, yet this seems to be precisely the tack the government has taken. Before the FTA was signed, economists warned the federal government to resist U.S. pressures to amend generally available advantages, such as social policies, that might affect production costs. In spite of this argument, the federal government revamped its unemployment insurance plan in 1990 to bring it more in line with the less generous U.S. system and cut all federal government contributions. In 1989 it cut unemployment payments to fishermen after the U.S. fishing industry filed a complaint that they were unfair subsidies. Similarly, Canada's deflationary macroeconomic policies have put severe pressure on wages, despite the fact that Canadian wages are not high by international standards. Although productivity is low (but not as low as in the United States), Canadian wages are lower than those in the United States, Germany, France, and Italy. Of course, this is in part a function of the exchange rate, but it is also a result of Canadian social policies. A report comparing wages in the Canadian and U.S.

automobile industries found that Canadian plants have an advantage of seven to eight U.S. dollars an hour in labor costs due to the exchange rate and the high cost of health care plans in the U.S. plants.[25]

It is not clear whether this sustained attack on social policies is a result of the FTA or simply a reflection of Tory ideology. Regardless, its misguided emphasis on getting the prices right could be catastrophic politically. One of the primary reasons for state intervention in Canada in the past was to cushion the Canadian economy from swings in the international market. Innis argued that to maintain national unity when these crises affect specific regions disproportionately, the federal government should intervene with adjustment efforts. Abandoning these adjustment efforts not only guarantees the exacerbation of regional disparities, it invites a nationalist "protectionist" reaction in the Polanyian sense. Failure to protect threatened firms and workers is bound to induce a nationalist backlash that could sabotage the trend toward greater cooperation between Canada and the United States. In any case, such cuts are ultimately self-defeating. Decreases in social spending adversely affect firms as well as workers. The restructured unemployment insurance plan actually increased corporate contributions, and Canada's national health care plan saves companies a lot of money.

Reich's recommendations for increased investment in the education of the labor force would also improve Canada's attractiveness to both foreign and domestic investors. A highly skilled labor force and competent researchers in high-technology industries are real drawing cards in terms of attracting new investment, both domestic and foreign. Yet Canada's record is poor in this regard too. The Labour Force Development Strategy introduced in 1989 increased the funds available for training programs merely by appropriating $775 million from the unemployment insurance fund and redirecting it to training. This strategy is likely to exacerbate the tendency of the labor market to polarize into high- and low-wage jobs, since it restricts the eligibility of beneficiaries by raising the minimum qualify-

25. *Globe and Mail*, January 5, 1991. The study was conducted by Professors Harry Katz and Noah Meltz for the International Motor Vehicle Program at MIT.

ing period.[26] Such policies are likely only to augment the growing trend toward wage polarization in Canada.[27]

These factors indicate that there is no political will to implement effective investment policies, at least at the federal level. Furthermore, in the absence of pressure from domestic capital, and with nationalism declining among the general populace, the political coalition that would support such policies is not in place. Yet greater promise is held at the provincial level. Although many provincial governments have no more desire to implement industrial strategies than the federal government does, Canada's own policy history demonstrates that for those with the political will to implement such programs, there is a high probability of success.

Mexico

Considerable political support for foreign-investment regulation exists in Mexico. But as the interests of the political groups that supported such policies changed during the 1980s, FDI policies began to change as well, and a trend toward liberalization has occurred. This deregulation occurred partly in response to the growth of a technocratic faction within the state apparatus, but it was also a response to the demands of local business groups that have changed their perspective on FDI regulation. As domestic capital, particularly in the industrialized north, has increased its international business activities, it has developed a greater interest in ensuring the free flow of international capital.

But Mexico's international *apertura* remains fragile; plenty of nationalist sentiment still exists within business and within the general populace. The country could witness a nationalist renaissance should current economic policies not meet with success. Even the MNEs that

26. Rianne Mahon, "Adjusting to Win? The New Tory Training Initiative," in Katherine Graham, ed., *How Ottawa Spends, 1990–91* (Ottawa: Carleton University Press, 1990).

27. According to the Economic Council of Canada, in 1967, 27 percent of the work force had earnings categorized as "middle-level." In 1986 only 22 percent of the labor force fit into this category. See Economic Council of Canada, *Good Jobs, Bad Jobs* (Ottawa: Supply and Services, 1990), p. 15.

invest in Mexico are not unilaterally opposed to investment regulations; in fact, some have an interest in ensuring that such policies survive. Combined with political splits within the PRI and the rise of the populist, nationalist coalition backing Cárdenas, the position of internationalist policies in Mexico is tenuous at best. Given the shallow nature of its transition to open investment policies, Mexico should exercise caution.

The liberalization of Mexico's investment regulations and the campaign to create a NAFTA are clearly designed to attract foreign direct investment to Mexico, and to a certain degree they have been successful. Foreign-investment inflows grew at a rate of 16.1 percent per annum from 1985 to 1989, compared with 11.6 percent from 1980 to 1985. It is difficult to distinguish how much of this growth is a response to the deregulation of foreign investment, however, and how much is due to the rebound of the Mexican economy. Foreign investment is far more responsive to underlying economic factors than it is to the changes in investment review policies, and it is unlikely that increased FDI would have occurred without greater economic growth. In addition, about half of the investment that entered the country in 1990 went into the stock market, a far less stable form of investment than setting up an actual branch plant.

Nevertheless, Mexican policies toward FDI mark a clever adaptation to changing economic circumstances. The new policies have drawn praise from MNEs and foreign governments alike because they eliminated many of the most obvious irritants: having to share ownership of subsidiaries in certain industries and dealing with numerous bureaucracies and delays. At the same time, the regulations ensure that foreign investors maintain a positive balance of payments, diversify their investments away from heavily industrialized areas, and institute new training programs. Mexico should seek to maintain this balance and resist further deregulation.

The Mexican quest for a NAFTA is an attempt to lock these liberalizations in and continue Mexico's reorientation toward export-led development. Presumably, involvement in an agreement would involve even further liberalization, particularly in the area of investment review. Although Mexico has clearly stated that areas such as oil will be excluded from the agreement, it will be pressured to do away with limits on foreign ownership in the approximately 130 sectors that remain restricted under the 1989 amendments to the foreign-investment laws. In addition, under the Canada–United States Free Trade Agreement, both countries agreed to refrain from making trade-related performance requirements of foreign investors. Since Mexico still requires that many foreign firms maintain a positive trade balance, it may be forced to make changes in this area. Only time will tell if such changes can be made in light of the numerous opposing pressures in Mexican society. Domestic companies, international companies, and state bureaucrats all have a stake in retaining at least some minimum of investment controls. If the kinds of investment concessions Canada made under the FTA come to pass in Mexico, they will constitute a true revolution in the way the economy is run. But two "revolutions" in a century may be too much for Mexico, and it is important to understand the economic and political constraints Mexico faces in negotiating the continentalization of its economy.

In economic terms, Mexico probably stands to benefit from a NAFTA agreement in the short run. Low wages in the *maquiladoras* (estimates range anywhere from US$0.60 an hour to US$2.40 per hour if benefits are included) are bound to attract major inflows of foreign investment. To date, the *maquiladoras* have shown impressive growth, attracting almost two-thirds of incoming foreign investment, and this trend can be expected to continue even if a NAFTA is not signed.[28] They have been excellent foreign-exchange earners and have increased employment from about 90,000 workers in 1980 to 500,000 workers in 1990.[29]

In the medium to long run, however, the shortcomings of this strategy are clear. The *maquiladoras* have not been effective in creating the kind of multiplier effects in the Mexican economy that are necessary for sustained growth, sourcing only 1.7 percent of their inputs from the Mexican economy. With the relaxed restrictions on *maquiladora* sales to the domestic economy, this situation could give Mexico the worst of both worlds if it is not improved. The new rules allow the *maquiladoras* further access to the domestic market without

28. Investment Canada, *Opportunities and Challenges* (Ottawa: Government of Canada, 1991), p. 37.

29. *Business Week*, November 12, 1990. These figures are from the Mexican National Statistics Institute and the Banco de México.

requiring that more inputs be sourced locally. Under these circumstances, they could begin to suck in imports at an unsustainable rate if export earnings are not increased proportionately.

In addition, although the *maquiladoras* do create jobs, most of these are "bad jobs" (that is, involving unskilled labor) and it is questionable how much they actually increase the overall buying power in the domestic market. Wages are still low and expenses are very high. According to one estimate, a *maquiladora* worker making the minimum wage earns only 28 percent of the basic food, clothing, shelter, and medical needs of a family of four.[30] Also, since employment creation has disproportionately been in the area of minimum wage, unskilled, female labor, it is questionable whether in-bond assembly in the *maquiladora* industry has had any major impact on unemployment in Mexico. Instead, it may have simply drawn more women workers out of the home without improving the options for higher-skilled and better-paid male labor. Because many of these women do not find themselves much better off after joining the work force, the gender-based benefits of the program are dubious.[31]

In general, the squalor that workers of the *maquiladoras* live in hardly make this a desirable model for development. Provisions for sewage and water treatment are practically absent, leading to nineteenth-century living conditions that affect both sides of the Rio Grande. Also, by relying on cheap labor as its chief advantage, Mexico risks falling prey to wage competition from other developing countries. If Mexican industrial strategy continues its current reliance on cheap labor without developing other comparative advantages, Mexico will not be in a position to deal with such competition without further wage cuts.

Another consideration is that if the NAFTA or liberalization is as great a success story as the Mexicans hope, it will create upward pressure on the peso. A major revaluation could significantly increase Mexican labor costs and decrease the competitiveness of Mexican capital, creating tensions among Mexican producers. The Canadian case study revealed that continentalization changed the

30. Latin American Working Group, "Open for Business: Canada-Mexico-U.S.," *LAWG Letter* (Toronto), no. 45, January 1991, p. 8.

31. See Susan Tiano, "Maquiladora Women: A New Category of Workers," in Kathryn Ward, ed., *Women Workers and Global Restructuring* (Ithaca: ILR Press, 1990).

interests of key economic actors; it created a group of subsidiaries that relied on close production and trade connections with U.S. parent companies and turned their focus away from the domestic Canadian market. This shift in attitude began among northern Mexican business interests during the debt crisis, as their fortunes became increasingly tied to U.S. financial and product markets. But it is not yet clear how solid these connections are. A significant change in the exchange rate could severely affect the continental aspirations of Mexican businesses and result in disaffection with export-oriented growth.

A major opening of the economy to foreign competitors could also result in a Polanyian protectionist response on the part of many domestic producers. Many industrialists have been protected by tariffs and restrictions on foreign investors, such as minimum Mexican ownership requirements, for decades. Joining the GATT resulted in the closing of an estimated 70,000 Mexican firms, and if a NAFTA brings increased competition from MNEs in the domestic market, the pressure may be too much for local producers to bear. Unlike Canada, where a large percentage of domestic production is already owned by foreign producers, Mexico still has a very large domestic manufacturing component. And since Mexican companies do not invest abroad nearly to the extent that Canadian firms do, a strong internationalist faction that might resist any future "reregulation" of foreign investment does not exist.[32]

External political threats to further continentalization also exist. The potential for a nationalist American backlash is much more evident in the Mexican case than the Canadian one. The AFL-CIO in the United States has made opposition to a NAFTA and the *maquiladoras* a top priority, and the more successful Mexican producers become, the more they can expect this resistance to spread to adversely affected U.S. businesses. The debate surrounding the renewal of fast-track negotiating procedures for the NAFTA talks revealed that this sort of threat is very real. Whether a NAFTA would actually protect Mexico from such challenges in the future is unclear. If anything, present conditions would seem to indicate that the

32. Mexican companies invested about US$1 billion in the United States in 1989, compared with US$35 billion by Canadian firms.

very success of a NAFTA from a Mexican perspective could create the seeds of its own destruction. The more upward pressure it places on the peso, the less popular it will be with Mexican producers. And the more it increases Mexican market share in Canada and the United States, the more likely it is to elicit a reaction from threatened Canadian and U.S. producers. Such a reaction would be most unfortunate for Mexico, given that over 86 percent of its exports are sold in these two countries (82 percent in the United States).

Measures must be taken to stabilize Mexico's relations with its northern neighbors, but it is not clear that a NAFTA would accomplish this end. As long as Mexico's strategy remains focused on prices—the exchange rate, cheap labor, and low social overhead—it risks getting caught up in a contradiction. Continued competitiveness depends on cheap labor costs and a devalued peso, but U.S. and Canadian labor is sure to pounce on the first point, and U.S. manufacturers will definitely resist the second. Regardless of whether a NAFTA is signed, therefore, these issues must be addressed if a political conflagration is to be avoided.

One response to this contradiction is to broaden the base of Mexican economic development. Observing some of the effects of continentalization on the Canadian economy can help guide policymaking in this area. One problem faced by Canada in the 1960s and 1970s was the "miniature replica" or branch plant phenomenon caused by MNE subsidiaries jumping tariff barriers to serve the domestic economy. This is one problem that the externally oriented *maquiladoras* and foreign subsidiaries designed for export have avoided in Mexico, and the deregulation of foreign investors could also alleviate this situation. The discussion of international capital in Chapter 5 reveals that many MNEs relied on investment regulations to provide them a guaranteed market share and keep competitors out. Mexican consumers have paid heavily for this, and opening up investment regulations should make most subsidiaries more efficient.

This suggestion is not a call for complete deregulation, however, but rather for re-regulation. Excessive foreign-ownership of high-technology industries in Canada led to an unimpressive innovation rate and to difficulty in enforcing sectorally based programs designed to increase Canadian R&D potential. Many multinationals were reluctant to join such programs because they have adequate R&D facilities on a global level and thus had little incentive to target Canadian operations. To counter this tendency, Mexico needs specific sectoral programs directed at technology sharing between foreign and domestic firms.

Such measures could be particularly effective if they are complimented by more sectoral policies. Mexico currently has sectoral policies in areas such as automobiles and electronics, but there are reports that it is considering stopping these endeavors. The evidence given in Chapter 2 indicates that completely abandoning sectoral policies would be a mistake. Mexico has used such policies to great effect in the past by molding the shape of production in the sector to suit Mexican interests. In the auto industry, for example, it managed to integrate local producers into the MNEs' production plans and reverse a growing balance-of-payments deficit in the industry. Through its negotiations with electronics companies such as IBM, it gained training facilities in exchange for concessions on the ownership issue.

Rather than organizing sectoral policies on a purely domestic level, however, Mexico should seek to join the auto pact between Canada and the United States and try to negotiate some of the production safeguards Canada did in the 1960s. United States labor is not fond of the auto pact signed with Canada, and it opposed its inclusion in the FTA. But with Mexico in the picture, the stakes change. Given the potential for a major exodus of jobs to the south, U.S. workers may be willing to sign a continental agreement that guarantees them greater job security.

Overall, however, sectoral policies must be supplemented by efforts to increase the size of the Mexican market by redistributing income and improving the buying power of the Mexican population. Sectoral agreements such as the auto pact could help in this regard by mandating wage increases for Mexican workers in exchange for jointly agreed-upon production quotas.[33] Multinational enterprises would gladly make concessions on training, R&D spending, and export performance for a share in a market of such potential. Ob-

33. Herzenberg suggests a gradual increase in the wages of Mexican auto workers over a ten-year period. See Herzenberg, "Continental Integration."

viously, such reforms are politically sensitive and would involve a major reorientation of Mexico's development trajectory. Until it realigns its consumption patterns to the growing industrial development of its economy, however, Mexico will not achieve broad based, sustained economic growth. Although it has a population of 85 million that is growing at twice the rate of Canada and the United States, GDP per capita remains at less than US$2,000, compared with US$21,000 in its neighbors to the north.

Mexico should not consider reinstituting its primary investment incentive program, the debt capitalization scheme. This program was suspended in 1987 because of several glaring flaws, but some swaps are still going through. The program was considered undesirable because it was inflationary—since the central bank essentially printed new pesos when debt was swapped, it increased the money supply. Also, the program unnecessarily subsidized foreign investors at the expense of domestic entrepreneurs. Since foreign investors swapped old debt to receive new pesos at discounts of up to 50 percent, they could reap the benefits of cheaper capital, while domestic entrepreneurs could not. In addition, there is always a danger that the investment attracted by debt conversions is offset by a decline in "real" foreign investment. Since the capital for "real" FDI is not provided at a discount and, in contrast to swaps, brings a fresh flow of foreign exchange into the economy, it is obviously preferable. Finally, by its very willingness to purchase its own debt, Mexico keeps the discount rate from rising, which in turn makes the program more expensive. Indeed, the major problem with debt conversions is that their very success drives up the prices debt may be purchased at on the secondary market, which makes conversions less attractive to debtor countries.[34]

Rather than reinstituting the debt swap program, Mexico should institute a system of incentives for foreign investors that does not involve the reduction of debt but does increase the inflow of foreign exchange. Given Mexico's cash shortage, these incentives should not

34. For a thorough analysis of debt conversion policies in several Latin American countries, see Eugenio Lahera, "The Conversion of Foreign Debt Viewed from Latin America," *CEPAL Review* 32 (August 1987), and Paul Krugman, "Private Capital Flows to Problem Debtors," in Jeffrey D. Sachs, ed., *Developing Country Debt and the World Economy* (Chicago: University of Chicago Press, 1989).

take the form of tax breaks or outright grants. It should offer the social subsidies discussed in the Canadian and U.S. case studies or guaranteed market shares through government procurement programs and the use of its remaining state-owned enterprises. Admittedly, this latter practice would risk replicating the inefficiency caused by foreign-investment review policies that guaranteed market share. Almost all countries use government procurement as a method to foster domestic industry, however, and so long as some sort of bidding process is in place, these side effects can be minimal. In return for granting firms lucrative contracts, the government should place performance requirements on foreign and domestic investors. This means that it should not make the same concessions that Canada did on trade-related performance requirements under the FTA.

The importance of performance requirements and the need for "sticks" to enforce firms to cooperate with such requests indicates that for the time being, Mexico should not agree to the complete removal of trade-related performance requirements agreed to in the Canada–United States Free Trade Agreement. It is difficult to see how it is in Mexico's interest to give up the option of demanding that firms balance their trade, given the country's need for foreign exchange to pay off external debts. It may be the case that trade-related performance requirements such as local content, however, can be achieved through an active strategic partnering program. If the state became involved as a shareholder, or even a negotiator in such deals, it would have the opportunity to mandate technology transfer and training programs from the inside. This position would reduce the state's need to impose limits on foreign ownership and other macrolevel requirements and would allow for sectoral and firm-related fine-tuning.

Even if Mexico decides it no longer needs the use of performance requirements, entering into free trade negotiations and liberalizing in one shot is simply a bad negotiating strategy. Mexico has a lot farther to go toward liberalization than Canada and the United States do, and it should use individual concessions on its part to extract compromises from its trade partners. This implies a far more gradual, prolonged approach to a trade and investment *apertura*, a strategy that would definitely be far more secure in a domestic political context as well.

223

CONCLUSION

This book does not constitute testimony to the unquestioned marvels of state regulatory policies. In many cases I have illustrated the weaknesses of state intervention. It does show, however, that carefully planned, strategic political intervention is a necessary and important element of successful market operations. This point is obviously not revolutionary, but it bears repeating in today's international political environment. The slowdown of economic growth that began in the 1970s, combined with the visible failures of social democratic policies such as those implemented by the French Socialists in 1981, have led many to give up on the notion that states can intervene effectively in international markets. The Keynesian economic management schemes that were hegemonic in the postwar period have been replaced by a neo-conservative agenda espousing deregulation and laissez-faire economic management schemes.

Given the current economic convention of assuming that deregulation and international competitiveness are coterminous, this question has relevance beyond the investment policy debate. These cases showed that the relationship between liberalization and competitiveness cannot be taken for granted and that often the relationship is the inverse. Although I did not produce evidence to show that the reduction of state involvement in investment policies was always bad, nor that regulation was always necessary, it seems clear that laissez-faire policies are not always the most obvious solutions to contemporary economic problems.

Current economic conditions do require changes in traditional state approaches to economic intervention, but these changes should not involve the wholesale rejection of regulatory and industrial policies that is dictated by the neo-conservative agenda. Instead, a more differentiated approach to state strategies is necessary. A wholesale rejection of state interventionist policies is far too extreme. As Cuauhtémoc Cárdenas noted, "Economic liberalization is not our objective, it is one of our tools. Development, social justice, a clean environment, and equality among nations are our objectives."[35] Current international economic conditions may require a rethinking of traditional state strategies, but national political interventions such as industrial policies or regulatory schemes continue to play an integral role in the operation of international markets.

35. Speech by Cuauhtémoc Cárdenas in Ottawa, Canada, April 17, 1991.

Canadian Decisions on Foreign-Investment Applications by Sector, 1978–1985

	Percentage allowed	Percentage disallowed	Percentage withdrawn	Total percentage disallowed per year
1978–79				
Resources	86.35	0	13.65	
Manufacturing	90.85	5.0	4.15	4.48
Services	86.7	8.45	4.85	
1979–80				
Resources	79.5	14.7	5.6	
Manufacturing	89.7	3.95	6.35	8.93
Services	85.5	8.15	6.35	
1980–81				
Resources	50.85	18.25	30.9	
Manufacturing	87.85	5.85	6.3	12.48
Services	71.2	13.35	15.45	
1981–82				
Resources	51.2	30.55	18.25	
Manufacturing	85.55	5.8	8.65	16.5
Services	65.85	13.15	21.0	
1982–83				
Resources	81.15	8.9	9.95	
Manufacturing	91.85	1.1	7.05	5.57
Services	84.25	6.7	9.05	
1983–84				
Resources	89.55	0	10.45	
Manufacturing	94.6	1.5	3.9	2.56
Services	86.5	3.65	9.85	
1984–85				
Resources	90.1	3.1	6.8	
Manufacturing	95.1	1.15	3.45	3.45
Services	93.0	.75	6.25	

Source: Calculated from Claire Sjolander, *Foreign Investment Policy-making: The Canadian State in the Global Economy* (Ph.D. diss., Carleton University, 1990), pp. 386–89.

Areas Restricted to Foreign Investors in Mexico

Category 1: Activities reserved exclusively for the Mexican state
   Oil and gas production
   Mining and refining of uranium and radioactive minerals
   Manufacture of basic petrochemical products
   Oil refining
   Treatment of uranium and nuclear fuels
   Coin minting
   Generation and transmission of electric energy
   Supply of electric energy
   Railroad transportation services
   Telegraph services
   Banking services
   Financial trusts and funds

Category 2: Activities reserved for Mexican nationals
   Forestry
   Forest nursery business
   Retailing of liquefied gas
   Building materials for transportation services
   Trucking
   Bus transportation services (intercity)
   Urban and suburban bus transportation services
   Taxi services
   School and tourism bus services
   Coastal transportation services
   Passenger air transportation services in aircraft with Mexican registry

Air taxi transportation services
Credit union services
Public warehouse services
Foreign-exchange house services
Financial consulting and promotion
Nonbank savings and loan services
Other credit services
Brokerage firm services
Investment company services
Stock market services
Bonding
Insurance services
Independent pension fund management
Private transmission of radio programs
Notary public services
Customs brokers and representative services
Management of sea, lake, and river ports

Category 3: Activities that allow up to 34 percent foreign ownership
Mining and refining of coal
Mining and refining of iron ore
Mining and refining of phosphoric rock
Mining of sulphur

Category 4: Activities that allow up to 40 percent foreign ownership
Manufacture of secondary petrochemical products
Manufacture of parts and accessories for automotive electrical systems
Manufacture and assembly of bodies and trailers for automobiles and
    trucks
Manufacture of automobile and truck motors and their parts
Manufacture of automobile and truck transmission parts
Manufacture of automobile and truck suspension system parts
Manufacture of parts and accessories for automobile and truck brake
    systems
Manufacture of other parts and accessories for automobiles and trucks

Category 5: Activities that allow up to 49 percent foreign ownership
Fishing
Fish breeding
Mining and refining of minerals containing gold, silver, and other
    precious minerals and metals

Mining and refining of mercury and antimony
Mining and refining of industrial minerals with lead and zinc content
Mining and refining of minerals containing copper
Mining and refining of other nonferrous metallic minerals
Mining and refining of feldspar
Mining of gypsum
Mining and refining of barite
Mining and refining of fluorite
Mining of other minerals to obtain chemical products
Mining and refining of salt
Mining and refining of graphite
Mining and refining of other nonmetallic minerals
Manufacture of explosives and fireworks
Manufacture of firearms and cartridges
Retailing of firearms, cartridges, and ammunition
River and lake transportation services
Telephone services
Other telecommunications services
Financial leasing

Category 6: Activities that require prior authorization if a majority foreign ownership is desired
Agriculture
Stock breeding and hunting
Gathering of forestry products
Timber harvesting and processing
Newspaper and magazine publishing
Manufacture of coke and other coal products
Residential or housing construction
Nonresidential construction
Construction of urban works
Construction of industrial plants
Construction of power generating plants
Construction and laying of power transmission networks and lines
Concrete structure erection or installation
Steel structure erection or installation
Construction of ocean and river works
Construction of streets and highways
Construction of railroad tracks
Construction of hydraulic and sanitary systems for buildings
Electric system construction for buildings

Telecommunications installations
Other special installations
Earth moving
Foundation construction
Excavation
Construction of underwater works
Installation of traffic and protection signals
Demolition
Construction of water treatment plants
Drilling of oil and gas wells
Drilling of water wells
Other construction services
High-seas transportation
Tourism ship chartering
Investment company services
Private pre-school or kindergarten services
Private primary school services
Private secondary school services
Private middle school services
Private university services
Private commercial and language school services
Private technical and handicrafts training school services
Private music, dance, and other special private instruction services
Private special education services
Legal services
Accounting and auditing services
Management of passenger bus terminals and auxiliary services
Management of toll highways, international bridges, and auxiliary
    services
Towing of vehicles
Other ground transportation services
Air navigation support services
Management of airports and heliports
Securities and investment consulting services
Insurance and bonding agency services
Pension consulting services
Representatives of foreign financial entities services
Other services related to financial, insurance, and bonding institutions

Source: National Commission on Foreign Investment, "Areas Restricted to Foreign
Investors in Mexico," 1991.

Index

adjustment assistance, 3–5, 111, 112, 205–7; and free trade, 28, 32, 35, 36, 195, 196, 214. *See also* Polanyi, Karl: "protectionist reaction"
antitrust, 204
apertura, Mexican, 155–56, 157–59, 188, 190, 215, 223
Apple Computer, 183
Atkinson, Michael, 140, 141, 146
automobile industry, 201; and duty remission, 211; in Mexico, 69–72, 221
autopact (Canada-U.S.), 221

Baldwin, Robert, 205
Bargaining school, 44–46
Bartlett Díaz, Manuel, 187
Becker, David, 50–51
Bellamy, Edward, 74
Belzberg family, 107
Biersteker, Thomas J., 49
Block, Fred, 12, 13, 16–17, 26–27, 34, 36, 64
Brady Plan, 168, 170–71
Bryant, John, 78
Bryant Amendment, 78, 93, 105
Bryant-Harkin bill, 105
BTR PLC, 107
Burroughs, 183
Bush, George, 79
Business Council on National Issues, 132, 133–34
business cycles, 53, 61, 64
Business Round Table, 104, 134

Cameron, David, 14
Campeau, Robert, 107
CANACINTRA, 176, 178, 179–80, 181
Canadian Federation of Independent Business, 135
Canadian Labour Congress, 139
capital, domestic: in Canada, 132–38, 215; in Mexico, 66, 173–81; and the state, 20, 50–51; in the United States, 100–106
capital, international: in Canada, 138–39; in Mexico, 182–85; and the state, 20, 51–52
Cárdenas, Cuauhtémoc, 188, 189, 224
Casar, José, 61
CCE, 176, 178
CEMAI, 180
Chambers of Commerce: Canadian, 135; U.S., 104
Clark, Joe, 130
clase política, 173, 190
Coleman, William, 133, 140, 141, 146
Collins, Cardiss, 79
Committee on Foreign Investment in the United States (CFIUS), 77, 79, 80–83, 93, 96, 105; and Commerce Department, 79, 81, 83, 93, 94, 96–97; and Treasury Department, 79, 80, 81, 82, 93, 94–97
CONCAMIN, 176, 177, 181
CONCANACO, 176, 177, 178
Confederación de Trabajadores Méxicanos (CTM), 172, 189

Connaught Laboratories, 145, 150
continentalization, 2, 5, 35, 44, 113, 122, 126–27, 156–57, 195–97, 217, 218–19, 220; of sectoral policies, 201, 221; of social policies, 202, 207. *See also* social expenditures
Cooper, Richard, 9
COPARMEX, 176, 178
corporate taxes, 4, 15, 16, 101, 106, 175, 180, 196–97
corriente democrática, 188–89
Crown corporations, 119

Danforth, John, 104
debt-equity swaps, 56–57, 66, 68, 167–68, 223
de la Madrid, Miquel, 56, 61, 158, 162, 163, 168, 170, 187
Department of Regional Industrial Expansion (DRIE), 142–43, 144, 147–48
Destler, I. M., 90
Dobb, Maurice, 25
Doern, Bruce, 142, 143
domestic politics: and state intervention, 18–21, 193–95. *See also* foreign direct investment regulation: and domestic politics
Dukakis, Michael, 74, 107

Ebert, Michael, 203
Echeverria, Luis, 57, 161, 174, 187
Elson, Diane, 22
Emergency Committee for American Trade (ECAT), 104
Encarnation, Dennis, 47
European Community, 27
Evans, Peter, 51
exchange rates, 4, 6, 29, 36, 101–2, 127, 137–38, 152, 174, 196, 197, 207, 210, 213, 219, 220
Exon-Florio Amendment, 78, 90, 92–93, 96, 97, 104, 105, 121, 153, 200, 210
export-oriented industrialization, 156, 158

fast-track procedures, 91, 92
Ford, Gerald, 77
foreign direct investment regulation, 6–7, 38, 41–43, 65; in Canada, 57–60, 61–65, 113–21; deregulation of, 43–44; and diversion of foreign investment, 54–61, 64; and domestic politics, 46–55, 89–94, 127–32, 185–90, 209–10; in Mexico, 54–57, 61–65, 159–68, 215; and public opinion, 90, 130, 131; re-regulation of, 220; by subnational governments, 106–8, 121, 146–48; as takeover defense, 103–4, 105–8, 135, 153; in the United States, 75–80, 86, 88, 202–4. *See also* Committee on Foreign Investment in the United States; Foreign Investment Review Agency; Investment Canada; National Commission on Foreign Investment
Foreign Investment Review Agency (FIRA), 58, 60, 63, 113, 114, 115, 117, 118, 119, 123, 124, 125, 126, 130, 131, 134, 136
Free trade agreement (Canada-U.S. FTA), 2–6, 63, 68, 92, 119–21, 126, 132, 133, 137, 140, 153, 199, 200, 201, 211, 212–13, 217, 223

General Agreement on Tariffs and Trade (GATT), 31, 84, 125, 126, 158, 159, 178, 179, 192, 198, 199, 200, 208, 219
General Motors, 184
Gephardt, Richard, 80
Gereffi, Gary, 51
globalization: of industries, 39, 44, 46, 65; of markets, 2, 38
Globerman, Steven, 63
Gordon, Walter, 113, 128
Gourevitch, Peter, 19
Graham, Edward K., 198, 203
Gray, Herb, 116, 130, 131
Gray Report, 114
Guisinger, Stephen, 66–67, 79
Gunder Frank, André, 9

Hall, Peter, 25
Hamilton, Alexander, 75
Hewlett-Packard, 183
Howe, C. D., 127
Hymer, Stephen, 40

import substitution industrialization, 70, 158, 178, 208–9
Innis, Harold, 111
institutional fit, 36
Institutionalist school, 44, 46–47
Institut Mérieux, 145
International Business Machines (IBM), 9, 182–84, 221

Investment Canada, 60, 63, 117–18, 119, 133, 142–47
investment incentives, 5, 57, 66–69, 204–8; and prisoner's dilemma, 67; by subnational governments, 106, 146–47
investment policies: and adjustment, 3–5, 201; international negotiations on, 198–99, 206. *See also* adjustment assistance

Japan, 22–23

Katzenstein, Peter, 110
Kindleberger, Charles, 9
Korea, South, 22
Krugman, Paul R., 198, 203

labor training, 214
Lall, Sanjaya, 47
Lalonde, Marc, 130
Law to Promote Mexican Investment and to Regulate Foreign Investment, 56, 159, 161
Laxer, Gordon, 139
Levine, Mel, 79
Lindblom, Charles, 12, 14, 15
Lipietz, Alain, 37
López Portillo, José, 174, 175, 186, 187

McNeill, Robert L., 104
Mahon, Rianne, 141
maquiladoras, 29, 56, 156, 165–66, 179, 209, 217–20
market-as-prison, 10–17, 193–94
market constraints, 12, 13, 14, 18, 20, 53
Ministry of Finance (Canada), 141
Ministry of Industry, Science, and Technology (Canada), 142
Moran, Theodore, 51
Mulroney, Brian, 117, 151
Murkowski, Frank, 93
Murray, Robin, 9

National Association of Manufacturers (NAM), 102, 104, 105
National Commission on Foreign Investment (NCFI), 161, 163, 164, 165, 167
National Cooperative Research Act, 98
National Energy Program (NEP), 58, 60, 63, 115–16, 117, 124, 130, 131, 137, 153
National Foreign Trade Council, 104

nationalism, 195–96; and business cycles, 63–64; in Canada, 64, 123–25, 127–31, 153–54, 209–10; in the United States, 83, 89, 152–53. *See also* protectionism, U.S.
National Policy of 1879, 29, 112, 126
national security: and investment review, 76, 78, 81, 86, 88, 92, 104, 105
national treatment, 27, 82, 84, 92, 108, 119, 120, 121, 151, 153
Nixon, Richard, 124
non-tariff barriers, 91
North American Free Trade Agreement (NAFTA), 3–6, 29, 92, 156, 159, 160, 197, 216, 218, 219, 220
Norton Company, 107

Offe, Claus, 13, 14
Okun, Arthur, 22
Olsen, H. A., 131
Omnibus Trade and Competitiveness Act, 78, 87, 91, 121, 153
OPEC, 77

paradox of production, 2, 7–10, 193
Partido Acción Nacional (PAN), 174, 175, 190, 191, 192
Partido Revolucionario Democrático (PRD), 189, 190, 192
Partido Revolucionario Institucional (PRI), 158, 171, 173, 174, 175, 176, 180, 185–88, 189, 190, 191, 192, 216
Pentagon, U.S., 79, 96, 105
performance requirements, 68–69, 207–8, 217, 223
Polanyi, Karl, 28; "protectionist" reaction, 30–31, 32, 35, 86, 113, 128, 195, 214, 219
Political Economy school, 44, 47–50
políticos, 186, 187, 188
Porter, Michael, 35, 39
Prestowitz, Clyde V., Jr., 199
Protectionism, U.S., 74–75, 83–89
Przeworski, Adam, 13, 14
Puche, Jaime Serra, 186

Reich, Robert, 35, 65, 151, 198, 202, 203, 204, 214
research and development: in Canada, 114, 146–51, 220–21; and MNEs, 39–41, 65–66; and subsidies, 205; in the United States, 88–89, 97–100, 201
Ruggie, John Gerard, 31

Rugman, Alan, 149

Salinas de Gortari, Carlos, 63, 71, 157, 158, 159, 163, 170, 187, 191
Schneider, Ben Ross, 190
SECOFI, 186
Shapiro, Helen, 70, 71, 72
Sharp-Lent-Exon bill, 79, 90, 93
Sjolander, Claire Turenne, 129
Sklar, Richard, 50
Smith, Adam, 21
Smith, Miriam, 140
Smith, Murray, 210
social expenditures: cuts in, 5, 213–14; as protection, 32, 196; as subsidies, 207
strategic partnerships, 22, 40, 43, 212
state legitimacy, 29–32
Streeten, Paul, 47
subsidies, 5, 72, 205–7
Super 301 clause, 87, 109

Technology Transfer Law (Mexico), 56, 161, 165
técnicos, 157, 186, 187, 188, 191

third option, 210
trade deficit, U.S., 84–85
Trading with the Enemy Act, U.S., 42, 123
Trudeau, Pierre, 113

United States Congress: and trade politics, 89–92
United States Council for International Business, 104
United States Trade Representative (USTR), 77, 91, 92

Velazquez, Fidel, 189
venture capital, 211

wages, 4, 5, 101, 106, 166, 189, 196, 205, 213, 214, 217, 218, 221
wage vouchers, 206
Walgren, Doug, 79, 94
Wallerstein, Immanuel, 9
Watkins Report, 113, 128
Wells, Louis T., 47
Wolf, Frank, 79
Workers' Ownership Program, 211

Cornell Studies in Political Economy

EDITED BY PETER J. KATZENSTEIN

Collapse of an Industry: Nuclear Power and the Contradictions of U.S. Policy, by John L. Campbell

Power, Purpose, and Collective Choice: Economic Strategy in Socialist States, edited by Ellen Comisso and Laura D'Andrea Tyson

The Political Economy of the New Asian Industrialism, edited by Frederic C. Deyo

Dislodging Multinationals: India's Strategy in Comparative Perspective, by Dennis J. Encarnation

Rivals beyond Trade: America versus Japan in Global Competition, by Dennis J. Encarnation

Democracy and Markets: The Politics of Mixed Economies, by John R. Freeman

The Misunderstood Miracle: Industrial Development and Political Change in Japan, by David Friedman

Patchwork Protectionism: Textile Trade Policy in the United States, Japan, and West Germany, by H. Richard Friman

Monetary Sovereignty: The Politics of Central Banking in Western Europe, by John B. Goodman

Politics in Hard Times: Comparative Responses to International Economic Crises, by Peter Gourevitch

Closing the Gold Window: Domestic Politics and the End of Bretton Woods, by Joanne Gowa

Cooperation among Nations: Europe, America, and Non-tariff Barriers to Trade, by Joseph M. Grieco

Pathways from the Periphery: The Politics of Growth in the Newly Industrializing Countries, by Stephan Haggard

Rival Capitalists: International Competitiveness in the United States, Japan, and Western Europe, by Jeffrey A. Hart

The Philippine State and the Marcos Regime: The Politics of Export, by Gary Hawes

Reasons of State: Oil Politics and the Capacities of American Government, by G. John Ikenberry

The State and American Foreign Economic Policy, edited by G. John Ikenberry, David A. Lake, and Michael Mastanduno

The Paradox of Continental Production: National Investment Policies in North America, by Barbara Jenkins

Pipeline Politics: The Complex Political Economy of East-West Energy Trade, by Bruce W. Jentleson

The Politics of International Debt, edited by Miles Kahler

Corporatism and Change: Austria, Switzerland, and the Politics of Industry, by Peter J. Katzenstein

Industry and Politics in West Germany: Toward the Third Republic, edited by Peter J. Katzenstein

Small States in World Markets: Industrial Policy in Europe, by Peter J. Katzenstein

The Sovereign Entrepreneur: Oil Policies in Advanced and Less Developed Capitalist Countries, by Merrie Gilbert Klapp

International Regimes, edited by Stephen D. Krasner

From Welfare Capitalism to Neoliberalism, by Paulette Kurzer

Power, Protection, and Free Trade: International Sources of U.S. Commercial Strategy, 1887 – 1939, by David A. Lake

State Capitalism: Public Enterprise in Canada, by Jeanne Kirk Laux and Maureen Appel Molot

France after Hegemony: International Change and Financial Reform, by Michael Loriaux

Economic Containment: CoCom and the Politics of East-West Trade, by Michael Mastanduno

Opening Financial Markets: Banking Politics on the Pacific Rim, by Louis W. Pauly

The Limits of Social Democracy: Investment Politics in Sweden, by Jonas Pontusson

The Fruits of Fascism: Postwar Prosperity in Historical Perspective, by Simon Reich

The Business of the Japanese State: Energy Markets in Comparative and Historical Perspective, by Richard J. Samuels

In the Dominions of Debt: Historical Perspectives on Dependent Development, by Herman M. Schwartz

Europe and the New Technologies, edited by Margaret Sharp

Europe's Industries: Public and Private Strategies for Change, edited by Geoffrey Shepherd, François Duchêne, and Christopher Saunders

Ideas and Institutions: Developmentalism in Brazil and Argentina, by Kathryn Sikkink

Fair Shares: Unions, Pay, and Politics in Sweden and West Germany, by Peter Swenson

Union of Parts: Labor Politics in Postwar Germany, by Kathleen A. Thelen

Democracy at Work: Changing World Markets and the Future of Labor Unions, by Lowell Turner

National Styles of Regulation: Environmental Policy in Great Britain and the United States, by David Vogel

International Cooperation: Building Regimes for Natural Resources and the Environment, by Oran R. Young

Governments, Markets, and Growth: Financial Systems and the Politics of Industrial Change, by John Zysman

American Industry in International Competition: Government Policies and Corporate Strategies, edited by John Zysman and Laura Tyson

Library of Congress Cataloging-in-Publication Data

Jenkins, Barbara (Barbara L.)
  The paradox of continental production : national investment policies in North
America / Barbara Jenkins.
    p.   cm. — (Cornell studies in political economy)
  Includes bibliographical references and index.
  ISBN 0-8014-2676-6
    1. United States—Commercial policy.   2. Canada–Commercial policy.
3. Mexico—Commercial policy.   4. North America—Economic integration.
5. Investments, Foreign—United States.   6. Investments, Foreign—Canada.
7. Investments, Foreign—Mexico.   8. Foreign trade regulation—United States.
9. Foreign trade regulation—Canada.   10. Foreign trade regulation—Mexico.
I. Title.   II. Series.
HF1456.5.C2J46   1992
332.6'73'097—dc20   92-52761